Understanding AS-Level Government and Politics

UNDERSTANDINGS

Series editor **DUNCAN WATTS**

Following the review of the national curriculum for 16–19-year-olds, UK examining boards introduced new specifications, first used in 2001 and 2002. A-level courses are now divided into A/S level for the first year of sixth-form studies, and the more difficult A2 level thereafter. The **Understandings** series comprehensively covers social science syllabuses of all major examination boards, featuring dedicated A/S and A2 level textbooks. The books are written in an accessible, user-friendly and jargon-free manner and will be essential to students sitting these examinations.

Already published:

Understanding criminal law
Caroline Buckley and Stephen Buckley

Understanding political ideas and movements
Kevin Harrison and Tony Boyd

Understanding British and European political issues (2nd edition)
Neil McNaughton

Understanding A/S accounting for AQA
Jeremy Renals

Understanding American government and politics (3rd edition)
Duncan Watts

Understanding US/UK government and politic (2nd edition)
Duncan Watts

Understanding A/S level government and politics
Chris Wilson

Understanding AS-Level Government and Politics

Second edition

Moyra Grant

The right of Moyra Grant to be identified as the author of this work has been asserted by her in accordance with the Copyright, Designs and Patents Act 1988.

Published by Manchester University Press
Oxford Road, Manchester M13 9NR, UK
and Room 400, 175 Fifth Avenue, New York, NY 10010, USA
www.manchesteruniversitypress.co.uk

Distributed in the United States exclusively by
Palgrave Macmillan, 175 Fifth Avenue, New York,
NY 10010, USA

Distributed in Canada exclusively by
UBC Press, University of British Columbia, 2029 West Mall,
Vancouver, BC, Canada V6T 1Z2

British Library Cataloguing-in-Publication Data
A catalogue record for this book is available from the British Library

Library of Congress Cataloging-in-Publication Data applied for

ISBN 978 0 7190 8654 0 paperback

First published 2013

Typeset by Servis Filmsetting Ltd, Stockport, Cheshire
Printed in Great Britain
by Bell & Bain Ltd, Glasgow

Contents

List of tables, figures and boxes   vii

1   Political power and participation   1

2   The UK constitution   17

3   Electoral systems and referenda   37

4   Political parties and MPs   63

5   Public opinion and pressure groups   87

6   Parliament   105

7   The executive   123

8   Rights and liberties   143

9   Local government and devolution   163

10   The European Union   181

Glossary   201

Index   211

List of tables, figures and boxes

Tables

1.1	Voting ages in different states (some examples)	5
1.2	The extension of the franchise in the UK	9
3.1	Winning parties' votes and seats in UK general elections, 1974–2010	41
3.2	Voting results in the UK 2010 general election	42
3.3	General election results, 1970–2010	43
3.4	UK general election turnouts, 1945–2010	45
3.5	Estimated results of 2010 general election using diverse electoral systems (number of seats out of 650)	49
3.6	Summary of key election turnouts, 2001–10	54
3.7	UK referenda, 2011–1973	55
4.1	The major and minor parties taking part in the 2010 general election	66
4.2	Women candidates and MPs, 1983–2010	70
4.3	UK party membership (thousands)	74
4.4	Registered donations to some UK political parties in 2009	75
4.5	MPs' representation, 2010	77
7.1	Examples of ministerial resignations over collective responsibility	128
7.2	Examples of ministerial resignations over individual responsibility	129
7.3	UK Prime Ministers, 1945–2010	130
7.4	Cabinet committees, 2010	133
9.1	Local government elections, 2011	167
9.2	Local government elections, 2011, percentage of votes won	167
9.3	Greater London Authority election results, 2008	170
9.4	London mayoral election results, 2008	171
9.5	Scottish Parliament election results, 2011	173
9.6	Welsh Assembly election results, 2011	175
9.7	Northern Ireland Assembly election results, 2011	176
9.8	Summary of devolved powers, 2011	176
10.1	UK policy and EU power	184
10.2	Number of seats per state (2009–14 parliamentary term)	186
10.3	EU Parliament elections (UK), 2009	190

Figures

2.1	Types of constitution	21
2.2	The British system of government	22
2.3	Contrasting structures of government	23
2.4	The formation of parliamentary government in Britain	24
3.1	A first-past-the-post ballot paper	40
3.2	Imbalance between seats and votes	42
7.1	Civil service conventions	138
8.1	Civil and criminal courts in England and Wales	146
9.1	London local authorities	170
10.1	The European Union, 2011	182
10.2	Summary of EU decision-making processes	189

Boxes

6.1	Example of a private Bill	111
6.2	Example of a statutory instrument	113
7.1	Example of a government department and its ministers	123

1 Political power and participation

Aims of this chapter

- To explain the key concepts of 'power' and 'authority'.
- To explain 'direct' versus 'indirect' democracy.
- To assess the various criteria of democracy.
- To assess the main criticisms of democracy.
- To explain the concept of 'liberal democracy'.
- To examine the concept of citizenship in a liberal democracy.
- To outline diverse ideological interpretations of citizenship.

What is politics?

Politics is about the study and exercise of power. **Power** is the ability to make people do things by the means to reward or by the threat or use of punishment, force or violence. Power may take various forms – economic, political, military, social or personal – and is a matter of degree. The epitome of power is the lawless gang that rampages through the streets generating fear and terror, or – at national level – the brutal military junta or rebel militia men who impose arbitrary violence and death, such as in Burma since the 1960s. However, power need not involve violence, or even the threat of violence. If a strike by transport workers forces you to walk to school, that involves power because you have been made to do something unwillingly; whereas a persuasive publicity campaign by a pressure group such as Comic Relief or Greenpeace is simply influence.

Influence is a persuasive effect upon others' ideas or actions; it may or may not be intended, organised, or even consciously perceived, but it is based on respect or agreement (whether reasoned or unreasoned), and is therefore closer to authority than to power.

Authority is the ability to make people do things because they think the power holders have the right to do so. Authority involves legitimate power based on consent, respect and support. It may derive from election, but also from tradition (for example, the House of Lords or the monarchy); from intense personal magnetism and character – known as 'charisma' (e.g. Jesus Christ, Churchill, Gandhi or Hitler); or from the office rather than the character of the individual, that is, from due process, training, rules, laws and principles (e.g. the police or civil service, doctors or teachers).

Question...

1.1   Distinguish between 'power' and 'authority'.

(5 marks)

Authority is the basis of any democracy. Almost every country in the modern world – including Britain – claims to be a democracy. However, when countries as diverse as the USA and Cuba lay claim to the label, its meaning is obviously not clear cut. In Britain, most people would point to the ballot box as proof of democracy, but the concept goes much further than this.

What is democracy?

Democracy – from the Greek *demos kratos* – literally means 'people power , or self-government of the people, by the people, for the people. In its original form, it meant the right of all qualified citizens directly to decide upon matters of general concern. This form of government began in the ancient Greek city-state of Athens in the fifth century BC, where all qualified citizens would gather regularly to vote directly on issues of concern. (Famously, however, only adult, free men were qualified citizens – women, slaves and non-Athenians were excluded.)

Any form of direct decision making or direct action by the people which increases their own control over their own lives may therefore be 'democratic' in this literal sense of 'people power' – be it a vote on an issue at local, workplace or national level, a boycott, a strike, a riot or a revolution. 'People -power' may thus be legal or illegal, peaceful or violent.

This helps to explain why, until the nineteenth century, the very idea of 'people power' was often called 'mobocracy' or 'tyranny of the majority' and was feared by the ruling elites in countries like Britain, who asserted that the people – the 'mob' – were dangerous, unintelligent, fickle and incapable of making responsible political decisions. However, industrialisation and the factory system brought together an increasingly organised and educated workforce which used its collective economic power to demand a greater political voice, while at the same time the rising class of industrial owners and entrepreneurs, in competition for social dominance with the old landed aristocracy, was seeking a political power base. Industrial workers and employers, together with an emergent 'middle class', thus found some common cause in the extension of the **franchise** – that is, the right to vote. Hence the idea of 'democracy' has gradually become accepted – indeed, positively lauded – in most countries, though it is invariably practised in a limited form.

Scarcely any modern industrial society can claim to practise **direct democracy** in the way that the ancient Greeks did. Switzerland perhaps comes closest, with its very frequent **referenda** – direct public votes on political issues and policies – in a very decentralised political system. However, throughout much of the twentieth century, Switzerland kept holding referenda on whether women should have the right to vote – and, since only the men had the right to vote in those referenda, women did not get the vote at all until 1971.

It is widely argued that most modern industrial states are too big and complex for such direct democracy to be possible. This is debatable: large states can be subdivided into small political units, and modern technology could, in theory, enhance the capacity for direct political participation. Interactive TV and internet websites are now commonplace. This two-way media facility could easily be applied to the process of genuine political decision making – rather than to mere expressions of opinion – if the political will were there. Perhaps, however, political leaders are too reluctant to surrender their power, and/or most people are too apathetic to take it, for the possibility of more direct democracy to be considered seriously in countries like the UK.

Britain is not, therefore, a direct democracy. Like most other modern states, Britain claims to be an **indirect or representative democracy**. This involves the election by qualified citizens of representatives who govern over, and on behalf of, the people. Mere vote casting is, obviously, a limited form of 'people power' and participation. It actually involves the voters in giving away their political decision-making power to a few representatives who then make most of the key political decisions in society. All representative democracy therefore entails **oligarchy** or elitism: rule by the few. In Britain, representative democracy – the extension of the franchise – developed in the nineteenth and twentieth centuries under pressure from popular movements such as Chartism, the trades union movement and the suffragettes; and it was, in part, a conscious effort on the part of the political power holders to forestall radical demands for more direct or extensive political democracy. In the words of the twentieth-century Conservative politician Lord Hailsham, 'If you don't give them reform, they will give you social revolution.'

> # key term...
>
> **Indirect/representative democracy** The election by qualified citizens of candidates to political office to make decisions on behalf of the electorate.

> # key term...
>
> **Oligarchy** Political elitism, or rule by the few.

Question...

1.2 Distinguish between two different types of democracy. *(5 marks)*

Nevertheless, all modern states – whatever their type of economic or political system – have some valid claim to call themselves democratic if they contain elements of one or more of the following:

- **People power:** e.g. referenda, effective pressure groups, trades unions etc.
- **Participation:** democratic participation may take many forms, from voting and standing for political office to meetings, marches, demonstrations, peaceful law-breaking and violent political opposition. Even riots have democratic claims, since they are 'people power' in the literal sense – although all states and governments will deny those democratic claims when such activities are directed against themselves. (It was interesting to observe, in 2011, Western media and governments' support for the mass protests in Egypt's Tahrir Square, which would have been roundly condemned had they been happening in Trafalgar Square, London or in Times Square, New York.)

Participation in any kind of political activity beyond voting is very much a minority phenomenon in the UK. Surveys indicate that only about 10%

participate in politics through pressure group membership. Less than 5% undertake various forms of direct action, and under 2% are involved in a wide variety of political activities such as party campaigning and political protests. However, the more recent surveys do indicate that more people – especially under-25s – are becoming actively involved in public campaigns and protests.

analyse this...

Which of the following forms of political activity would you consider doing?

	Yes	No
Voting for a political representative		
Signing a petition		
Completing an opinion poll		
Contacting your MP		
Attending a political meeting		
Joining a political party		
Joining a pressure group		
Producing a leaflet or poster		
Setting up a website		
Going on a demonstration		
Going on strike		
Peaceful law-breaking (e.g. smoking a joint)		
Damaging property (e.g. painting protest graffiti)		
Rioting		

In the 2010 general election, thousands of people who were queuing to vote were turned away at 10 o'clock in the evening when the polling stations closed, prompting criticisms of constraints on political participation and possible distortions of the election results. The rules were unclear (or non-existent) and the actions of polling station staff were inconsistent. For the 2011 elections, for the first time it was stated on polling cards that 'You cannot be issued with a ballot paper after 10pm, even if you are at the polling station before then.'

E-democracy

E-democracy refers to the use of the internet, mobile phones and other electronic media as means of giving people access to information and to give their opinions in polls, surveys and commentaries on local or national policies. At best, however, e-democracy is informative or consultative. It rarely amounts to genuine decision making by voters.

Examples:

www.theyworkforyou.com — A website about the work of the UK's parliaments and assemblies.

www.writetothem.com — A website where you can find the name of your local councillor, member of the UK, European or Scottish Parliament, or member of the Welsh, Northern Ireland or London Assembly, and write to them by e-mail.

http://petitions.number10.gov.uk — The official government website for creating and signing online petitions.

talking point...

In the UK, people cannot vote until they are 18. Some people argue that, at 16, young people in Britain can work, pay taxes, marry or join the army and, therefore, they should also be entitled to vote. Voting at 16 is already the official policy of the Liberal Democrats, the Scottish and Welsh Nationalists and the Green Party.

Table 1.1 Voting ages in different states (some examples)

State	Voting age
Uzbekistan	25
Japan	20
Tunisia	20
France	18
UK	18
USA	18
Bosnia-Herzegovina	16 if employed, otherwise 18
Brazil	16, compulsory from 18
Serbia	16 if employed, otherwise 18
Indonesia	17
North Korea	17
Sudan	17
Austria	16
Cuba	16
Nicaragua	16
Iran	15

Note: Western European politicians regard many of the countries listed above as 'undemocratic' because of the illiberal nature of their political regimes. Does the age at which people are entitled to vote make any difference to this evaluation, or not?

- **Representation:** this can mean different things. The strongest interpretation of the concept of 'representative' is that of a delegate: an elected power holder who acts exactly as instructed by his or her voters, thus reflecting and implementing the voters' *views* on every issue. This does not apply to British MPs – and it would be difficult for them, in practice, to consult all of their voters on every issue.

Alternatively, representation can mean the reflection of voters' *interests*, even if the decisions are not popular (this form of representation is commonly claimed by politicians when they are, for example, increasing taxes or closing hospitals). This is sometimes called the 'trustee model' of representation, and it was first proposed by eighteenth-century Conservative MP Edmund Burke. It may apply to British MPs, but they are also closely tied to the aims and interests of their parties.

Finally, it can mean the reflection of voters' *social backgrounds* by the politicians: for example, the percentage of female, ethnic minority, young or gay MPs in Parliament. British MPs are now more representative of the wider public in this sense than ever before, but they are still quite atypical – for example, only 22% of MPs are female, and only 26 out of 650 (4%) are black or Asian, as compared with 8% of the wider UK population. The 2010 coalition Cabinet of 23 members contained 19 millionaires, 70% Oxbridge-educated ministers and just four women – again, not socially representative.

- **Responsibility:** this concept can also mean different things. **Responsible government** means, primarily, government which is answerable and accountable – either directly to the voters or, as in the UK, to Parliament, and, thereby, indirectly to the voters (hence the doctrines of collective and individual ministerial responsibility, discussed in Chapter 7). A secondary interpretation is the idea of wise and sound government in the national interests of the voters.

- **Consent:** most modern states rest on the general agreement of the people that the governors have the right to govern and that the people will accept and live by the decisions of the governors (even if many people did not vote for them or do not agree with the decisions made).

The problem with defining democracy in terms of consent is that, especially in the modern age of mass media, consent can be created by political power holders – through the manipulation of information and of public opinion – to legitimise their rule. In Nazi Germany, for example, there was undoubtedly a substantial degree of mass, active support for the regime; but there was also a well-developed and effective system of political indoctrination and propaganda in the schools and mass media, which made it difficult to distinguish real from manufactured political consent.

Most commentators would agree that the same point applies, to a greater or lesser degree, in every political system. People do not emerge from the womb as little flag-waving Nazis, or communists, or royalists, or parliamentarians; they learn to accept and support the system in which they live through a process of **political socialisation**. Through the various agencies of family, school, work, peer group (friends and colleagues), media and religion we each acquire the necessary attitudes and values to enable us to accept and adapt to the system in which we live, and to enable that system itself to survive. All individuals, in all states, are subject to this process of socialisation – sometimes by open indoctrination, often by more subtle, less honest and usually more effective methods.

> **key term...**
>
> **Representation** A form of indirect democracy reflecting the views, interests and/or typical social background of the electorate.

> **key term...**
>
> **Responsible (party) government** Executive accountable to Parliament and the public (through party system, manifesto and mandate); or wise and sensible government in the best interests of the people.

> **key term...**
>
> **Political socialisation** The instilling of political attitudes and values through agencies such as family, media, education, peer group, church etc.

The reliance of modern governments upon 'spin doctors' – advisers on positive public relations and policy presentation (or propagandists?) – is illustrative of this process.

The relationship between politicians, the media and public opinion is, therefore, a complex one, like a dog chasing its tail – it is often hard to know which is leading and which is following.

Anti-democratic philosophies would argue, anyway, that governments should *not* follow public opinion because it is uncertain, divided, manipulable, fickle, ignorant or selfish. The most cynical views would say that modern 'democracy', the world over, consists of the power holders telling people what they want (socialisation) and then duly giving it to them (representation).

Question...

1.3 What are the main criticisms of democracy? *(15 marks)*

Liberal democracy

Representative democracies take many forms: one-, two- or multi-party systems, etc. Britain, like the United States and most European countries, claims to be a **liberal democracy**. This is a representative system embodying the concepts of diversity, freedom of choice and individual rights and freedoms (as opposed to, for example, collective equality or mass participation). It asserts the following principles:

- **free and fair elections:** most adult citizens will have the right to vote in regular, competitive and secret ballots; diverse candidates and parties will be free to campaign in opposition to the government of the day; and the election results will be honestly counted, accepted and presented.
- **pluralism:** diverse centres of economic and political power; thus competitive private ownership in the economy and, especially, two or more parties in the political system, together with many pressure groups. This should generate competition, and, hence, freedom of choice and effective representation of many different views and interests.
- **political equality:** one person, one vote, one value – which implies a proportional system of voting, where the percentage of votes received by a party equates with the percentage of political seats (elected representatives) granted to them. It also implies equal opportunity to stand for political office and equal opportunity to be elected to office. There are, however, always restrictions on those qualified to stand for office: for example, in Britain, to stand as a Westminster MP, a person must be aged 18 years or over and must pay a deposit of £500. This last is intended to discourage 'frivolous' candidates, but it effectively excludes many serious contenders who do not have the financial backing of a large party.
- **constitutionalism:** government constrained by clear and enforceable rules which set limits to political power.

key term...

Liberal democracy A system of individual representation and protection of individual rights based on free, regular and competitive elections, constitutionalism and the rule of law.

key term...

Pluralism Diverse and competing centres of power – especially many parties and pressure groups.

- **the rule of law:** a fair, just and impartial legal system which should ensure legal equality – the principle that everyone (including the government) is equally subject to the same laws and has equal access to the law – with an independent and impartial judiciary.
- **limited government:** checks and constraints upon the power of government by various other bodies – e.g. the courts and pressure groups – to safeguard individual liberties.
- **open government:** non-secretive government, to ensure that government is honest and accountable to the people. This has, to some extent, been enhanced in the UK by the introduction in 2000 of a freedom of information law.
- **civil rights and liberties:** public entitlements and freedoms, preferably enshrined in law.

Note: Exam questions often ask: to what extent is the UK a liberal democracy? That is, how far do the above principles apply within the British political system? Later chapters will examine this question in detail.

British political culture and citizenship

The United Kingdom is a state. A **state** is an independent entity with ultimate political power and authority – that is, **sovereignty** – over all of the individuals and groups within its territorial boundaries. It is made up of all the formal institutions of political power such as the crown, legislature, executive, judiciary, army, and sometimes the church.

It has a legal monopoly on the use of violence, but will often use consensus – agreement – as well as coercion – force – to keep order within its boundaries, as well as against other states.

The **government** is the executive agent of the state; it decides and implements the policies by which the country is run (e.g. whether or not to impose student tuition fees). Whereas the state is said to be a permanent, abstract entity (e.g. the crown), the actual people and the institutions of government come and go (e.g. the Prime Minister).

Society is the body of people within and under the power of the state – both individuals and informal power bodies such as pressure groups and private businesses.

A **nation** is a group of people who share a sense of common culture, based on common ties of, for example, language, religion, race, territory and/ or history. One state may embrace many nations: for example, within the United Kingdom, the Scots, Irish, Welsh and English – even the Cornish and the Shetland Islanders – all have a separate and distinct sense of nationhood. Thus the UK – a sovereign state – contains at least four different nations. (Alternatively, one nation may be spread across many states: for example, the Jews were a nation without a sovereign state until the creation of Israel in 1948.)

key term...

State The formal, abstract, sovereign political power over a given territory, usually comprising legislature, executive and judiciary and usually possessing a legal monopoly of coercive power.

key term...

Sovereignty Ultimate legal and political power and authority.

key term...

Government The executive, policy-making branch of the state.

key term...

Society The body of people within and under the power of the state.

key term...

Nation A group of people who share a sense of common culture, based on common ties of e.g. language, religion, race, territory and/or history.

British political culture

The term '**political culture**' encompasses the predominant values and attitudes of the people within a particular state, which are both a cause and a consequence of the formal political system of that state. A political culture may encourage participation (e.g. small but strong democracies like Switzerland), passivity (e.g. authoritarian regimes like Burma or Singapore), conflict (e.g. countries with violent histories such as Ireland and Israel), compromise (e.g. very pluralist systems such as Sweden) – and so on.

The UK likes to call itself 'the mother of democracies'. It was the first country to industrialise and, until the twentieth century, it was the leading industrial power in the world. There is a fairly close correlation between industrialisation and the development of liberal democracy – with the significant exceptions of the fascist and communist regimes of the twentieth century.

British democracy can probably be said to originate from 1832, when the franchise – the right to vote – began to be extended to more and more people from male property holders and then male householders to all adult men and, in 1918, to older women (aged 30 years and over). Women gained the vote at this time largely because of their economic and occupational contributions (e.g. working in munitions factories) during the First World War (1914–18); although younger women were deemed too childlike to deserve a political voice. In 1928, however, almost all men and women aged 21 and over were given the vote; this established the principle of 'universal adult suffrage' in the UK. The voting age was lowered to 18 (under a Labour government) in 1969.

Table 1.2   The extension of the franchise in the UK

Date	Number of persons per 100 adults having the right to vote in the UK
1800	3
1832	5
1867	13
1884	25
1918	75
1928	100

Throughout the nineteenth and twentieth centuries, the UK had a comparatively stable democracy with relatively little use of domestic political violence – excepting in Ireland; no major political upheavals (such as the revolutions throughout Europe); relatively low levels of political extremism (neither fascism nor communism took strong hold in the UK); and substantial respect for individual rights and liberties, a largely independent judiciary and the acceptance of a legitimate political opposition.

Traditional conservative philosophy, especially, would attribute this stability to the pragmatic flexibility of key institutions such as the Church, Crown and House of Lords, which, by accepting gradual reductions in their own power, prevented major political conflicts and, at the same time, ensured their own survival and continuing political influence. Others would point to the relative social homogeneity – that is, social and cultural similarities – of the British people. Class has long been the dominant division in British politics because other factors such as religion, language, nationality and race – which have torn many other states apart – have had relatively limited impact in the UK.

From more critical perspectives, however, this view of British political culture, as a stable and harmonious example to the modern world, is rather smug, self-satisfied and complacent. Change is afoot within the UK. Critics might argue the following points:

- There has been a growing imbalance between the political institutions, with government becoming more centralised and powerful, and Parliament – the heart of British democracy – losing power and status.
- Growing nationalist sentiment in Scotland and Wales might not be 'bought off' with limited devolution; it might, conceivably, result in the actual break-up of the UK in the foreseeable future.
- As voters have become more disillusioned with mainstream politics, party memberships and voter turnouts have been falling and the politics of direct action have been increasing (see Chapters 3 to 5).

talking point...

Some countries today – e.g. Belgium and Australia – regard voting not only as a right but as a legal and civic obligation. Voting is therefore compulsory in these countries, and people may be fined if they do not vote. Perhaps this is one reason why, in the 2009 European elections, turnout in Belgium was 90%, while in the UK it was just 35%.

Would you advocate compulsory voting for the UK?
Why or why not?

- There have been significant incidents of public disorder and violence – especially, but not only, during the 'radical right' Thatcherite phase of government in the 1980s, when economic deprivation (and perceived injustices such as the poll tax) prompted widespread inner-city rioting.
- Since the 1990s, the growing politics of 'anti-capitalism' have sought to challenge the whole economic and political system upon which British political culture is based.
- There have been growing curbs on civil liberties in the UK in the last three decades (largely justified by references to terrorism, illegal immigration and asylum seeking) which, say critics, are threatening the rights and freedoms all of British citizens.

All of these issues and arguments will be examined more fully in later chapters.

True or false?

1. Authority requires election.
2. All representative democracy entails oligarchy.
3. Democracy simply means 'one man, one vote'.
4. Over 40% of Westminster MPs are women.
5. England is not a state.

British citizenship

> **key term...**
>
> **Citizenship** An individual's legal membership of, and recognition by, a state which grants mutual rights and obligations between state and citizen.

What does it mean to be a British citizen? Narrowly, **citizenship** is an individual's legal membership of, and recognition by, a state which grants mutual rights and obligations between state and citizen. Broadly, a citizen is an individual with rights in relation to the state – as distinct, for example, from the concept of a 'subject' subservient to the state and the monarchy. Since the UK is a monarchy, it is debatable whether its people are citizens, or subjects, or both.

British citizens have the right to live and work in the country and may apply for and receive a passport which gives them the right to travel out of and into the country. Usually the right to work entails the obligation to pay taxes. Similarly, an individual who is on the voting register may be called up for compulsory jury service as a civic responsibility. The concept of citizenship, therefore, implies both rights and duties for both the individual and the state.

Legal citizenship is not granted to everyone who lives in the UK. Non-citizens – so-called 'aliens' – are not granted the same rights to live, work and vote within the state as are British citizens. Since the 1960s, a succession of nationality and asylum laws have restricted rights of legal citizenship in the face of the UK's post-imperial heritage of immigration, unemployment and racialism. In this sense, the idea of 'citizenship' perhaps excludes, as much as it includes, many people.

Even among those who are granted legal citizenship in the UK, there are still widespread economic and social inequalities, with many people remaining poor and disadvantaged. This has led the various political philosophies and parties to develop different interpretations of citizenship.

The post-war (1945 onward) development of the welfare state embodied the modern liberal and socialist concept of 'social citizenship' and was intended to extend the social and economic rights of citizenship – such as a job, and access to free education, health and welfare services – to everyone. However, this liberal or social democratic version of citizenship, in practice, came to be seen – especially by many Conservatives – as requiring too much state involvement, bureaucracy and cost. Thatcherites spoke critically of the 'nanny state' fostering a 'dependency culture'. Hence the alternative New Right conservative (i.e. Thatcherite) interpretation of citizenship which emerged in the 1980s.

According to the ideology of the New Right, the 'good citizen' is an individual who makes an active and responsible contribution to the community: whether by joining their local Neighbourhood Watch scheme; by 'walking with purpose' (to quote former Conservative leader Michael Howard's much-mocked description of voluntary street patrols); by picking up litter; looking after the young, the old and the sick through family or 'care in the community'; by becoming a school governor or by running a profitable business. This concept of the 'active citizen' underpinned Conservative Prime Minister David Cameron's idea of the 'Big Society' in 2010. However, it is more about civil obligations than about civil rights, and it is at odds with the notion that the state has a duty to provide for the citizen in terms of welfare and protection against need or deprivation. This New Right approach, according to liberal and socialist critics, is employed to justify cuts in the state provision of services and is very divisive, with its sometimes outspoken disapproval of the passive, the dependent and the needy – the 'undeserving poor'.

Yet another, more personal and emotional, concept of citizenship is rooted in a sense of cultural identity and belonging associated with feelings of nationalism and patriotism. Thus, some people may feel as if they belong to a country even if that country is not a sovereign state (for example, Scotland or Wales), or even if they are denied legal citizenship by the state which they claim as their own (for example, asylum seekers within the UK).

The concept of citizenship also has an increasingly international dimension. For some, Europe is a common home and cultural identity. Article 8 of the European Union Maastricht Treaty (1992) established 'citizenship of the European Union' for every legal citizen and worker of a member state.

Finally, a growing perception of, and concern about, looming environmental crisis on a world scale (e.g. global warming) has given impetus to the rise of green politics, with an emphasis on our common citizenship of Planet Earth, with universal environmental rights and obligations which transcend geographical and political boundaries.

Quiz

1. Give examples to illustrate the difference between 'political power' and 'political authority'.
2. Where did democracy originate?
3. Name one European country which holds frequent referenda.
4. What percentage of the UK population is ethnic minority, e.g. black/ Asian?
5. Give three possible criticisms of democracy.
6. How many parties are currently represented in the House of Commons?
7. In what year was universal adult suffrage established in Britain?
8. Give one example of a right, and one example of a duty, accruing from British citizenship.
9. Name one country where voting is legally compulsory.
10. What – in political terms – is an 'alien'?

Answers to questions

Note: The following are notes for guidance only and are not intended to be taken as model answers.

1.1 *Distinguish between 'power' and 'authority'.* (5 marks)

Power is the ability to dictate others' behaviour through sanctions or coercion. Authority is the ability to shape others' behaviour through consent, respect and support – i.e. authority is rightful, legitimate power and is a feature of representative democracy, where the main source of authority is election. The nineteenth century German sociologist Max Weber distinguished three types of authority: traditional (e.g. House of Lords), charismatic (e.g. Churchill) and legal–rational (e.g. civil servants). Power may exist without authority (tyranny), or authority without much power (e.g. the British monarch). Authority tends to generate power, but power may generate authority through indoctrination. Conversely, misjudgement or misuse of power may mean the loss of authority, e.g. former Prime Minister Tony Blair's downfall in 2007. In a democracy, power should rest on authority.

1.2 *Distinguish between two different types of democracy.* (5 marks)

Good answer:
In a direct democracy, political decisions on all major issues are made directly by all qualified citizens, as in the ancient Greek city-states. However, it is often argued that this system is not feasible in large modern states. Therefore most societies today have a system of indirect or representative democracy, where representatives are elected to govern on behalf of the voters – that is, to reflect the voters' views, interests and/or social background. This may be a pluralist, multi-party system (e.g. Britain) or a single-party system (e.g. the former USSR), but it is inevitably oligarchic or elitist.

Weak answer:
Direct democracy is where people do it themselves, whereas with indirect democracy other people do it for them, which isn't really democratic at all.

Weak answer:
In direct democracy, everyone votes for everything, like in ancient Greece, though actually women and slaves didn't, so it wasn't really very democratic, and anyway it's not possible in big, complicated societies, whereas in Greece it was only in small cities, so it doesn't really happen now, except in some African tribes; and referenda such as that on the Alternative Vote in 2011 are a bit like direct democracy. Instead, voters vote for representatives to represent them, i.e. indirect, like Britain's two-party system which is called pluralist, or the old Soviet Union's one-party system which isn't democratic anyway, but anyway only a few people are doing the ruling, which is oligarchy.

Say why the above examples are good or bad. If you were the examiner, how many marks (out of 5) would you give to each?

Note: The 'weak' short answers are not factually wrong. The first is much too short and skimpy; it would be lucky to get one mark. The other is long-winded, repetitive, clumsy and colloquial in style, and it contains unsubstantiated value-judgements; but it would gain three marks for factual detail.

1.3   *What are the main criticisms of democracy?*   *(15 marks)*

Democracy – 'people power', whether direct or representative – can be criticised as a dangerous and inefficient form of government. Political philosophies with a negative view of human nature – such as traditional conservatism and fascism – argue that direct 'people power' is not desirable because it will be exercised in a selfish and irrational way. For example, some Fathers4Justice (F4J) campaigners have climbed high buildings and public landmarks (including Buckingham Palace) to publicise their protests, sometimes disrupting people and traffic, and endangering their own and others' safety.

Such pessimistic philosophies also argue against representative democracy, on the grounds that voters may be persuaded to vote for unsuitable people who seek power for its own sake, who are clever with words and who know how to appeal to popular emotions (such as Hitler).

'People power' may amount to 'mobocracy' or 'tyranny of the majority', ignoring or suppressing individual and minority views and rights.

'People power' may take illegal or even violent forms – for example, May Day 'anti-capitalist' protesters.

Alternatively, the result of 'people power' may be sheer apathy because most people are just not interested enough to take an active part in decision making.

All modern and supposedly democratic systems actually amount to rule by a small and powerful minority – a power elite – because, arguably, most voters are too uninformed, unintelligent or uninterested to take an educated and active part in decision making.

In representative democracies, elected politicians may favour popular short-term policies for their own political gain, which may actually be contrary to the long-term interests of the voters (for example, politicians may cut taxes and thus damage public services).

Finally, there are practical arguments against 'people power': it may be slow, costly, inefficient, inconsistent, dishonest and prone to corruption.

In summary, there is a view that democracy is the most dangerous and least efficient form of government: one in which the stability of the state is threatened by internal divisions; complex issues are distorted and simplified by self-serving politicians and ignorant voters; difficult decisions are delayed or avoided; and matters of high judgement are reduced to the lowest common denominator acceptable to a majority of the voters at any given time.

Note: This is a one-sided question. Stick firmly to that side in your answer.

True or false?
1. False.
2. True.
3. False.
4. False.
5. True.

Quiz

1. If a strike by transport workers forces you to walk to school, that involves power because you have been made to do something unwillingly; whereas an elected MP voting on a Bill in the House of Commons is exercising legitimate authority.
2. The ancient Greek city-state of Athens in the fifth century BC.
3. Switzerland.
4. 8%.
5. 'People power' may amount to 'tyranny of the majority'; voters may be uninformed, selfish or emotional rather than rational; elections and referenda are costly and time consuming.
6. Ten.
7. 1928.
8. British citizenship allows people the right to a passport and obliges them to do jury service if summoned.
9. Belgium, Australia.
10. A non-citizen.

Sample questions

Short

- Distinguish between direct and representative democracy.
- Distinguish between power and authority.
- Define 'liberal democracy'.

Medium

- What are the features of representative democracy in the UK?
- How do elections promote democracy?
- How does government acquire its legitimacy?

Long

- Assess the limitations of the UK democratic system.
- Evaluate the arguments for and against direct democracy.
- Evaluate advantages and disadvantages of representative democracy in the UK.

References

Burke, E. (1774) 'Letter to Constituents in Bristol' in *Edmund Burke: Selections from his Political Writings and Speeches*, T. Nelson and Sons, London.

Hailsham, Q. (1976) Elective Dictatorship: The Dimbleby Lecture in *The Listener*, 21 October.

Weber, M. (1948) *Essays in Sociology*, (Gerth, H.H. and Mills, C.W., eds), RKP, London.

Useful websites

www.bbc.co.uk/news
An excellent, wide-ranging and impartial source for topical news items and archive articles.

www.historylearningsite.co.uk/democracy.htm
A useful introductory article on the concept of 'democracy' and its application in the UK.

news.bbc.co.uk/democracylive/hi/default.stm
Democracy Live. A BBC website with a host of useful video extracts on UK and European politics.

www.positech.co.uk/democracy
A political strategy game where your aim as Prime Minister is to stay in power for as long as possible.

www.google.co.uk
Hundreds of thought-provoking images are also available by performing a Google image search on the concept of 'democracy'.

The UK constitution

Aims of this chapter

- To outline the various types of constitution.
- To examine the sources and main features of the UK constitution.
- To explain UK 'parliamentary government'.
- To explain UK 'parliamentary sovereignty'.
- To outline recent reforms of the UK constitution.
- To outline the arguments for and against a codified constitution.

What is a constitution?

If you have played or watched a good game of football or rugby recently, you will have understood and enjoyed it all the more because it was played according to certain rules which were (usually!) followed by the players and firmly enforced by the referee. If a state is to be run successfully, it also needs rules.

A **constitution** is the set of rules and principles by which a state is governed. If a constitution is outlined in a single, legal document it is described as **written** – for example, the US constitution.

The British constitution is described as **unwritten** because there is no single, legal document called *The British Constitution* which we can pick up and browse through. This is mainly because the UK has had no major political upheavals or revolutions in the last couple of centuries which might have required it to write out a clear statement of new rules. There are rules – but they have evolved gradually and piecemeal, over centuries; and they derive from many different sources – some are written and some are not, some have the force of law and some do not.

Sources and features of the UK constitution

Many – but not all – of the rules of the British constitution are **laws**, that is, rules of state which are enforceable by the courts and judges. There are, in turn, several different types of law:

- **European Union law (since the UK joined the EU in 1973):** this takes precedence over UK law; for example, the worldwide ban on the sale of British beef which was imposed by the EU during the BSE ('mad cow disease') crisis in the 1990s.
- **Acts of Parliament (statute law):** for example: the Human Rights Act 1998; the Freedom of Information Act 2000; and the Parliamentary

key term...

Constitution The set of rules and principles by which a state is governed.

key term...

Written constitution A set of state rules outlined in a single, legal document.

key term...

Unwritten constitution A set of state rules not contained in a single, legal document but deriving from many different sources (some written and some not, some with the force of law and some not).

key term...

Laws Rules of state which are enforceable by the courts and judges.

Voting System and Constituencies Act 2011, which paved the way for the referendum (a direct vote on an issue by the electorate) on reform of the Westminster electoral system and the proposed reduction of the number of MPs from 650 to 600.

- **Common law:** ancient, unwritten law; for example, the powers of the Crown.
- **Case law (judge-made law):** judicial interpretations of common and statute law, in new court cases, which then set a precedent for future cases. For example, the law on privacy in the UK has been developed by judges in key test cases, because there is no specific statute law on privacy.

talking point...

'Naomi goes to Lords in battle with Mirror over privacy'

Telegraph, 19 February 2004

www.telegraph.co.uk/news/uknews/1454764/Naomi-goes-to-Lords-in-battle-with-Mirror-over-privacy.html

Other rules of the constitution are not laws, but may still be very important:

- **Historical documents** and **constitutional writings:** for example, Magna Carta (1215), and Walter Bagehot's book *The English Constitution* (1867). These are not legally binding, but are very influential.
- **Conventions:** these are unwritten customs which are traditionally regarded as binding, but which have no legal force; for example, the practice that the queen chooses, as Prime Minister, the leader of the majority party in the House of Commons. Some of the most important rules of the UK constitution are simply conventions, not laws.

key term...

Conventions Unwritten customs which are traditionally regarded as binding, but which have no legal force.

analyse this...

Some key conventions of the UK constitution
The tradition that the queen chooses, as Prime Minister, the leader of the majority party in the House of Commons . . .
It is law that the monarch appoints the Prime Minister and, according to law, she could choose anyone (such as the leader of Her Majesty's Opposition, the Leader of the Liberal Democrats, or her gardener) but the government is granted some democratic legitimacy if the head of government also heads the majority party in the elected House of Commons – if there is a majority party. All of the powers of the Prime Minister, by law, largely still belong to the monarch, but have by convention passed to the Prime Minister – again, to give them democratic legitimacy.

The very existence, structure and powers of the cabinet . . .
The doctrines of collective and individual ministerial responsibility (explained in Chapter 7), by which government ministers should resign if they cannot publicly defend their own government policies, or if they make mistakes.

The concept of parliamentary sovereignty (see below) . . .
This only exists because UK judges have always accepted that the will of the elected House of Commons should prevail over that of the non-elected judges.

The above illustrate the fact that some of the most important and 'democratic' rules of the UK political system do not have the force of law, but are merely long-standing customs and practices – highlighting the potential danger that they can, quite easily, be bent or broken.

Questions
a   What is meant by 'conventions' of the constitution?
b   What may be the benefits of conventions over laws?
c   What may be the disadvantages or dangers of conventions?

---

key term...

Unconstitutional action An action which breaks any part – that is, any rule – of the constitution.

key term...

Manifesto Booklet of policy proposals issued by every party before each general election.

An action is **unconstitutional** if it breaks any part – that is, any rule – of the constitution. This usually refers to government action. A government action or decision may break a law and be ruled illegal in the courts – *ultra vires* (Latin for 'beyond their legal powers'): for example, in 2004 the Law Lords ruled that the indefinite detention of foreign terror suspects without any charge or trial was illegal. In 2010 the government called a halt to random police stops and searches, following a ruling by the European Court of Human Rights (ECHR).

Alternatively, an unconstitutional action may break a convention rather than a law: for example, in 1998, Labour Prime Minister Tony Blair appointed his friend the Scottish media tycoon, Gus MacDonald, as a junior industry minister in his government, although MacDonald was neither an MP nor a peer. This breached the important convention that government ministers should be chosen from within Parliament so as to give them democratic legitimacy. In another example: the 2010 coalition government has broken some key pre-election pledges – such as on raising student tuition fees, despite a promise to the contrary in the Liberal Democrat party's **manifesto** (that is, its booklet of policy proposals issued before the general election). However, manifesto promises – like many of the important rules of the UK constitution – are not legally binding, and are especially problematic for a coalition government which must, necessarily, make compromises. It is therefore often hard to know what *is* 'unconstitutional'.

It is even possible that a rule of the constitution may, itself, break the 'spirit', if not the letter, of the constitution. Acts of Parliament are laws which, by definition, add to the rules of the constitution. However, a series of new laws on anti-terrorism, law and order and asylum seekers that have been passed since 2000 are – though perfectly legal – very illiberal and potentially constraining of civil liberties. A prime example is the Anti-Terrorism, Crime and Security Act 2001, which allowed for the indefinite detention without charge or trial (i.e. internment) of foreign terror suspects. Many critics regard such laws as undermining the basic principles of British liberal democracy.

Another problem with the UK's unwritten constitution is that, because it derives from so many different sources and types of rules – which have developed, piecemeal, over many centuries – the rules may, sometimes, be downright contradictory. Here are two examples:

- According to eminent (this usually means dead) constitutional commentators, such as A.V. Dicey (1835–1922), the 'twin pillars' of the British constitution are 'the rule of law' – the principle that everyone is equal under the law – and 'parliamentary sovereignty' – the principle that Parliament is above the law.
- A second example: in British elections for the Westminster Parliament, voters choose one local MP to represent a single geographical area (a 'constituency') and voters are, therefore, said to have a one-to-one, personal relationship with that MP. For this reason, if an MP defects from one political party to another between general elections, no new election is held – on the grounds that the electorate voted for the person and not for the party label. However, a conflicting principle of the UK constitution is the 'doctrine of the mandate'. This is the idea that the winning party at a general election has been granted the authority – mandate – by the voters, to govern according to the promises in its manifesto. This theory rests on the assumption that the electorate are voting *not* for the individual candidate but for a party label and package of party proposals. Two wholly contradictory principles are at work here.

The British constitution is thus, in many ways, uncertain, inconsistent and even unknowable. This is a problem for a political system which claims to be a liberal democracy operating within clear and enforceable rules.

The British constitution is also **flexible** (or '**unentrenched**'), i.e. it requires no special procedures for amendment, but can be changed by an ordinary Act of Parliament. This means that even a major change to the British political system – such as the abolition of the monarchy – could be implemented by a one-vote majority in the House of Commons (in the same way as any minor change, such as a law on littering). Thus, there is no distinct or higher body of constitutional law. A **rigid** (or '**entrenched**') constitution, by contrast, requires a special process for change: for example, the US constitution requires two-thirds of Senate and House of Representatives' votes, plus three-quarters of all of the state legislatures' (law-making assemblies); and the Irish constitution legally requires a referendum for major change. Because an entrenched constitution is based upon a distinct and 'higher' body of law, it is also 'judiciable': that is, any disputes about its meaning are decided by the judiciary rather than by the politicians in a Parliament.

Note that a constitution may be written but *also* flexible, e.g. New Zealand's, and thus there is no necessary connection between these two concepts. The British constitution is rare in being both unwritten and flexible.

Codified constitution (e.g. USA)	Uncodified constitution (e.g. UK)
Written	Unwritten
Rigid/entrenched	Flexible/unentrenched
Higher law	Ordinary law
Judiciable	Non-judiciable

The British constitution is also **unitary**: that is, it has one sovereign legislature – namely, the UK Parliament at Westminster, which has ultimate legal authority

key term...

Mandate The authority of the government, granted by the voters, to govern according to the promises in their manifesto.

key term...

Flexible/unentrenched constitution A constitution which requires no special procedures for amendment, but can be changed by an ordinary Act of Parliament.

key term...

Rigid/entrenched constitution A constitution which requires a special legal process for change.

key term...

Codified constitution A written, entrenched constitution which has the status of higher law and is judiciable.

key term...

Uncodified constitution An unwritten, unentrenched constitution which has the status of ordinary law and is non-judiciable.

key term...

Unitary constitution A constitution of a state with one sovereign legislature which has ultimate law-making power and authority over all other bodies within the state.

over all other bodies within the UK. Although there are local government councils and there are now also national parliaments throughout the UK, these bodies are still subordinate to the central, sovereign, Westminster Parliament; and their existence and powers are wholly determined by the Westminster Parliament, which can limit the powers of the local or national bodies or, indeed, abolish them altogether at any time. (This does not mean that the law must be exactly the same throughout the whole of the UK; but differences – for example, between the Scottish and English laws on university tuition fees – are only those allowed, or ordered, by Westminster.)

This unitary system contrasts with a **federal** constitution such as that of the USA or Australia, where the state executive and/or legislative bodies have strong and autonomous powers within their own defined areas of responsibility. The centre has decision-making power over matters such as national security, defence and foreign affairs, but it cannot impose on the powers of the state bodies – nor vice versa. The central and state power bodies are, in theory, equal and autonomous, and there are mutual checks and balances between them. A federal system is, therefore, more decentralised.

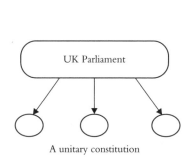

A unitary constitution   A federal constitution

Figure 2.1   Types of constitution

Questions...

2.1 What is an uncodified constitution?   *(5 marks)*

2.2 What are the main sources of the UK constitution?   *(10 marks)*

2.3 Why has the UK constitution been criticised?   *(25 marks)*

Note: The best technique is *not* to make a few points at length but, rather, to make several points in a very precise and concise way, adding real, topical examples to illustrate each point.

Try it!

In theory therefore, the British constitution is unwritten, flexible and unitary. In practice – *de facto* – however, all of these features are changing.

The British constitution is, in practice, becoming more written and legally codified: mainly because of the growing quantity and impact of EU laws and regulations, which take legal precedence over all other sources of the UK constitution; and also because of the large number of constitutional reforms introduced by law within the UK since 1997 – such as devolution, reform of the House of Lords and the introduction of a UK Human Rights Act. This trend will continue.

Again, in practice rather than theory, the British constitution is gradually becoming more rigid or entrenched as the principle becomes increasingly accepted and expected that referenda (direct votes by the people) should be held on issues of major political change such as devolution and electoral reform. Although, in theory, such referenda in the UK are invariably merely 'advisory', so as to maintain the semblance of 'parliamentary sovereignty' (see later), no government could, in reality, ignore a referendum result.

Finally, the unitary nature of the UK is already challenged by the power of the EU over the UK Parliament; and it is likely to come under more challenge from below as the Scottish Parliament and the Welsh and Northern Ireland assemblies become more established and assertive in their roles.

The British system of government

Back to our analogy of a football game. If it is to be understood and played successfully, it needs rules, it needs officials to implement those rules fairly and consistently – raising and spending money in the process – and it needs a referee or association to enforce the rules if they are broken. Similarly, any state has three branches:

- A **legislature**, which makes the laws.
- An **executive**, which implements the laws and policies.
- A **judiciary**, which interprets and enforces the laws.

The UK executive, or government, decides and carries out the policies by which the country is run – whether that means raising taxes, cutting welfare benefits, imposing university tuition fees or going to war. However, all of these policies must be lawful. Therefore, every year the government must submit its new policy proposals to the legislature to be passed into law. If Parliament – the legislature – defeats a government Bill (draft law), the government cannot implement that policy.

> **key term...**
>
> **Legislature** The branch of state responsible for the making of laws (or 'legislation').

> **key term...**
>
> **Executive** The branch of state responsible for running the country through the execution and administration of laws and policies; often also called the 'government'.

> **key term...**
>
> **Judiciary** The branch of state responsible for the interpretation and enforcement of the laws – that is, the judges.

Legislature	Executive	Judiciary
Parliament	*Government*	*Courts*
Crown	Crown	Crown
House of Lords	Prime minister	Judges
House of Commons	Cabinet	Magistrates
	Junior ministers	
	Civil service	
	(Local government)	

Figure 2.2   The British system of government

key term...

Bicameral legislature A legislature with two houses or 'chambers'.

talking point...

In the UK, the legislature is called 'Parliament' and it has two houses or 'chambers', the House of Commons and the House of Lords; thus it is a **bicameral legislature**. The Lords is a wholly unelected House – an extreme rarity in twenty-first-century liberal democratic politics.

In the USA, the legislature is called 'Congress' and it also has two chambers, the House of Representatives and the Senate – both elected.

In Russia, the legislature also has two chambers, the State Duma and the Federation Council – again, both elected.

States such as Denmark and Sri Lanka, by contrast, are 'unicameral' – that is, their parliaments have only one (elected) chamber. The Scottish Parliament is also unicameral.

What advantages or disadvantages might arise from a bicameral system?

key term...

Separation of powers Non-overlapping personnel and powers of the legislature, executive and judiciary.

If the three branches of state – legislature, executive and judiciary – are completely united, the system may be a tyranny. Liberal democratic theory advocates the **separation of powers** – non-overlapping personnel and powers of the legislature, executive and judiciary – in order to ensure checks and balances between the different parts of the system and hence more freedom for the citizen. The United States has a substantial degree of separation between the legislature (Congress), the executive (president and cabinet), and the judiciary. Britain, however, does not practise extensive separation of powers.

Contrasting structures of government

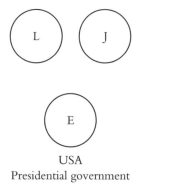

USA
Presidential government

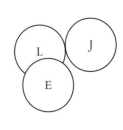

UK
Parliamentary government

Figure 2.3 Contrasting structures of government

The main overlap in the British system is between the legislature and the executive. The term **parliamentary government** refers to this overlap between Parliament and government: that is, the executive (government, i.e. Prime Minister and ministers) is chosen from within the legislature (MPs and peers) and is, in theory, subordinate to the legislature.

Step 1

At each general election, the voters elect 659 MPs into the House of Commons, usually on the basis of a party label. Assuming that one party wins over 50% of the seats...

Step 2

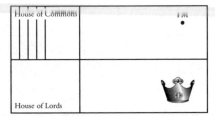

The Queen appoints, as Prime Minister, the leader of the majority party in the Commons.

Step 3

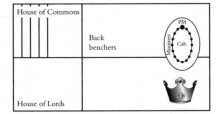

The PM then appoints his/her senior Cabinet ministers, and wider team of junior ministers, from within both the Commons and the Lords.

Figure 2.4   The formation of parliamentary government in Britain

The main example of the government's subordination to Parliament is an important convention of the constitution that, if a government is defeated in a 'vote of no confidence' (or 'vote of censure') in the House of Commons, it should resign. The last time that this happened was in 1979, when Prime Minister James Callaghan's Labour Government was defeated by just one vote in the Commons (rumour has it that one MP refused to come out of the loo to vote!). However, it is important to note that this defeat was inflicted upon a **minority government** with less than 50% of the seats in the Commons. It is highly unlikely that the backbench MPs of a majority government would risk political suicide by bringing down their own leadership in a vote of no confidence.

Government is also responsible – i.e. accountable – to Parliament through Question Time, debates and votes on government Bills, parliamentary committees and financial scrutiny. Thus, through its link with Parliament – and especially with the elected House of Commons – Britain is said to have gov-

key term...

Representative government
Political decision-making reflecting the views, interests and/or typical social background of the electorate.

ernment which is both **representative** – reflective of the voters' views and interests – and **responsible** – that is, accountable and answerable for its actions to Parliament and, thus, indirectly, to the voters.

The United States and many other countries, by contrast, have a **presidential system**. This does *not* (confusingly) refer to the fact that they have presidents and Britain does not. It means that the executive – who is the president – is directly elected by the voters, quite separately from Congress (the American legislature); the president is not allowed to be a member of Congress and he is, in theory, equal (rather than subordinate) to the legislature, with mutual checks and balances between them.

Questions...

2.4 What is parliamentary government? *(5 marks)*

2.5 In what ways does parliamentary government differ from presidential government? *(10 marks)*

key term...

Responsible government
Government accountable to Parliament and the public.

key term...

Presidential system A system where the executive is separately elected from the legislature and the two bodies are, in theory equal, possessing checks and balances against each other.

analyse this...

The UK constitution: reasons for controversy and change

- The long-term dominance of the Conservative Party in post-1945 governments, and hence limited constitutional change until 1997.
- Deficiencies of representative democracy – e.g. lack of proportional representation in the House of Commons, and unelected House of Lords.
- Perceived 'elective dictatorship', especially after 1997 (see below).
- Lack of checks and balances within the UK system e.g. weaknesses of Parliament versus executive, of Opposition versus government, of Lords versus Commons, of Cabinet versus Prime Minister, of local versus central government.
- Improper use of the royal prerogative powers (by Prime Ministers and ministers).
- On-going secrecy of governments.
- Perceived 'politicisation' e.g. of judiciary, civil service, police, church and education.
- Regional inequalities and imbalances, compounded by differential devolution.
- Loss of civil liberties.
- The uncertainty, flexibility and breakability of constitutional rules.
- The impact of the European Union.

Questions

a What is a 'constitution'?

b Why may it be dangerous to have one party in power for very long periods of time?

c Can you think of any reasons why the basic freedoms of citizens might be limited by governments?

Parliamentary sovereignty

Sovereignty is unrestricted power and authority. It applies to a body which can act or take decisions without hindrance from any institution above, below or within it. A body has internal sovereignty if it has the power to make decisions binding on all of its own citizens. A body has external sovereignty if it can control its own affairs without being blocked by outside bodies and states. And, to complicate matters, there are different kinds of sovereignty – for example, legal, political and economic.

key term...

Sovereignty
Ultimate power and authority.

talking point...

Parliament can pass **retrospective law**, that is, backdated law, which may have effect for days, months or years before it was even passed. At its most extreme, this means that Parliament could – in unlikely theory – pass a law which says 'As from now, it was illegal for you to have been walking down that particular road last week. Which you did. You are therefore nicked.' This breaches the principle (in an important theory called the 'rule of law', outlined later) that the law should be 'knowable' at the time that someone is breaking it.

In 1998, for example, retrospective law stopped tax exemptions for overseas earners (which prompted the Rolling Stones to cancel their British tour). Also, after 11 September 2001, Parliament hastily imposed a retrospective increase in the criminal penalty for terrorist hoaxes, from six months to seven years; and in 2003 it effectively abolished the 800-year-old 'double jeopardy' rule – the principle that you could not be tried twice for the same crime – and this change was backdated to apply to people who had been tried and acquitted years ago. The first case in which a man was convicted of murder after having previously (1991) been acquitted occurred in 2006.

key term...

Retrospective law
Backdated law.

In federal states, internal sovereignty is divided between national and local powers; they are, therefore, based upon the paradoxical idea of shared sovereignty. However, the UK is a unitary state. Therefore, perhaps the main pillar of the British constitution is, in theory, the **legal sovereignty** or **supremacy of Parliament**. This suggests that Parliament is the supreme law-making body in the UK, and that no institution in the country can override its laws. Thus no Parliament can bind its successors – that is, any future Parliament may amend or repeal any previous law passed by any previous Parliament. Also, Parliament is not bound by its own laws (statutes), but instead by a special body of law known as parliamentary privilege. (This exempts MPs from some ordinary law; for example, they cannot be sued for slander for words spoken in Parliament.)

Parliament's external sovereignty is now limited in practice by the European Union, whose laws have formal sovereignty over all member states – e.g. fishing quotas, the worldwide ban of the export of British beef (imposed in 1996 and lifted in 2006) and the 48-hour working week. This is the only formal over-ride upon the Westminster Parliament's legal supremacy. In theory, however, Parliament could legislate to withdraw from the EU at any time, and therefore it remains technically sovereign – although, in practice, withdrawal from the EU seems unlikely.

There are also many other, *informal* constraints on parliamentary sovereignty, both external and internal:

- Other international courts and laws, such as the European Court of Human Rights (which, in 2005, ruled against the UK government's ban on votes for all prisoners. This was still provoking controversy in 2012).
- Big business, the City and other economic power bodies, such as the international currency dealers, commodity speculators and credit-rating agencies.
- Pressure groups (e.g. the huge extra subsidies given to beef farmers in the 1990s to compensate them for lost sales due to the BSE crisis; and the Labour Government's decision in 2010 not to privatise the Royal Mail, in the face of strong opposition from the Communication Workers Union).
- The media (for example, most tabloid newspapers consistently urge Parliament to limit the numbers and rights of asylum seekers).

Ultimately, Parliament is constrained by the **political sovereignty of the electorate**, who may occasionally simply refuse to obey the law of Parliament (e.g. the mass refusal to pay the poll tax in 1989/90); and who both choose and remove MPs via the ballot box.

Most importantly, Parliament tends to be dominated, from within, by a 'majority' government (that is, an executive whose party holds over 50% of the seats in the Commons) which, with strong party discipline and backbench support, can usually ensure that its legislative proposals are passed by Parliament. No *majority* government has been forced to resign by a vote of no confidence in the House of Commons since the 1880s.

In his 1976 Dimbleby Lecture, Lord Hailsham (a former Conservative Lord Chancellor) therefore used the term '**elective dictatorship**' to suggest that a majority government, in control of a sovereign Parliament, with a flexible constitution, could effectively change the constitution at will. This argument gained renewed strength after the general election of 1997, when Labour won a massive 179 majority of seats over all the other parties combined in the House of Commons (on a minority of the votes cast – see Chapter 3) and seemed, to

---

key term...

Parliamentary sovereignty
Parliament has supreme law-making power, and can make, amend or repeal any law without challenge from any other UK body or institution.

---

key term...

Political sovereignty The ultimate electoral power and authority of the voters.

---

key term...

Elective dictatorship Lord Hailsham's thesis of excessive executive (government) power, between elections, over Parliament and the public.

many critics, virtually unstoppable. Labour's majority was almost undented in the 2001 general election, but much reduced in 2005, after which it suffered its first ever Commons defeat (on 90-days' detention without charge or trial for foreign terror suspects).

The (rare) exceptions to this balance of power within Parliament are:

- A minority government: e.g. the Conservative government, by 1996.
- A coalition government: e.g. the Conservative–Liberal Democrat coalition 2010. (Within its first six months in office, this government suffered 59 backbench rebellions out of its first 110 votes in the Commons; though none of these amounted to an outright defeat, the government was persuaded to make U-turns on, for example, providing money for school sports and free school books.)
- A successful backbench revolt against a majority government: e.g. in 2005, MPs blocked the Labour government's attempt to introduce 90-days' detention without charge or trial for foreign terror suspects.
- Defeat by the House of Lords: e.g. peers in 2008 blocked the Labour government's attempt to introduce 42 days' detention without charge or trial for foreign terror suspects.

Questions...

2.6 Outline the main principles of the constitution. *(20 marks)*

2.7 Examine the weaknesses of having an unwritten constitution. *(20 marks)*

Recent reforms of the UK constitution

Labour's constitutional reforms 1997–2010

A wide-ranging series of constitutional reforms under three successive Labour governments amounted to the most significant changes to the UK constitution in recent political history.

Democracy
- Greater use of referenda.
- New, often proportional electoral systems for the devolved assemblies, the European Parliament and local mayors.
- The Political Parties, Elections and Referendums Act 2000, which regulated party funding and spending, and created an independent Electoral Commission to regulate elections and referenda.

Parliament
- The removal of all but 92 hereditary peers from the Lords (1999).
- Reform of Prime Minister's Question Time and the timetable of the House of Commons.
- Independent Parliamentary Standards Authority created (2009) to supervise MPs' expenses.

Devolution
- Election of select committee chairs by backbenchers, and creation of a Backbench Business Committee (2010).
- A Scottish Parliament with primary legislative and tax-varying powers (1999).
- A Welsh Assembly with secondary legislative and executive powers (1999).
- Power-sharing institutions in Northern Ireland following the 1998 Good Friday Agreement: a Northern Ireland Assembly with primary legislative powers.

Local government
- An elected Mayor and London Assembly for London, and elected mayors in other towns and cities.

Executive
- Independence granted to the Bank of England (1997).
- Civil Service ethics protected by statute (2010).

Judiciary
- Effective abolition of the office of Lord Chancellor.
- Independent appointments process for senior judges
- Separation of the Law Lords from the House of Lords and creation of a Supreme Court (2009).

Rights
- Opting in to the EU Social Chapter.
- The Human Rights Act 1998, which incorporated the European Convention on Human Rights into UK law.
- The Freedom of Information Act 2000.

Each of these recent reforms will be explained and analysed in future chapters. The list above contains only the proclaimed and 'progressive' changes enacted by the Labour governments from 1997 to 2010. Other changes perceived by (often critical) observers during that time – such as the centralisation of the executive, the politicisation of the civil service, former Prime Minister Blair's '**presidentialism**' and growing curbs on the civil liberties of UK citizens – were perhaps equally real, but less legitimate, examples of changes to the UK constitution.

key term...

Presidentialism A style of government leadership (often attributed to former Prime Minister Tony Blair) that is populist and personalised, aloof from Cabinet and dismissive of Parliament.

Coalition government's constitutional reform proposals since 2010:

Democracy
Referendum on Alternative Vote electoral system for the House of Commons (2011).
Elected police commissioners.

Parliament
Upper chamber mainly elected, by PR.
Fixed-term Parliaments.
Reduction in number of MPs from 650 to 600.
Equalisation of constituency sizes.
Recall by voters of MPs found guilty of serious misconduct.

Devolution
Further devolution of powers to the Scottish Parliament.
Referendum on further devolution in Wales.

EU
'Referendum lock' on any treaty transferring power to EU.

On the one hand, the constitutional and political reforms enacted since 1997 are the most far-reaching in many decades. On the other hand, they have been piecemeal, sometimes contradictory and often motivated by the vested party interests of all three main parties.

Also, some of the 2010 coalition government's proposals have been obstructed: fixed-term Parliaments and elected police commissioners were – at least temporarily – rejected by the Lords in 2011; and the national referendum on the Alternative Vote for Westminster elections was roundly defeated.

A more far-reaching and genuinely 'liberal democratic' programme of reforms might include:

- A codified constitution.
- An entrenched Bill of Rights.
- Proportional representation for the House of Commons.
- A fully elected upper chamber.
- Federalism across the UK, including legislative assemblies for England.
- More frequent use of referenda, subject to clear rules.
- Stronger local government.
- Reform or abolition of the monarchy.

The case for a codified constitution

- A document of written rules would be more knowable, accessible and educative.
- A document of legal rules would be more enforceable.
- A special legal process for changing the rules would make them less flexible and changeable, especially by an 'elective dictatorship' to suit its own interests.
- Independent and impartial judges would be the ultimate guardians of the constitution, rather than self-interested and short-sighted politicians.
- The rights of citizens would be better protected by an entrenched Bill of Rights.

Case against a codified constitution

- An unwritten constitution allows for more natural and organic evolution.
- A flexible constitution allows for easier adaptation to changing times and circumstances.
- Elected and accountable politicians are the ultimate arbiters of the constitution, rather than unelected and unaccountable judges.
- There is no agreed process for creating a codified constitution.
- There is no consensus on the content of a codified constitution.

Questions...

2.8 What is meant by 'sovereignty'? *(5 marks)*

2.9 What is meant by calling British government 'parliamentary government'? *(5 marks)*

2.10 Define the word 'control' in the phrase 'parliamentary control of government'. *(5 marks)*

2.11 What is meant by 'the rule of law'? *(5 marks)*

True or false?

1. In Britain, the law is made by the judiciary.
2. A constitution is basically a set of rules.
3. In a state, the government is often referred to as 'the executive'.
4. In Britain, the government is the legally sovereign body.
5. Governments are required by law to fulfil their manifesto promises.
6. Parliament could pass a law abolishing the monarchy by the same procedure as it can pass any other Bill.
7. In the UK, certain people can be imprisoned indefinitely without charge or trial.
8. England has its own Parliament.
9. British voters directly elect the Prime Minister.
10. If a constitution is written, it must also be rigid.

Quiz

Say what is wrong with each of the following statements, and why.

1. The legislature – Parliament – is elected by the people.
2. The two elements in 'parliamentary government' are the House of Commons and the House of Lords.
3. In parliamentary government, the executive is elected from the majority party in the legislature.
4. In parliamentary government, the Cabinet and ministers are taken from the House of Commons.
5. The legislature is often, in theory, subordinate to the executive.
6. The British constitution is unwritten, therefore flexible.
7. The British constitution is flexible, therefore Britain has no constitutional laws.
8. A minority government has a minority of the votes but a majority of the seats.
9. A coalition government is where two or more parties have merged to form a single governing party.
10. A manifesto is what the government proposes to do, and the mandate is what it actually does when it gets in.

Answers to questions

Note: The following are notes for guidance only and are not intended to be taken as model answers.

2.1   *What is an uncodified constitution?*   *(5 marks)*

An uncodified constitution is a set of rules by which a state is governed but which is not contained in a single legal document. Instead, the rules derive from many different sources – some written, some not, some with the force of law, some not. This type of constitution is also unentrenched, that is, it can be changed by the ordinary parliamentary process rather than requiring a special process such as a referendum. Hence there is no higher body of constitutional law, and thus it is also non-judiciable. The UK has an uncodified constitution.

2.2 *What are the main sources of the UK constitution?* *(10 marks)*

Many – but not all – of the rules of the UK constitution are laws, that is, rules of state which are enforceable by the courts and judges. There are, in turn, several different types of law:

- European Union law (since the UK joined the EU in 1973); this takes precedence over UK law, e.g. on fishing quotas.
- Acts of Parliament (statute law), e.g. the Voting System and Constituencies Act 2011, which paved the way for the referendum on electoral reform for Westminster.
- Common law: ancient, unwritten law, for example, the powers of the Crown.
- Case law (judge-made law): judicial interpretations of common and statute law, in new court cases, which then set a precedent for future cases – e.g. recent UK privacy rulings.

Other rules of the constitution are not laws but may still be very important:

- Conventions: these are unwritten customs which are traditionally regarded as binding but which have no legal force; for example, the practice that the monarch chooses, as Prime Minister, the leader of the majority party in the House of Commons. Some of the most important rules of the UK constitution are simply conventions, not laws.
- Historical documents and constitutional writings: for example, Magna Carta (1215) and Walter Bagehot's book *The English Constitution* (1867). These are not legally binding, but are very influential.

2.3 *Why has the UK constitution been criticised?* *(25 marks)*

- The rules are often unclear and uncertain, even unknowable.
- The rules may be contradictory.
- The rules are often too bendable and breakable.
- An uncodified constitution is an ineffective check on the government of the day and thus may allow an over-powerful government to develop – what Lord Hailsham called an 'elective dictatorship'.
- An uncodified constitution is an ineffective protector of citizens' rights and freedoms.

Note: Topical examples should be given to illustrate all of these points.

2.4 *What is parliamentary government?* *(5 marks)*

In a system of parliamentary government, the executive – government – is chosen from within the legislature – Parliament – and is, in theory, subordinate and accountable to the legislature. Thus the legislative and executive branches of the state are fused rather than separate, and government takes place through Parliament. The UK is a parliamentary system.

2.5 *In what ways does parliamentary government differ from presidential government?* *(10 marks)*

In a presidential system there is clear separation of powers, functions and personnel between the legislature and the executive. Members of the executive cannot, at the same time, be members of the legislature. The head of government is separately and directly elected by the voters and is directly accountable to the voters. The legislature cannot normally dismiss the executive, nor can the executive dissolve the legislature. In a parliamentary system, by contrast, Parliament can dismiss the government by a vote of no confidence, and the government can dissolve Parliament by calling a general election. Executive power is exercised collectively in a cabinet system, whereas in a presidential system executive power is concentrated in the office of President and the members his 'cabinet' are mere advisers. In a pure presidential system, such as in the USA, the head of government – the president – is also head of state. In a parliamentary system, however, the head of government is a Prime Minister (appointed from within Parliament) and the head of state is a hereditary monarch (e.g. the UK) or elected president (e.g. Ireland), often with largely ceremonial functions.

2.6   *Outline the main principles of the constitution.*   *(20 marks)*

Principles include: parliamentary sovereignty, the rule of law (see question 2.11 below) and representative democracy. Also the uncodified – unwritten, flexible and unjudiciable – nature of the constitution and its unitary and parliamentary (versus presidential) nature.

2.7   *Examine the weaknesses of having an unwritten constitution.*   *(20 marks)*

Weaknesses include: no clear, easily understood or accessible statement of the powers, functions and duties of the various institutions of the state or government, or of the rights of the citizen; even fundamental and hard-won features of the constitution can be changed relatively easily; the rules can be broken quite easily; an unwritten constitution is an ineffective check on the government of the day and thus makes 'elective dictatorship' more likely.

However, statutory changes such as devolution and reform of the House of Lords have helped to clarify the constitution and provide more checks and balances within it; the Human Rights Act and Freedom of Information Act have enhanced citizens' rights; the recent creation of a coalition government precludes the danger of a single-party elective dictatorship; and an uncodified constitution is ultimately controlled by elected politicians rather than by unelected judges.

Note: 'Examine' means that both sides of the question must be evaluated. Topical examples should be given to illustrate all points.

2.8   *What is meant by 'sovereignty'?*   *(5 marks)*

Sovereignty resides in that body which has supreme or ultimate decision-making power. It also implies authority, that is, consent and legitimacy. A state has sovereignty over all individuals and groups within its boundaries. In Britain, Parliament at Westminster is said to have 'legal sovereignty', i.e. it can pass, amend or repeal any law without challenge. In practice it is subject to constraints, e.g. the EU, other international bodies, economic and business powers, pressure groups, the media, and the electorate, which has ultimate 'political sovereignty'. Thus, sovereignty is divided between the state (exercised by the executive), Parliament (which has 'legal sovereignty') and the voters (who have 'political sovereignty'); it is therefore debatable where, or whether, it exists at all.

2.9 *What is meant by calling British government 'parliamentary government'?* *(5 marks)*

In British 'parliamentary government' the executive (that is, government) is chosen from the majority party within the legislature (Westminster Parliament), and the government is therefore dependent on Parliament's support. Hence the government is, in theory, subordinate and accountable to Parliament (unlike in the US presidential system, where the executive is separately elected and is, in theory, equal to the legislature, with mutual checks and balances between the two, and the principle of separation of powers is generally followed). In practice in Britain, the executive tends to dominate the legislature because the electoral and party systems usually produce a strong 'majority' government which can control Parliament from within; Lord Hailsham has described this an 'elective dictatorship'.

2.10 *Define the word 'control' in the phrase 'parliamentary control of government'.* *(5 marks)*

In 'parliamentary government', the executive is chosen from within the legislature (Parliament) and is, in theory, subordinate and accountable – responsible – to the legislature. Parliament is therefore supposed to scrutinise, debate, criticise and check the activities of government, to publicise executive actions, to convey public opinion to government and to authorise the raising and spending of money by government – through, for example, debates, votes, Question Time and parliamentary committees.

The ultimate form of control is a vote of no confidence in the government by the House of Commons, which would (by convention) oblige the government to resign. However, some see parliamentary control of government as inadequate: hence the concept of 'elective dictatorship' (Hailsham) – that is, the excessive power of a majority government over the legislature.

2.11 *What is meant by 'the rule of law'?* *(5 marks)*

The '**rule of law**' (A.V. Dicey, 1885) is a paramount principle of any democratic constitution which seeks to equate law and justice. Its main principle is legal equality: everyone should be equally subject to the same laws – but in the UK, for example, the Crown, diplomats, MPs and, often, the government are not equally subject to the same laws (see Chapter 8). There should also be a clear statement of people's legal rights and duties; fair and consistent trial and sentencing; and no arbitrary law or government. Justice should be an end in itself and always be impartial. However, all of these principles are breached in practice in the UK: for example, by the UK's lack of a codified constitution and by its often ambiguous laws; by the reintroduction 2001–4 of **internment** (indefinite detention of some suspects without charge or trial); by inconsistent sentencing, high legal costs, and by police and judicial 'bias' (see Chapter 8).

key term...

Rule of law A principle which seeks to ensure fair and just law which is applicable to all; thus there should be legal equality, clear, consistent and impartial laws and an independent judiciary.

key term...

Internment Indefinite detention of suspects without charge or trial (introduced in the UK in 2001).

True or false?

1. False.
2. True.
3. True.
4. False.
5. False.
6. True.
7. False.
8. False.
9. False.
10. False.

Quiz

1. Only the House of Commons is elected; not the House of Lords or the Crown.

2. The two elements in 'parliamentary government' are the legislature (Parliament) and the executive (government).

3. The executive is not directly elected; the Prime Minister is appointed by the Crown and s/he appoints the other ministers.

4. Ministers may be appointed from the House of Lords as well as from the House of Commons.

5. The legislature is often, in practice, subordinate to the executive; but always sovereign in theory.

6. There is no necessary connection between an unwritten and a flexible constitution.

7. Britain does have constitutional laws. They are passed in the same way as other laws.

8. A minority government has less than 50% of the seats in the House of Commons; its percentage of the vote is irrelevant.

9. A coalition government consists of two or more parties (either in a 'hung' Parliament where no party has over 50% of the seats, or in a crisis, such as war) – they do not merge to form a single party.

10. A manifesto is the list of policy proposals issued by any party prior to a general election. A 'mandate', strictly speaking, is the authority, or even duty, granted to the government by the electors to govern along the policy lines indicated in the manifesto. *However*, voters rarely read manifestos and cannot pick and choose between specific policies; above all, UK governments invariably win under 50% of the votes cast (see Chapter 3). The authority of government to do anything is, therefore, questionable.

Sample questions

Short

- Define 'parliamentary government'.
- What is an uncodified constitution?
- What is sovereignty?

Medium

- What are the main sources of the UK constitution?
- Outline the constitutional reforms proposed by the 2010 coalition government.
- How have Conservative Party views on constitutional reform changed since 1997?

Long

- Discuss the view that further constitutional reform is needed in the UK.
- How adequate is the British constitution in constraining executive power?
- Discuss the view that the British system of government would be better if there were greater separation of powers.

References

Bagehot, W. (1867) *The English Constitution*, Fontana, London.
Dicey, A. V. (1885) *Law of the Constitution*, Macmillan, London.

Useful websites

www.bbc.co.uk/news
  An excellent, wide-ranging and impartial source for topical news items and archive articles.

www.ucl.ac.uk/constitution-unit
  University College London's Constitution Unit. A leading research centre and source of excellent articles on constitutional change in the UK.

www.re-constitution.org.uk
  The Constitution Society. An independent educational trust and another good source of articles as well as videos about UK constitutional reform.

www.guardian.co.uk/politics/constitution
  The *Guardian* newspaper's website on constitutional reform; source of many topical articles and useful further links.

www.usconstitution.net/const.pdf
  The US Constitution – read it here.

3 Electoral systems and referenda

Aims of this chapter

- To outline the development of the right to vote in the UK.
- To explain and evaluate the different types of electoral system in the UK.
- To evaluate the advantages and disadvantages of proportional representation.
- To outline the factors influencing voting behaviour.
- To outline the results of past referenda in the UK.
- To evaluate the advantages and disadvantages of referenda.

The right to vote

The right of all adults to vote for elected representatives in free, fair, secret and competitive elections is widely regarded as the defining feature of a liberal democracy, such as Britain claims to be. However, even this apparently basic criterion begs questions: for example, who is defined as 'adult'? At present, most people over the age of 18 years can vote in the UK – but 16-year-olds may work, pay taxes, get married and join the army, yet cannot vote. The Liberal Democrats have long advocated giving the vote to 16-year-olds, and the former Labour government began to consider this idea. This was mainly because of falling turnouts in recent elections. In the 2001 general election, only 59% of qualified voters actually voted – the lowest turnout since the 1920s. If voting numbers decline in future elections, this could damage any government's claim to democratic legitimacy.

Even 18- to 21-year-olds were only granted the right to vote in the UK as late as 1969. The gradual extension of the **franchise** (the right to vote) from a very few male property owners dates from the 1832 Reform Act. Those still not allowed to vote are members of the House of Lords, most non-British citizens, under-18s, certified mental patients and people disqualified for corrupt electoral practices such as bribery or dishonesty. An example of an MP disqualified for corrupt electoral practice was Labour's Phil Woolas, who was stripped of his seat after the 2010 election for lying about an election opponent in his campaign literature (the first such case since 1911). All prisoners under sentence were also disqualified from voting from 1870. In 2005, the European Court of Human Rights ruled this blanket ban illegal. The then Labour government chose simply to ignore the ruling; the 2010 coalition government proposed giving short-sentence prisoners the vote, but MPs voted overwhelmingly against giving any prisoner the vote.

For the Westminster Parliament (2011), there are 650 single-member constituencies in the UK: England has 533, Scotland 59, Wales 40 and Northern Ireland 18 (roughly in proportion to their populations). Constituencies are geographical areas, each represented by one Member of Parliament (MP).

The 2010 coalition government plans to reduce the number of MPs to 600. Labour opposed the changes, fearing that the government would 'gerrymander' the boundaries, i.e. manipulate them for party advantage. For example, the Conservative Party set up a special unit at its party headquarters to ensure that no Conservative MP lost out in the boundary changes; and it split the Isle of Wight into two, thus creating two safe Conservative seats out of one.

A **general election**, to choose the entire House of Commons, involving all UK constituencies, must be held when Parliament has run its full five-year term (under the Parliament Act 1911); or when it is dissolved earlier if the Prime Minister of the day calls for a general election; or when the government loses a vote of no confidence. The 2010 coalition government proposed to introduce five-year fixed-term parliaments, with 55% or more of all MPs' votes needed to trigger an early election – partly so that neither the Conservatives nor the Liberal Democrats could force the collapse of the coalition government. To most constitutional commentators, this looked unworkable: 'I simply do not see how such a rule is credible or can be enforced; a majority is a majority is 51%, not 55% or 60% or 80%' (Styles, 2010).

A **by-election** takes place in a single constituency when the MP dies, loses the seat through disqualification (e.g. for corrupt electoral practice or by being granted a peerage – a seat in the House of Lords) or quits for other reasons. By-elections are inevitably used as pointers to the current popularity of the government and other parties but they are, by definition, singular events where factors come into play which do not feature in general elections. Very few seats are 'safe' in by-elections. The Conservatives did not win a single by-election between 1988 and 1997 – a factor which led to the loss of Prime Minister John Major's slim majority by the time of the 1997 general election.

> **key term...**
>
> **General election** The election of all Westminster MPs to the House of Commons at intervals of no more than five years.

> **key term...**
>
> **By-election** An election in a single constituency when an MP dies, loses the seat through disqualification or quits for other reasons.

Question...

3.1 Why is voting behaviour often so different in by-elections from general elections?

(10 marks)

Electoral systems

Of the record low 59% who voted in 2001, only 41% voted Labour – and yet the Labour Party won 63% of the seats in the House of Commons. This was because of the particular electoral system used for UK general elections.

There are many different electoral systems in use around the world, and even for different bodies within the UK. Some electoral systems are designed to produce just one winner (locally or nationally); all votes for losing candidates do no not count – thus, they are 'wasted' votes. These are non-proportional systems. Other electoral systems are designed to produce seats in the legislature which are (more or less) in proportion to the votes cast for each party (locally or nationally). These systems are called **proportional representation (PR)**.

key term...

Proportional representation
An umbrella label for systems of election which produce seats in proportion to the parties' share of votes cast.

Types of electoral systems

Non-PR systems	PR systems (mixed or full)
First-past-the-post	Additional Member System (AMS)
Alternative Vote (AV)	Alternative Vote Plus (AV+)
Supplementary Vote (SV)	Single Transferable Vote (STV)
Second ballot	Party List System (a) Closed/bound or (b) Open/free

Electoral systems used in the UK

System	PR or not	Elections
First-past-the-post	Non-PR	Westminster Parliament
SV	Non-PR	Local mayors (e.g. London)
AMS	Partial PR	Scottish Parliament, Welsh Assembly, Greater London Authority
STV	PR	Northern Ireland Assembly, Scottish local councils
Closed Party List	PR	European Parliament

key term...

Electoral deposit The sum of money required from each candidate who stands in an election.

talking point...

Electoral deposits

These are the sums of money required from each candidate who stands in an election. They are intended to deter frivolous candidates. The danger is that they may deter poor but serious candidates. The deposit is returned to those candidates who win over 5% of the votes cast.

Westminster deposit: £500 per candidate.

European Parliament deposit: £5,000 per candidate.

London mayoral election deposit: £10,000 per candidate.

Political equality, this is not.

First-past-the-post

This is the system used for elections to the Westminster Parliament. It entails one vote per elector in single-member constituencies – that is, one MP is elected to represent a single local area; and the one candidate with the most votes wins the constituency, with *or without* an **absolute majority** (over 50% of the votes cast).

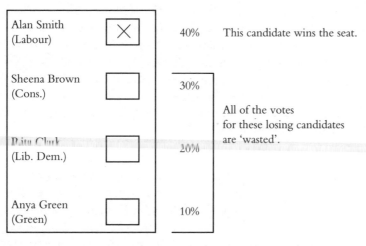

Alan Smith (Labour)	☒	40% This candidate wins the seat.
Sheena Brown (Cons.)	☐	30%
		All of the votes for these losing candidates are 'wasted'.
Ritu Clark (Lib. Dem.)	☐	20%
Anya Green (Green)	☐	10%

Figure 3.1 A first-past-the-post ballot paper: % votes won by each candidate

Advantages and disadvantages of first-past-the-post

The first-past-the-post system is simple, quick and cheap. One person, one vote is a basic form of political equality.

It is said to favour the two-party system, as it usually produces a single-party, majority government and a second, strong opposition party in the House of Commons; hence, strong and stable government which is clearly accountable to the voters. However, this must be qualified: the system produced minority governments – with under 50% of the seats in the Commons – in the 1970s, and a coalition government in 2010; and a two-party system has both advantages and disadvantages – the latter including lack of choice and diversity (especially in **safe seats**, where one particular party is virtually certain to win every time), unfair representation of minority parties and their voters, and a majority-seat government with a minority of votes cast. The rise of the Liberals – now Liberal Democrats – since the 1970s has undermined the two-party system; as have the marked regional differences in party support, e.g. in Scotland, and in northern versus southern England, producing a clear north–south, Labour–Conservative political divide and, critics say, two Britains.

It is also sometimes said that the two-party system created by the first-past-the-post electoral system reflects a 'natural' political divide between conservatism and radicalism. However, the substantial third-party vote since the 1970s belies this argument (35% of votes in the 2010 general election were cast for parties other than the 'big two', compared with just 3% in 1951), as do the substantial policy similarities between the two main parties since the 1997 election.

It is also often said that contact between MP and constituents is closer than in large, multi-member constituencies. In principle there is, indeed, a one-to-one relationship; but, in practice, MPs need not even live in their constituencies, and contact with voters is often negligible, especially in safe seats (though these are now declining as the electorate becomes more volatile). Do you know the name of your own MP?

Crucially, since any vote for a losing candidate is 'wasted', i.e. not directly represented at all in the House of Commons, all votes do not carry equal weight; i.e. the system does not grant one person, one vote, *one value*, and political equality is denied. Voters may therefore be discouraged from voting for minority parties, or from voting at all.

In the 2010 general election, just one third of MPs secured over 50% of the votes cast in their constituencies. This illustrates how no government since the 1930s has had an absolute majority (over 50%) of votes cast across the country, though most have had an absolute majority of seats in the House of Commons. This usually produces a powerful government which the majority of people voted *against* – arguably, an 'elective dictatorship' (to use Lord Hailsham's phrase) of an unrepresentative kind. Opinion polls suggest that around 60% of voters now favour a system of PR.

Table 3.1 Winning parties' votes and seats in UK general elections, 1974–2010

Date	Winning parties	% votes	Overall majority of seats
(Feb.) 1974	Labour	37	−33
(Oct.) 1974	Labour	39	3
1979	Conservative	44	43
1983	Conservative	42	144
1987	Conservative	42	102
1992	Conservative	42	21
1997	Labour	44	179
2001	Labour	41	167
2005	Labour	35	66
2010	Conservative and Liberal Democrat	59	78

Until the 1997–2005 general elections, when the Conservatives were underrepresented in the House of Commons, the two main parties had both been consistently over-represented; while the Liberal Democrats, especially (because of the geographical dispersal of their votes) have been consistently under-represented.

Occasionally, a government may have more seats but fewer votes than the 'losing' party: e.g. the Conservatives in 1951 and Labour in February 1974 (because of unequal constituency sizes and winning margins).

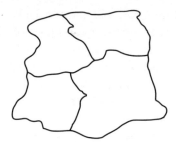

The party with the most *seats* becomes the government –

Although another party may have more *votes*

Figure 3.2 Imbalance between seats and votes

First-past-the-post also creates many safe seats – in effect, little one-party states which rarely change hands and which consequently disenfranchise most voters. A think-tank, the Institute for Public Policy Research, estimated that the 2010 general election result was determined by just 1.6% of voters, that is, the 460,000 whose votes made up the margin of victory in seats which actually did change hands.

Independent candidates (with no party attachment) have very little chance of success. This may exclude quality and diversity from the system.

Finally, in the period of economic boom from the 1950s to mid-1970s, the two-party system was based on 'consensus politics', when the two main parties shared very similar, centrist policies in support of the mixed economy, welfare state, full employment and nuclear defence. This was praised by some for producing moderation and stability, but was criticised by others for its lack of innovation and choice. Conversely, the recessions of the 1980s were said to have produced 'adversary politics' with more right-wing Conservative governments and a more influential left-wing in the Labour Party. The opposite merits and demerits of consensus politics were advanced: namely, more diversity and choice, but also more risk of a 'pendulum swing', i.e. sharp policy reversals between different governing parties.

However, after four successive election defeats, in the 1990s Labour shifted increasingly to the right in pursuit of disaffected Conservative voters. The post-1997 period has witnessed a new kind of political consensus based upon a more right-wing agenda of low taxation and inflation, privatisation of services and authoritarian law-and-order policies.

key term...

Independent candidate
A candidate who is not a member of any political party.

2010 general election

Table 3.2 Voting results in the UK 2010 general election

	Votes	**%**	**Seats**	**%**	**change**
Conservative	10,726,614	36	307	47	+98
Labour	8,609,527	29	258	40	−91
Liberal Democrat	6,836,824	23	57	9	−5
Other	3,518,415	12	28	4	−2

'Other' includes first Westminster Green Party MP (Caroline Lucas).
Scotland: Labour: 41; Liberal Democrat: 11; Scottish National Party: 6; Conservative: 1
Wales: Labour: 26; Conservative: 8; Plaid Cymru: 3; Liberal Democrat: 3
Northern Ireland: Democratic Unionist Party: 8; Sinn Fein: 5; Social and Democratic Labour Party: 3; Alliance: 1; Independent: 1 Ulster Unionist Party: 0
Turnout: 65%
Labour to Conservative swing: 5%

Notes and novelties
- 10 parties in the Commons, and one independent MP.
- 142 female MPs (22%) – including 81 Labour, 49 Conservative, 7 Liberal Democrat.
- 26 ethnic minority MPs (4%).
- 20 openly gay MPs.
- 231 new MPs.
- Average age of MPs fell very slightly, from 51 to 50.
- Over one-third of MPs had private schooling, as compared to 7% of voters; and 90% of MPs were university graduates (versus 31% of the electorate), including over 25% Oxbridge.
- First televised 'leader debates' in UK general elections.
- First hung/balanced Parliament elected since 1974.
- Out: Northern Ireland Democratic Unionist Party First Minister Peter Robinson (personal scandal).Jacqui Smith, Charles Clarke, Tony McNulty, Ann Keen (expenses).Lembit Opik (Liberal Democrat); George Galloway (Respect).
- In: Caroline Lucas (first Green Party MP at Westminster).
- No UKIP or BNP MPs.
- Controversies over voters barred when polling stations closed at 10pm.
- Controversies over lost postal votes (because of the Icelandic volcanic ash cloud) and fraudulent postal votes.

analyse this...

Table 3.3   General election results, 1970–2010

Date	Party	% Votes	Seats	% Seats
1970	Cons.*	46.4	330	52.4
	Lab.	42.9	287	45.6
	Lib.	7.5	6	1.0
	Others	2.2	7	1.1
1974 (Feb.)	Cons.	37.9	297	46.8
	Lab.*	37.1	301	47.4
	Lib.	19.3	14	2.2
	Others	5.6	23	3.6

Table 3.3 (continued)

Date	Party	% Votes	Seats	% Seats
1974 (Oct.)	Cons.	35.8	277	43.6
	Lab.*	39.2	319	50.2
	Lib.	18.3	13	2.1
	Others	6.6	26	4.2
1979	Cons.*	43.9	339	53.4
	Lab.	36.9	268	42.2
	Lib.	13.8	11	1.7
	Others	5.5	17	2.7
1983	Cons.*	42.4	397	61.0
	Lab.	27.6	209	32.2
	Lib./SDP	25.3	23	3.6
	Others	4.6	21	3.2
1987	Cons.*	42.3	376	59.4
	Lab.	30.8	229	36.1
	Lib./SDP	22.6	22	3.5
	Others	4.3	23	3.5
1992	Cons.*	42.0	336	51.6
	Lab.	35.4	271	41.6
	Lib. Dem.	17.9	20	3.1
	Others	5.6	24	3.7
1997	Lab.*	44.4	419	63.6
	Cons.	31.5	165	25.0
	Lib. Dem.	17.2	46	7.0
	Others	8.5	29	4.4
2001	Lab.*	40.6	413	62.7
	Cons.	31.6	166	25.2
	Lib. Dem.	18.3	52	7.9
	Others	9.1	28	4.2
2005	Lab.*	35.2	355	55.1
	Cons.	32.3	197	30.6
	Lib. Dem.	22.1	62	9.6
	Others	10.4	31	4.6
2010	Cons.*	36.1	307	47.2
	Lab.	29.0	258	40.0
	Lib. Dem.*	23.0	57	8.8
	Others	1.9	28	4.3

* = governing party

Questions

a Check the percentages of votes and seats gained by the Labour and Conservative parties in February 1974. Which party became the governing party and why?

> **b** Check the percentages of votes and seats gained by the Labour and Liberal/Social Democrat parties in 1983. How would you explain the discrepancies?
>
> **c** Compare the number of votes cast, and seats won, for the Liberal Democrats in 2005 and 2010. How did they manage to win more votes, and yet fewer seats, in 2010?

Table 3.4   UK general election turnouts, 1945–2010

Year	% of electorate
1945	73
1950	84
1951	83
1955	77
1959	79
1964	77
1966	76
1970	72
1974 (Feb.)	79
1974 (Oct.)	73
1979	76
1983	73
1987	75
1992	78
1997	71
2001	59
2005	61
2010	65

The twenty-first century has been characterised by sharply declining voter turnouts. These call into question a government's 'mandate' (authority) to do anything.

Other non-proportional voting systems

Alternatives to first-past-the-post are many and varied; they need not involve proportional representation.

The Alternative Vote (AV)

Voters list candidates in order of preference; in the count, the candidate(s) with the lowest number of votes are eliminated, one at a time, and their votes are redistributed according to the second choices marked on the ballot papers until one candidate has an absolute majority (over 50%) of the votes (e.g. in Australia). This is the method which Labour used to elect its party leader in 2010. This was the only alternative proffered by the government in the 2011 referendum on

key term...

Majoritarian representation
Electoral system in which the winning candidate must get over 50% of votes cast.

voting reform for Westminster. Despite the fact that it was not PR – and could, indeed, produce even more disproportionate results than first-past-the-post – it was supported by smaller parties such as the Liberal Democrats and the Greens, in the hope that it might be a step towards a more proportional system.

The Supplementary Vote (SV)
Similar to AV: preference voting, but with the voter allowed only *two* preferences; in the count, all candidates except the first and second are eliminated; the losers' second preferences are redistributed and the candidate with over 50% of first and second preferences combined is the winner. This is the system used to elect the London Mayor.

The Second Ballot
Voters vote for one candidate; if no candidate gets 50% of the votes, the candidate(s) with the lowest numbers of votes are eliminated and new ballots are held until one candidate has over 50% (e.g. France). This is the method which the Conservative Party uses to elect its leader.

These three non-PR systems, unlike first-past-the-post, all produce a single winner with *over* 50% of the votes cast. They may, therefore, have more claim to democratic legitimacy than first-past-the-post. However, critics question the legitimacy of a winning candidate's leapfrogging others on the basis of second preference votes; and the repeated votes required under the Second Ballot system tend to produce falling turnouts.

Proportional representation
This label covers a wide variety of electoral systems where seats are won more or less in proportion to votes cast. PR, in one form or another, is used throughout Europe, is advocated by the Liberal Democrats and support for it has grown in Britain since the 1970s – partly because the first-past-the-post system failed in the 1970s to produce majority governments and partly because the increasing third-party vote since the mid-1970s has highlighted the distortions of first-past-the-post. The 1997 Labour Party's manifesto promised a referendum on the issue, but the Labour government did not hold one – presumably because of its landslide victory under first-past-the-post in 1997.

Advantages of PR
All forms of PR are said by supporters to share the same basic advantages: they are more representative of voters' wishes as expressed at the ballot box; fewer votes are 'wasted', therefore greater participation may be encouraged; minority parties are more fairly represented; there are less likely to be 'safe seats' with low turnouts and poor-quality MPs; voters may have more choice and therefore candidates may be of better quality; the two-party system (which may have both pros and cons) is usually eliminated and the end result is more 'pluralist'; and the possibility of single-party 'elective dictatorship' is greatly diminished.

It is sometimes argued against PR that it generally demands more knowledge and activity on the part of voters (e.g. to rank candidates in order of preference), and hence may discourage participation. Conversely, however, voters may welcome the opportunity to be better informed and to exercise greater choice, and turnout may actually increase.

Above all, if there are more than two main parties competing, a proportional allocation of seats to votes will tend to produce a '**hung Parliament**' where no party has over 50% of the seats. The consequences (and pros or cons) of a hung Parliament are not clear-cut. For one thing, a hung Parliament in post-war Britain is rare; and, given the nature of the British constitution, when it does happen the 'rules' are uncertain – e.g. who may be chosen as Prime Minister, which parties should form a government, and when and whether a fresh election should be called. This was manifest after the 2010 general election, when several days of negotiations ensued before Gordon Brown conceded defeat. The result was a Conservative–Liberal Democrat **coalition government**.

However, a hung Parliament need not result in a coalition government. Occasionally in Britain the result has been a single-party minority government with less than 50% of the seats in the House of Commons. For example, from February 1974 Labour under Harold Wilson hung on for eight months as a minority government, boosting its own popularity with pension increases and rent freezes before calling a new election in October 1974 and winning a small overall majority.

The Liberal Democrats argue in favour of coalitions. They prefer to call a hung Parliament a 'balanced Parliament'; they favour centrist coalitions, arguing that these would curb 'elective dictatorship', encourage moderation and continuity, promote greater stability of national direction and policy and therefore be more efficient than the present potential 'swing of the pendulum'. Certainly a hung Parliament usually ensures better attendance in the House of Commons and harder-working MPs, while coalition governments can draw on a wider pool of talent and may be quite stable. Equally, a one-party government may be 'unstable' if it adopts sudden or unpopular policy changes: e.g. John Major's forced withdrawal from the ERM in 1992, and Tony Blair's decision to invade Iraq in 2003.

Disadvantages of PR

The case against these arguments, and against PR, is that no one votes for a coalition; there is no clear authority (or mandate) for compromise politics. Coalition government may also give disproportionate power to small parties and may therefore be as unrepresentative, in its own way, as the first-past-the-post system.

talking point...

The Liberal Democrats came fourth in the Scottish parliamentary elections (behind Labour, the Scottish Nationalists and the Conservatives) in both the 1999 and 2003 elections but they were, nevertheless, in a coalition government with Labour in Scotland from 1999 until 2007. This is sometimes cited as an example of 'proportional representation producing disproportional power'.

Nor is there any inherent virtue in centrism, which, from a critical or radical standpoint, may be seen as stagnation. If the Liberal Democrats' goal of a permanent, centrist consensus or coalition were to be achieved, it could amount to a new form of 'elective dictatorship' and a retreat from pluralism.

It is now necessary to examine the main types of PR individually, because each has its own particular characteristics, merits and demerits; *beware* of over-generalising in exam answers.

Mixed proportional systems

Some electoral processes combine two systems (one PR and one not) in one procedure, in an attempt to produce the best of both worlds. In these arrangements, each voter has two votes and two different kinds of MP are produced – one with a local, single-member constituency and one who is a regional or national representative. Two such systems are described here.

Additional Member System (AMS)

This combines first-past-the-post and PR. The ballot paper has two parts and the elector has two votes. One vote is cast for a candidate to win a seat in a single-member, first-past-the-post constituency. The second vote is cast for a party label, and a number of set-aside or 'top-up' seats in the legislature are filled by non-constituency candidates (additional members) chosen through the Closed Party List PR system (see below) in exact proportion to the votes cast for each party on the second part of the ballot paper. This retains single-member constituencies but also provides top-up proportionality for parties which would otherwise be under-represented by first-past-the-post alone. The Scottish Parliament, Welsh Assembly and London Assembly are elected by AMS on a ratio of about 60% first-past-the-post seats to 40% 'top-up' PR seats.

Alternative Vote Plus (AV+)

This is a novel combination of electoral systems, devised and recommended by the Jenkins Commission in 1998 for future Westminster parliamentary elections. It would combine the alternative vote for 80% of the (single-member constituency) seats at Westminster with 20% of (non-constituency) top-up PR seats to be chosen by a Closed Party List system. This system is not actually used anywhere.

Proportional systems

The Single Transferable Vote (STV)

STV is based on multi-member constituencies. Voters list candidates in order of preference. Any candidate obtaining the necessary quota (*not* necessarily a majority) of first preference votes is elected. (The quota is a formula designed simply to ensure that there are *not* more winners than there are seats available within each shared constituency.) Any winners' surplus votes are redistributed among the other candidates in proportion to the second preferences on the winning candidates' ballot papers and so on until all seats are filled. If too few candidates achieve the quota by that process, the last candidate(s) are eliminated and their votes are redistributed in proportion to the second preferences on their ballot papers. This system is used in Ireland and also for the Northern

Ireland Assembly and Scottish local council elections; and it was long advocated by the Liberal Democrats.

The Party/Regional List system

This is the most common, and purest, form of PR. The elector votes for a particular party list of candidates, and seats are allocated to each party in exact proportion to votes received. The party seats are then allocated to specific candidates (e.g. Switzerland, Israel).

There are two varieties of the party list system:

- **Bound/Closed list:** the elector simply votes for a party label and then the party chooses the candidates to fill the seats. This system was employed in Iraq's first 'free' election (after the overthrow of Saddam Hussein) in 2005. The obvious criticism of this system is that the voter has no say in who are the actual MPs, who are likely to be loyal party placemen. Shortly after it came to power in 1997, the Labour Government introduced the Closed Party List system for elections to the European Parliament, generating protest from some left-wing Labour MPs who feared that they would be frozen out by the process. The House of Lords rejected the closed list system for European elections a record *six* times, but the government pushed the measure through the Commons nevertheless. By 1999, some independent-minded and popular MEPs (e.g. Labour's Christine Oddy, Coventry and North Warwickshire) were pushed so far down the party lists as to be effectively deselected by the leadership, with the voters having no say in the process.
- **Free/Open list:** the elector may have several preference votes, and may vote for many candidates within one party list or even across different party lists. Each party wins seats in proportion to its total votes received, and those seats are then given to the candidates with the most personal votes within each party list. This may be quite complicated, but it allows the voter much more choice, together with very close proportionality.

analyse this...

Table 3.5 Estimated results of 2010 general election using diverse electoral systems (number of seats out of 650)

	% vote share	FPTP	AV	AV+	AMS	STV	Party list
Conservative	36	307	281	275	299	246	234
Labour	29	258	262	234	204	207	189
Lib. Dems	23	57	79	110	114	162	149
Others	12	28	28	31	33	35	78

Zvl y̧ l A̶Ł$ ȷ {vy̧hṣ¥l mẏt ₤Zvȷ p̧ {¢

Questions

   a Calculate the percentages (out of 650 seats) represented by each of the figures above.

> **b** Compare these with the percentage of votes won by each party in 2010.
> **c** Which electoral system is (a) least representative and (b) most representative of votes cast?

Quiz

Briefly answer the following questions.

1. Which system seems to give the most power to the parties in choosing MPs?
2. Which system seems to produce the closest proportion of seats to votes?
3. Which system does not have single-member constituencies? List three advantages and three disadvantages of multi-member constituencies.
4. Which system(s) produce one winning candidate with more than 50% of the votes cast?
5. Which system(s) produce two types of MP, one with a local constituency and one without? Suggest two advantages and two disadvantages of this arrangement.
6. Which system requires the electorate to turn out to vote more than once? Give one advantage and one disadvantage of such a system.
7. Which system(s) allow for cross-voting between parties and/or candidates? Give two possible advantages and two disadvantages of cross-voting.
8. Which system(s) are likely to give more accurate representation to minority parties? Give two advantages and two disadvantages of such systems.
9. Suggest one reason why STV is not purely proportional.
10. List four reforms to the *present* first-past-the-post system (other than the various other electoral systems discussed above) which might make it more 'democratic'.

Consequences of PR in the UK

- More accurate reflection of voters' views as expressed at the ballot box.
- Fairer representation of parties, especially smaller parties – e.g. the Green Party and the UK Independence Party (UKIP) have won several seats in the devolved assemblies and European Parliament. Indeed, UKIP came second in the 2009 European election, with 13 seats. Ironically, the Conservative Party, too, has benefited in Scotland from AMS, although it does not support PR on principle.
- A more pluralist, multi-party system in various parts of the UK.
- Fewer 'safe seats'.
- More frequent minority and coalition governments. In 2010, Scotland had a minority SNP government, Wales had a Labour–Plaid Cymru coalition and Northern Ireland had a five-party coalition led by the Democratic Unionist Party (DUP) and Sinn Fein – the first time that the nationalist parties had ever been represented in all three governments.

- Voting behaviour has become more complex and sophisticated, with split-ticket and often more tactical voting.
- More complex voting systems have sometimes resulted in more spoilt ballot papers – e.g. 146,000 in the 2007 Scottish Parliament election.
- Variable turnouts. Whether low turnouts are due to PR or are typical of second-order elections is hard to gauge.
- More representation for 'extremist' parties – e.g. the British National Party (BNP) won a seat on the Greater London Assembly in 2008, and two seats in the European Parliament in 2009.
- Tensions between constituency and list MPs in Scotland and Wales, where the former often regard the latter as less hard-working and less legitimate.

talking point...

Initiatives allow the voters themselves to trigger a referendum by collecting the required number of signatures in a petition. Many US states and other countries allow such voter initiatives; in New Zealand, only 10% of voters' signatures are required to initiate a referendum.

Recall allows the voters themselves to sack an elected representative between official elections. Again, many US states have recall provisions. Their effectiveness and desirability depend on the precise terms: for example, whether the representatives are deemed to have broken any rules, or whether they can simply be removed by voters who never liked them in the first place. The 2010 coalition government proposed to introduce a recall process for MPs found guilty of serious misconduct, but the details were unclear.

Primaries allow the voters themselves to choose the candidates who will contest the official election. In 'closed primaries', only party members are allowed to vote; in 'open primaries', all registered voters in the constituency are allowed to vote. David Cameron introduced a system of open primaries to the UK for the first time in 2009 (in a by-election in Totnes, where the party sent out postal ballots to all 68,000 voters at an estimated cost to the party of £38,000).

What might be the merits and demerits of introducing such provisions in the UK?

Some factors influencing voting behaviour

Social class and occupation

These have long been the most important influences on voting in Britain. Historically, the wealthier upper and middle classes were more likely to vote Conservative and the working class were more likely to vote Labour, while centrist parties such as the Liberal Democrats have suffered from their lack of class identity. However, there have always been exceptions. Lower-income Conservative voters used to be classified by sociologists either as 'deferential' voters (regarding the Conservatives as superior governors) or as 'secular' or 'instrumental' voters (seeking personal advantages such as tax cuts).

This analysis is now regarded as too simplistic. Since the 1970s, voters have become more volatile and quicker to change sides, and the old class allegiances are weakening – a process known as **class or partisan dealignment**. There are several suggested reasons for this process.

The traditional, manual working class has markedly declined in size, as a result of structural changes in the economy and rising unemployment in the 1980s. Trade union membership has also fallen for the same reasons and, with it, some of the traditional working-class values of equality, collectivism, solidarity and 'old' Labour support. Rising living standards for those in work, together with increasing home and company-share ownership, geographical mobility (often due to the break-up of traditional working-class communities e.g. after coal-pit closures), population shifts to the South and privatised and non-unionised work have also weakened traditional working-class values and voting patterns.

Many workers looked to the Conservatives in the 1980s for promised tax cuts and council house sales. Other key policy issues, e.g. defence, law and order and local government, also caused problems for Labour at that time.

As the Conservative and Labour parties were seen to be polarising throughout the 1980s, growing support for the centre and smaller parties increased the distortions of the first-past-the-post electoral system.

In the 1997 election, as 'new' Labour adopted almost wholesale the Conservatives' tax and spend policies, it won over many middle-class voters for the first time. Since then, the link between social class and voting has weakened further, as both main parties have sought to become 'catch-all' parties with appeal across the classes, and as more voters have deserted both main parties completely. In the 1950s, over 90% of the electorate voted either Labour or Conservative; by 2010 this was down to 65%.

Other important factors also cut across class divisions.

Regional variations

Labour is stronger in inner city areas, and in Scotland and Wales, where the Conservatives won no Westminster seats at all in 1997. The Conservatives are stronger in rural areas and in southern England. These patterns are linked to both class and local culture. The Liberal Democrats have pockets of support in Wales, South-West England and the Scottish Isles and Borders.

Sex, age and race

Historically, women tended to vote Conservative more than Labour, but, by 2001, the figures were identical for both sexes. More young people in 2001 voted Labour: 57% of first-time voters, as opposed to 19% for the Conservatives and 18% for the Liberal Democrats. However, voting turnout is lowest among young people: only 44% of 18- to 24 year-olds voted in the 2010 general election. Surveys of ethnic minorities consistently show around 70% support for Labour, 25% for the Conservatives and 5% for the Liberal Democrats.

Religion

Roman Catholics and nonconformists tend to support the Conservatives less than do Anglicans; but this influence is declining and, again, may be linked

key term...

Class or partisan dealignment
The breakdown, since the 1970s, of long-term patterns of consistent voting for a political party, which were based mainly on social class.

to class. The invasion of Iraq undermined support for Labour among Muslim voters in 2005.

Mass media

TV and newspapers both create and reflect public opinion and can highlight particular political issues (e.g. education, unemployment), party images and personalities as a basis for voting. For several decades the national press in Britain was largely Conservative (hence the *Sun*'s notorious front-page headline after the 1992 Conservative victory, 'It's The Sun Wot Won It').

Uniquely, however, Blair courted and won over the Rupert Murdoch stable – the *Sun*, *The Times*, the *Sunday Times* and the *News of the World* as well as his Sky TV and other international broadcasting media – before the 1997 election. Whether it helped to swing the result or simply anticipated the inevitable is a matter of conjecture. It swung back to the Conservatives before the 2010 election.

Personal experience

Family, friends and work associates can help to shape a person's political opinions; parental influence is particularly strong (and is, of course, linked again to social class).

Party image and party policy

Because of the first-past-the-post and parliamentary systems (when we vote for a single, local MP we are indirectly voting for a national government) electors tend to vote for a party label more than for an individual candidate. Some voters look closely at the parties' past records and present policies; many vote on the basis of a broad party image (united or divided, pro-spending or cuts, pro- or anti-welfare, helping the poor or the wealthy etc.), although this may not always correspond to the parties' actual policies when in power. For example, much is made of the economic 'feel good' factor; but, paradoxically, the economy was in serious decline when the Conservatives won for a fourth consecutive time in 1992, and was recovering well when they lost in 1997.

Party leaders

Growing emphasis has been put upon the image and popularity of the party leaders – especially since the mid-1990s, when the main parties' policies have been quite similar. In 1992, the 'Kinnock factor' clearly put off a significant number of voters, who felt that he lacked stature and gravitas; he was also the object of a sustained campaign of character assassination by the *Sun* newspaper. Conversely, in 1997 Tony Blair was perceived to be leading an increasingly moderate and disciplined party, in contrast to the feuding Conservatives; and he was careful not to repeat Neil Kinnock's over-exuberance and premature triumphalism. In 2001, William Hague was widely perceived as a rather weak leader heading a party which was still divided, old and out of touch. Michael Howard's unpopular record as a Cabinet minister in the Conservative governments of the 1980s and 1990s told against him in 2005. Gordon Brown's perceived character flaws undermined him in 2010.

Abstentions

Qualified voters may choose not to vote for many reasons: lack of information about, or interest in, the election (especially in local council elections, by-elections and European elections; and also in safe seats where campaigning may be minimal and the outcome is a foregone conclusion); dislike of all available parties or candidates, or lack of effective choice (again, especially in safe seats); difficulty in getting to the polling station (though the local parties may provide transport for some voters). In sum, the main reasons are apathy, disillusionment, protest or practical difficulties. The young, the poor, ethnic minorities and the unemployed are the most likely to abstain – or not to register at all – which tends to hit the Labour vote hardest.

This is an increasingly important issue, given the low turnouts for all recent elections. Some new methods of vote-casting are being tried in various parts of the country to see if they encourage higher voter turnout, including all-postal ballots in some regions.

Table 3.6 Summary of key election turnouts, 2001–10

Election	Turnout (%)
General election, June 2001	59
General election, May 2005	61
Scottish Parliament, May 2007	52
Welsh Assembly, May 2007	44
Northern Ireland Assembly, May 2007	62
London Mayor and Assembly, May 2008	45
English local elections, May 2009	39
European Parliament, June 2009	35
General election, May 2010	65

True or false?

1. Democracy has existed in Britain ever since Saxon times.
2. The Reform Act 1832 gave the vote to all men over the age of 21.
3. General elections must normally be held at least every five years.
4. The Prime Minister decides when a general election is to be held.
5. A by-election is held to elect local councillors.
6. Judges and police officers are legally disqualified from voting.
7. In a general election, the winning party is the one with the most votes.
8. A 'coalition' is a government composed of people from more than one party.
9. Only 23% of the qualified electorate in the UK voted Conservative in the 2010 general election.
10. The influence of social class upon voting behaviour in the UK is declining.

Referenda

A **referendum** is a direct vote by the electorate on a policy issue offered by the government, usually in the form of a question requiring a 'yes' or 'no' answer. Switzerland – a very small and decentralised country with only 5 million voters – is the world record holder in the number of referenda which it holds, accounting for an estimated half of the referendum ballots worldwide.

Table 3.7   UK referenda, 2011–1973

Year	Issue	Question	Result (%)	Turnout (%)
2011	UK	At present, the UK uses the 'first past the post' system to elect MPs to the House of Commons. Should the 'alternative vote' system be used instead?	Yes 32.1 No 67.9	42
2011	Wales	Do you want the Assembly now to be able to make laws on *all* matters in the 20 subject areas it has powers for?	Yes 63.5 No 36.5	35.4
2004	English regional devolution	Do you support an elected regional assembly for the North East of England?	Yes 22.0 No 78.0	48.0
1998	Northern Ireland	Do you support the agreement reached at the multi-party talks on Northern Ireland and set out in Command Paper 3883?	Yes 71.7 No 28.9	81.0
1998	London	Are you in favour of the Government's proposals for a Greater London Authority, made up of an elected mayor and a separately elected assembly?	Yes 72.0 No 28.0	34.1
1997	Wales	1) I agree that there should be a Welsh Assembly or 2) I do not agree that there should be a Welsh Assembly	Yes 50.3 No 49.7	50.1
1997	Scotland	1) I agree that there should be a Scottish Parliament or 2) I do not agree that there should be a Scottish Parliament	Yes 74.3 No 25.7	60.4
		1) I agree that a Scottish Parliament should have tax-varying powers or 2) I do not agree that a Scottish Parliament should have tax-varying powers	Yes 63.5 No 36.5	
1979	Wales	Do you want the provisions of the Wales Act 1978 to be put into effect?	Yes 20.3 No 79.7	58.8
1979	Scotland	Do you want the provisions of the Scotland Act to be put into effect?	Yes 51.6 No 48.4	63.8
1975	UK/EEC	Do you think that the UK should stay in the European Community (Common Market)?	Yes 67.2 No 32.8	64.5

Table 3.7   (continued)

Year	Issue	Question	Result (%)	Turnout (%)
1973	Northern Ireland	1) Do you want Northern Ireland to remain part of the UK?, or	1) 98.9	58.6
		2) Do you want Northern Ireland to be joined with the Republic of Ireland, outside of the UK?	2) 1.1	

There have also been many more local referenda throughout the UK in recent years: for example, on whether to introduce a city congestion charge in Edinburgh in 2005 (74% 'no') and in Manchester in 2008 (79% 'no'). These examples highlight one possible problem with direct democracy: that socially beneficial but personally costly policies are too easily rejected.

Advantages and disadvantages of referenda

Referenda provide an element of 'direct democracy' in a representative system (even though, in Britain, they are invariably only 'advisory', so as to maintain the semblance of parliamentary sovereignty). They can be educative, increasing public awareness and understanding of an issue, because all sides are likely to bombard the voters with information and arguments. They help to legitimise the resulting policy decision and to promote consensus on within both the government and the public. Thus they may be used to unify a governing party that is deeply divided on a core issue (as Labour was in 1975 over whether to remain in the European Community – now the EU). In practice, though not in theory, they effectively entrench constitutional changes such as devolution, meaning that no future government or Parliament could simply reverse the policy at will without another affirming referendum of the people.

On the other hand, referenda may result in a 'tyranny of the majority' (or even of a minority, if turnout is low). They may also oversimplify a complex issue by limiting the available options and by reducing voter choice to a simple 'yes' or 'no'. For example, the coalition government's referendum in 2011 on electoral reform (first-past-the-post or AV) was a limited choice which did not include PR at all.

talking point...

Considering what you now know about the many different electoral systems available – including the many possible forms of PR – what do you think about the Labour government's (broken) 1997 manifesto promise of a 'yes/no' referendum on PR for Westminster elections? Could you have given an informed answer to such a question before you had studied the topic? Could you do so now?

Referenda may also reduce voter choice by merging two or more issues in one question – for example, in the referendum on an elected London council and mayor in 1998. Voters may also be subjected to very one-sided campaigns – e.g. in the 1975 European and 1998 Scottish referenda; or to misleading propaganda rather than informative facts – e.g. the 2011 'no to AV' campaign was criticised for overstating the cost of a new voting system. Even the wording of a referendum question may be perceived as 'leading' or biased, although in UK practice this is now unlikely because the wording must be approved by the independent Electoral Commission. The vote may be so close as to call into doubt the legitimacy of the policy; e.g. the 1997 referendum on Welsh devolution was won by under 1%.

Cynics may go so far as to suggest that UK governments will only offer referenda when it suits them and when they are sure that they are going to win – hence the timing of the Northern Ireland referendum. This argument was, however, undermined by the 'no' votes in the 2004 referendum on devolution for the North-East of England and the 2011 referendum on AV – but these raised another possible problem: namely, that many voters may have used the referenda to express their broad dissatisfaction with the government of the day, rather than focusing on the specific issue in question.

In sum, referenda may be used simply to legitimise what governments intend to do anyway, whilst at the same time allowing governments to evade responsibility and to blame the voters for any unpopular consequences. When Irish voters did not supply the 'yes' vote which their government wanted on the EU Lisbon Treaty in 2008, the Irish government simply held a second referendum the following year to achieve the desired result, much to the fury of Eurosceptics. Referenda are also, of course, quite time consuming and costly. In UK practice, if not in law (*de jure*), they undermine parliamentary sovereignty.

Given the UK's flexible constitution, there are no legal rules at all about when and how referenda should be held. In 1998 the Neill Committee on Public Standards recommended that there should be equal state funding for both sides in referenda campaigns and that the government of the day should remain neutral. The government promptly rejected both ideas.

Questions...

3.2 Outline two differences between a referendum and an election. *(5 marks)*

3.3 Describe the circumstances of three referendums held in the UK. *(10 marks)*

3.4 What are the disadvantages of referendums? *(25 marks)*

Answers to questions

Note: The following are notes for guidance only and are not intended to be taken as model answers.

3.1   *Why is voting behaviour often so different in by-elections from general elections?*   *(10 marks)*

- Voters know that they are not voting for a whole new government, therefore their voting behaviour often changes.
- Turnout therefore usually falls quite sharply.
- Local issues may matter more than in a general election.
- The individual candidates and their personalities may matter more.
- Media attention is focused on a single constituency, therefore many more small parties may stand candidates and the voter may have much more choice.
- Voters often use a by-election to register a protest vote against the government.
- Support for third and smaller parties often increases markedly – if only temporarily.

In sum, by-election results are not a good basis for predicting the results of general elections.

Note: Illustrative examples should be given wherever possible.

Quiz

1.   The 'closed'/'bound' party list system.
2.   The party list system (both types).
3.   STV; and the party list system may be based on multi-member, regional constituencies, or may treat the whole country as a single constituency (e.g. Israel).

Advantages of multi-member constituencies:
   a.   Voters have a choice of MPs to represent them.
   b.   Competing MPs may work harder for their constituents.
   c.   Different shades of thinking in one party can be represented by different MPs in one constituency.

Disadvantages:
   a.   Constituencies would probably be larger, less homogeneous and less easy to represent.
   b.   Blurring of accountability between different MPs.
   c.   MPs may work less hard if others are there to do the work.
4.   The Alternative Vote, Supplementary Vote and the Second Ballot systems.
5.   AMS and AV+.

Advantages:
   a.   Non-constituency MPs can concentrate on 'national' issues and on parliamentary versus constituency work (e.g. committees).
   b.   Maintains one-to-one relationship between constituency MPs and voters, whilst also giving a greater degree of proportionality.

Disadvantages:
  a. Non-constituency MPs are not personally elected by voters.
  b. Closed party list element gives greater power to party machines.
6. The Second Ballot.

Advantage: produces one winner with absolute majority of votes, while also allowing sophisticated recasting of votes, or second thoughts.

Disadvantage: prone to apathy and low turnout on second ballot.
7. Alternative Vote, Second Ballot, AMS, AV+, STV, 'free' party list.

Advantages:
  a. More choice for voters.
  b. Allows electorate to vote for personalities as well as parties – may improve quality of representatives.

Disadvantages:
  a. Complexity.
  b. Undermines 'the doctrine of the mandate' – the theory that the link between voters and policies is party.
8. STV, party list and AMS.

Advantages:
  a. Fairer and more representative.
  b. More 'pluralist'.

Disadvantages:
  a. May produce coalitions where small parties have disproportionate power.
  b. May produce fragmented and inefficient legislature.
9. Second and third preference votes are given the same weight as first preference votes; minority parties may have disproportionate balance of power.
10. Initiative, recall, referenda, fixed-term elections, primaries, votes for 16- to 18-year-olds, a presidential system, an elected second chamber, lower (or no) deposits, more devolution . . . and many others.

True or false?
 1. False.
 2. False.
 3. True.
 4. True.
 5. False.
 6. False.
 7. False.
 8. True.
 9. True.
10. True.

3.2   *Outline two differences between a referendum and an election.*   *(5 marks)*

A referendum is a form of direct democracy where qualified voters can vote on a specific policy issue, usually with a 'yes' or 'no' answer. There are no strict rules or laws in the UK about the timing, wording or financing of referenda.

An election, however, is a form of indirect democracy where qualified voters elect parties and/or candidates on a package of issues to make policy decisions on behalf of the voters. There are legal stipulations about timing, financing and procedures.

3.3   Describe the circumstances of three referendums held in the UK.   (10 marks)

In 1975 a referendum was held on whether or not the UK should remain in the (then) European Community – the UK's first national referendum. It was called because Harold Wilson's Labour Cabinet was very divided on the issue. Wilson wanted to stay in but the left-wingers (e.g. Tony Benn) did not. Wilson wanted the outcome to be popular and legitimate, so called a referendum. The convention of collective ministerial responsibility (where ministers must demonstrate public unity) was suspended. All of the main parties and newspapers supported a 'yes' vote, which received a two-thirds majority.

In 1997, two referenda were held on devolution – for Scotland and for Wales. Nationalist sentiment in Scotland was strong (led by the Scottish Nationalist Party) due to the discovery of North Sea oil, the perceived economic benefits of EU membership and the poor treatment of Scotland by long-serving Conservative governments. The Scots were offered both a devolved Parliament and tax-varying powers (+/-3%) for that Parliament. The result was strongly 'yes/yes'.

In Wales, nationalist sentiment was less strong, with the Welsh mainly wanting to preserve and promote their distinctive language. The result was 'the little yes', with just over 50% voting 'yes' on a 50% turnout. The weaker Welsh Assembly – created with no primary legislative or tax-varying powers – reflected this.

3.4   What are the disadvantages of referendums   (25 marks)

The UK is a representative democracy with a sovereign (ultimate law-making) Parliament. Referenda undermine the principle of parliamentary sovereignty; MPs should make decisions as voters have elected them to do – especially according to traditional conservative theory. (Although in theory, referenda in the UK are merely advisory, in practice no Parliament or government could ignore the result.) Referenda also enable politicians to absolve themselves of responsibility for making difficult decisions.

Often, the issues involved are too complex to be reduced to a simple 'yes/no' answer. One example is a possible future referendum on whether the UK should join the euro. It is a complex economic, political and social issue, but much media coverage has simplified it to 'losing the pound' (emotive).

The result is not always decisive, as seen in the very close Welsh referendum in 1997. This undermines its legitimacy.

Too many referenda may result in voter apathy, and hence low turnouts, which distort the results and undermine their legitimacy. For example, the 1998 referendum on whether London should have an elected mayor and assembly had only a 34% turnout. Also, in this referendum, two quite different issues were combined in a single question, which limited voter choice.

Finally, there are no rules or laws in the UK about the holding of referenda. The financing and information (or propaganda) on each side of the issue may, therefore, be very unbalanced – e.g. in the 1975 European referendum, where huge sums were spent on the 'yes' side. In the 1990s, the Labour government was criticised for using state funds to support the campaign for a 'yes' vote in the referenda on devolution. There are no guidelines about which issues are important or controversial enough to warrant referenda (why not moral issues, such as abortion or hanging?). UK governments can hold referenda at whim, when they believe that public opinion is on their side – to legitimise what they want to do anyway.

Sample questions

Short

- Outline *two* functions of a general election.
- Why are marginal seats important under the first-past-the-post electoral system?
- Describe *three* different elections regularly held in the UK.

Medium

- Explain the merits and demerits of 'fixed term' elections.
- In what ways do elections differ from referendums?
- Explain the workings of the Additional Member System and the Single Transferable Vote in the UK.

Long

- Evaluate the arguments for and against the increased use of referendums in the UK.
- To what extent has the use of more proportional electoral systems affected the political processes in the UK?
- Evaluate the case for electoral reform for Westminster elections.

References

Hailsham, Q. (1976) Elective Dictatorship. The Dimbleby Lecture. In: *The Listener*, 21 October.

Styles, S. (2010) senior lecturer, Aberdeen University, quoted at: www.guardian. co.uk/politics/2010/may/12/fixed-five-year-parliamentary-term (15 May).

Useful websites

www.bbc.co.uk/news
An excellent, wide-ranging and impartial source for topical news items and archive articles.

www.electoralcommission.org.uk/elections
The website of the Electoral Commission, an independent body set up by the UK Parliament to oversee and inform people about electoral processes in the UK.

http://news.bbc.co.uk/1/hi/uk_politics/election_2010/default.stm
    A BBC website containing the results, analysis and memorable moments of
    the 2010 general election.

www.bbc.co.uk/news/uk-politics-12913122
    A BBC website containing the results and analysis of the AV referendum
    and elections across the UK in 2011.

www.cses.org
    Comparative Study of Electoral Systems. An international academic
    research forum for comparative electoral studies.

4

Political parties and MPs

Aims of this chapter

- To outline the functions, advantages and disadvantages of political parties.
- To examine the nature of the UK's party system.
- To examine the principles and policies of the major UK parties.
- To outline the organisation and financing of the major UK parties.
- To assess the diverse roles and responsibilities of MPs.

Political parties

A **party** system implies political decision making and representation on the basis of formal, organised groups of (more or less) like-minded people who stand candidates for election on a common policy programme. A party system may contain only one party (which would widely be seen as a dictatorship), or two, or many. A party system, of any type, has merits and demerits as compared with, for example, representation and political decision making by independent individuals. The issues involved include representative and responsible government, pluralism and 'elective dictatorship'.

talking point...

Try to imagine an electoral system where no political parties exist. Instead, voters must choose between a number of independent candidates, each with their own, individual manifesto – probably several thousand of them across the whole country. What difficulties – or advantages – might this present?

Advantages of a party system
- Parties provide the basis for the choice of a Prime Minister and the formation of a legitimate and unified government.

- Parties provide the basis for a coherent and comprehensive body of policies for government.
- Parties organise and crystallise public opinion into coherent blocks.
- Parties educate public opinion through their activities inside and outside of Parliament, and through the media (though they may also try to manipulate and mislead public opinion for party advantage).
- Parties provide effective organisation, financing and campaigning for candidates.
- According to the 'doctrine of the mandate', an elected government is authorised, or even obliged, to implement the policy proposals contained in its party manifesto; the party system is therefore essential for representative government.
- The convention of collective responsibility, whereby government is accountable to Parliament, and hence to the electorate, assumes an executive united around a common body of policy. The party system therefore enhances responsible government.
- The party system provides stability and consistency of government.

Disadvantages of a party system

- A single-party, majority government based on strong party discipline may amount to 'elective dictatorship'.
- Parties may encourage partisan conflict for its own sake, undermining effective government.
- Voters have no choice between the policies of any one party.
- Voters have no say in the parties' candidates (though 'open primaries' could be introduced, as held in the USA and, very occasionally, by the Conservative Party).
- The party system discourages close, personal contact between MPs and voters.
- The party system undermines MPs' independence and individualism.
- The national or local party machines may have excessive power (e.g. over MPs) at the expense of the voters.
- The party system may permanently exclude some minority views, or may neglect important issues which cut across orthodox party lines (e.g. moral issues such as abortion or capital punishment).
- The party system excludes able independents.

Party methods

In their search for political power – or, for most small parties, mere political support and publicity – parties employ many diverse methods, including:

- Recruiting members.
- Compiling an ideological platform and an election manifesto (a booklet of policy proposals).
- Seeking finance, through membership fees and donations.
- Campaigning, through public meetings, posters and leaflets, door-to-door canvassing, use of the mass media, internet and opinion polls.
- Putting up candidates for election, whether at central or local level.
- Seeking a 'mandate' to govern – see below.

talking point...

The doctrine of the mandate is a theory which gives the winning party the authority, granted via the ballot box, to implement its manifesto proposals. It is thus intended to underpin representative and responsible party government. Problems:

- No party since 1935 has won 50% of votes cast, which calls into question the real extent of any government's authority.
- Very few voters ever read the parties' manifestos.
- A manifesto is a 'job lot' – voters cannot pick and choose between the policies contained in it, though not all of them may be popular. For example, the Conservative government's infamous poll tax of the 1980s was in the election manifesto but was hugely unpopular and eventually contributed to Prime Minister Margaret Thatcher's downfall.
- Manifesto wording may be ambiguous – often deliberately.
- The doctrine of the mandate imposes no legal obligation on any government to fulfil its promises.
- Changing political or economic circumstances may require changing policies and, hence, beneficial breaches of the mandate. Hence the broader concept of a 'doctor's mandate', which grants a government authority to do whatever it believes to be necessary for the country's welfare and security. This may be perceived by critics as a 'blank cheque'.
- The doctrine of the mandate is barely relevant to a coalition government, which must, of necessity, compromise on diverse manifesto promises. (The 2010 coalition government produced a detailed Coalition Agreement document a couple of weeks after the election – in effect, a post-election manifesto, with no electoral mandate.)

How valid or useful is the doctrine of the mandate in modern UK politics?

The UK party system

talking point...

There are currently ten parties in the House of Commons (including the Scottish and Welsh Nationalists and the Northern Ireland parties), and about 140 'parties' stood candidates in the 2010 general election. Many of them, of course, were very small groups indeed – often, in reality, pressure groups pursuing a single cause and standing candidates merely for publicity. Some of them, as you can probably guess from their labels, were rather frivolous – but even these serve a valuable function in a pluralist democracy by providing a channel for political participation and protest.

Table 4.1 The major and minor parties taking part in the 2010 general election

Parties with one or more MPs in the House of Commons

Conservative	Alliance Party
Labour	Green Party of England and Wales
Liberal Democrats	Sinn Fein
Plaid Cymru	Social Democratic and Labour Party
Scottish National Party	Ulster Democratic Unionist Party

Parties with representatives in either the Scottish Parliament, Welsh Assembly, London Assembly or European Parliament

Green Party of England and Wales	British National Party
Green Party of Scotland	UK Independence Party

Parties that are registered by the Electoral Commission

21st Century Conservative Democrats
A
A BEE C
Adam Lyal's Witchery Tour Party
Alliance for Green Socialism
Alliance Party of Northern Ireland
B
Beyond
British National Party
British Public Party
C
Christian Peoples Alliance
Church of the Militant Elvis Party
Citizens' Action Party (UK)
Common Good
Community Action Party
Community Alliance
Communist Party of Britain
Community Representatives Party
Consensus
Co-operative Party
Countryside Party
Cymru Annibynnol
D
Democratic Party
Dorset Stop The War
E
England First Party
English Democrats Party
English Progressive & Liberty Party
Englishindependenceparty.com
Equal Parenting Alliance
Esher Residents Association
F
Firefighters Against Cuts
First Democrat Party [The]
Free Scotland Party

Freedom Party
G
Glossopdale Independent Party
H
Havering Residents Association
Hawkwell Residents
Henley Residents Group
Highlands & Islands Alliance – Càirdeas
I
Idle Toad
Imperial Party
Independent Green Voice
Independent Working Class Association
Iranian Civil Rights Committee
J
John Marek Independent Party
L
Legalise Cannabis Alliance
Liberal Party
Libertarian Party
Ligali Party
Local Education Action By Parents
Local Government Reform
M
Mebyon Kernow – The Party for Cornwall
Men's Representative Party
Middlewich First
Molesey Residents Association
Motorists Equity & Unity Party
MP3 Party
N
N9S
National Democrats
National Front
Nationalist Alliance
Natural Law Party

Table 4.1   (continued)

Parties that are registered by the Electoral Commission

New Party

No Candidate Deserves My Vote!

Nork Residents' Association

Northern Ireland Unionist Party

Northern Ireland Women's Coalition

O

Official Monster Raving Loony Party

Operation Christian Vote

Organisation of Free Democrats

P

Pensioners Party

Pensioners Party (Scotland)

People Against Bureaucracy Action Group

Popular Alliance

Populist Party

Progressive Union Party of Northern
     Ireland

ProLife

Protect Rural Scotland Party

R

Real Democracy Party

Reform UK Party

Residents Associations of Epsom and Ewell

Revolutionary Communist Party Britain
     (Marxist-Leninist)

Rochford District Residents

Rock 'n' Roll Loony Party

S

Scottish Green Party

Scottish Independence Party

Scottish Senior Citizens Unity Party

Scottish Socialist Party

Scottish Unionist Party

Social Justice Party

Socialist Alliance

Socialist Environmental Alliance

Socialist Labour Party

Socialist Party of Great Britain

Socialist Party (Northern Ireland)

Southport Party

St. Albans Party

Swindon Org UK Party

T

Thames Ditton/Weston Green
     Residents' Association

Third Way

True English Poetry

U

UKpopdems – popular democrats

Ulster Third Way

United Kingdom Unionist Party

U.K.U.P.

Upminster and Cranham Residents
     Association

V

Veritas

Vivamus

Vote 2 Stop The War

Vote For Yourself

W

Walton Society

Welsh Socialist Alliance

Wessex Regionalists

West Ewell and Ruxley Residents'
     Association

Whitnash Residents Association

Workers' Liberty

Workers' Party

Workers Revolutionary Party

World

www.xat.org

Y

Your Party

Registered parties without known websites are: Alternative Party; Save St John's Wood Adventure Playground; Unrepresented Peoples Party; Welsh Socialist Alliance.

Source: bbc.co.uk/news

There are several possible ways of describing the party system in the UK – and all of them have some validity, depending upon which part of the political system, and which time period, is under scrutiny.

A multi-party system is one where many parties exist and there is a fairly even balance of power between them. Clearly, as shown above, many parties exist in the UK and even within Parliament. There are also clear regional differences in the parties' strengths: for example, in Scotland the Scottish Nationalist

Party is in government. In local government, too, the small parties, such as the Greens and the BNP, do better than at national level. Finally, because of its unique history, there is a completely different party system in Northern Ireland, based upon nationalist and unionist parties. The main British parties, such as the Labour and Conservative parties, usually do not even stand candidates in Northern Ireland.

A two-and-a-half party system is one where two parties dominate but a third party plays a significant role. The Liberal Democrats won 23% of the votes cast in the 2010 general election; they were in coalition government with Labour in Scotland from 1999 to 2007 and are currently in coalition with the Conservative Party at Westminster.

A two-party system is one where, although many parties exist, only two dominate the legislature and have any real prospect of winning government power. The first-past-the-post system of election transforms – or deforms – a multi-party system in the country into a two-party system in Westminster. Until 2010, only the Labour and Conservative parties had formed (single-party) governments since 1945; almost 90% of Westminster MPs are Labour or Conservative; the constitution historically recognises only 'Her Majesty's Government' and '**Her Majesty's Opposition**'; and Westminster parliamentary procedures such as pairing and Opposition Days – and even the two-sided layout of the House of Commons' chamber – assume and reinforce the two-party system.

A dominant party system is one where one particular party is in executive power for significantly longer periods of time than any other party (whether with a small or large majority). The Conservatives, by 1997, had been in power for the previous 13 years, for two-thirds of the post-war era and, indeed, for over two-thirds of the twentieth century. However, three consecutive terms in office for the Labour Party after 1997 – a historic first – modified this pattern.

The main disadvantages of a dominant party system are:

- The governing party becomes complacent, arrogant and even corrupt.
- Government becomes stagnant and runs out of useful ideas.
- Alternatively, government casts around for new ideas for their own sake, which may generate policy instability.
- The Opposition lacks information and experience over the long term, especially in a system as secretive as Britain's.
- Institutions such as the civil service, police and judiciary may become 'politicised'.
- Large sections of the electorate are long excluded from representation by government and may become apathetic or angry; they may turn to direct action. Even supporters of the governing party may get fed up and develop the 'time for a change' sentiment that was so evident in the 2010 general election.

'**Elective dictatorship**' is the phrase used by Lord Hailsham to describe periods of time in the UK when the governing party has such a large majority in the Commons that it can overwhelmingly dominate it and push through almost any decision it wants. Within its first year in office in 1997, Labour had pushed through many unpopular policies which were not in its manifesto, such as lone parents' benefit cuts, disabled people's benefit cuts, students' tuition fees, a five-year public sector pay squeeze and increased taxation of pension funds.

key term...

Her Majesty's Opposition
The second-largest party in the legislature and an official part of the constitution.

Question...

4.1 Distinguish between two types of party system. *(5 marks)*

Principles, policies and organisation of the major parties

The Conservative Party

This is the oldest of the three main parties. Under Margaret Thatcher in the 1980s, it was led by economic **neo-liberals** – the **New Right** – who emphasised private property, the free market, individual enterprise and self-help, and reducing inflation, public spending and taxation (at the expense of employment, if necessary). This ideology was inherited from eighteenth-century 'classical' liberals. Paradoxically, within New Right ideology – known in the UK as Thatcherism – the stress on 'rolling back the frontiers of state' in the economy was combined with a very illiberal, **neo-conservative** agenda of growing political centralisation and authoritarianism, e.g. in law and order, anti-immigration and strict social and moral policies reflecting 'Victorian values'. The New Right tended also to be strongly **Eurosceptic** – that is, hostile to the European Union to a greater or lesser degree. It came to the fore in the late 1970s as a reaction against: the 'consensus politics' of the post-war period (see later); 'excessive' state intervention in the economy – e.g. the many nationalised industries and the welfare dependency of the 'nanny state'; the influence of the trade unions in 1970s politics, perceived by the New Right conservatives as excessive; and the 'permissive society' of lax moral values since the 1960s.

There is also, however, a still older school of more **traditional political conservatives** in the party (e.g. Lord Howe) who emphasise 'natural' hierarchy, social stability and consensus, traditional institutions (e.g. the monarchy, the Church and the House of Lords), the nuclear family and public duty. These 'wets' (a derogatory label coined by Margaret Thatcher) combine traditional Toryism with a Keynesian approach to economic policy, favouring some state intervention, a mixed economy, public spending, welfare and pro-European policies – e.g. Michael Heseltine and Kenneth Clarke. Successive leaders from the 1990s until 2005 (John Major, William Hague, Iain Duncan Smith and Michael Howard) leant more towards the Thatcherite wing of the party, which caused continuous internal party conflict, especially over Europe, and kept the party out of power for many years.

All Conservatives advocate private property, hierarchy, strong defence and law and order.

After the party's 2005 general election defeat, David Cameron was elected as the new party leader, partly on the strength of an impressive party conference speech performed without notes, and partly because he presented himself as a youthful moderniser intent on rebranding the Conservative Party, much as Blair had done for the Labour Party. In his first three years,

key term...

New Right neo-liberals
Economic Conservatives (Thatcherites) who emphasise private property, the free market, individual enterprise and self-help, low inflation, public spending and taxation, and minimal welfare.

key term...

New Right neo-conservatives
Social Conservatives (Thatcherites) who emphasise authoritarian social structures, punitive law-and-order policies and Victorian moral family values.

key term...

Eurosceptics People doubtful about, or quite hostile to, the UK's involvement in the EU and further European integration (largely neo-conservatives).

key term...

Traditional political conservatives Older school of Conservatives who emphasise organic hierarchy, social stability and consensus, traditional institutions (e.g. the monarchy, the Church and the House of Lords), the nuclear family and paternalist public duty.

Cameron determinedly rejected much of Thatcherite ideology, with sound bites such as 'There *is* such a thing as society, it's just not the same as the state', and 'Vote blue, go green'. He vowed to make the party more inclusive and representative, especially by recruiting more women and ethnic minority candidates via a controversial 'A-list'. As a result in the 2010 general election, the number of Conservative women MPs almost trebled. (The number of Labour women MPs was hugely boosted in 1997 by the introduction of all-women shortlists of candidates, but in 2010 the number of Labour women MPs actually fell.)

Table 4.2   Women candidates and MPs, 1983–2010

Year	Conservative		Labour		Liberal Democrat		Total women MPs
	Candidates	MPs	Candidates	MPs	Candidates	MPs	
1983	40	13	78	10	75	0	23
1987	46	17	92	21	106	2	41
1992	63	20	138	37	143	2	60
1997	69	13	157	101	140	3	120
2001	92	14	146	95	135	5	118
2005	118	17	166	98	142	10	128
2010	151	49	189	81	137	7	143

Note: Total of women MPs includes MPs from other parties.

Cameron's early emphasis on policy areas such as the NHS, social justice, constitutional reform and the environment, his 'hug a hoodie' speech in 2006 and his enrolment of Bob Geldof as an adviser on global poverty signalled an attempt to create a more centrist party. Conservative London Mayor Boris Johnson described his own party's leadership as 'the namby-pamby, tree-hugging, solar-powered, bicycle brigade'. However, by 2007 there was more stress on tax cuts, law and order, family values, anti-immigration and Euroscepticism. In 2008, the party abandoned its commitment to matching Labour's spending levels on health and education.

During the 2010 election campaign, Cameron promoted the concept of a 'Big Society', perhaps implying an inclusive social agenda or an active and involved public. His acceptance speech outside No. 10 Downing Street reflected an emphasis on 'compassionate conservatism': 'Freedom, fairness and responsibility . . . We will look after the elderly, the frail and the poorest.'

Once in government, however, the party pursued a neo-liberal economic agenda of £81 billion of cuts in spending, welfare and jobs in order to reduce the national deficit rapidly. In October 2010, even Conservative London Mayor Boris Johnson described the government's housing benefit cuts as 'Kosovo-style social cleansing from the capital'. The 'Big Society' concept was perceived by critics as seeking to substitute government obligations with charity, community, personal and private services 'on the cheap'. Whether this government agenda was an economic necessity or an ideological choice was a matter of political debate and disagreement.

In 2011 Cameron also said in a controversial speech that 'multiculturalism in the UK has failed', signalling a more neo-conservative direction – and perhaps, according to his critics, confusing multiculturalism and extremism.

The Labour Party

Labour, founded in 1900, historically was similarly divided between the more radical left-wing **democratic socialists** (e.g. Tony Benn), who sought extensive collective ownership, workers' democracy, welfare, social equality, greater political participation and political reform (e.g. abolition of the House of Lords), unilateral nuclear disarmament and withdrawal from NATO and the EU; and a more centrist, **social democratic** leadership which favoured 'freedom, fairness and fraternity' in a mixed, mainly private enterprise economy, combined with some state control and planning, welfare and multilateral nuclear disarmament within international bodies such as NATO and the EU.

In 1995, Labour abandoned Clause Four of its founding constitution – the section which advocated common ownership and which was the most sacred totem of 'old' Labour values. This was the most symbolic moment in the shift from 'old' to 'new' Labour, which was pioneered by Neil Kinnock and then John Smith before Tony Blair took over as leader in 1994.

Clause Four of the Labour Party constitution (1918):
This was emblazoned on all Labour Party membership cards until 1995:

> 'To secure for the workers by hand or by brain
> the full fruits of their industry, and the most equitable distribution thereof
> that may be possible, upon the basis of the common ownership
> of the means of production, distribution and exchange
> and the best obtainable system of popular administration and control
> of each industry or service.'

The key phrase here is 'common ownership' – that is, collective or state (as opposed to private-for-profit) ownership of businesses and industries – a central principle of socialism.

By contrast, as then Trade Secretary Stephen Byers said in 1999, 'new' Labour is about 'wealth creation, not wealth distribution'. Blair's 'third way', as he called it, was more right wing than either of the old Labour schools of thought: although it had elements of social democracy within it, it chose largely to continue New Right neo-liberal economic and taxation policies, combined with the 'wet' Conservatives' pro-European stance, a liberal programme of constitutional reforms and an authoritarian stance on law and order, anti-terrorism and immigration.

Senior Conservative Lord Onslow said of the 'new' Labour government in its early days, 'They're buggering up the constitution and ruining fox hunting. Otherwise, it's a perfectly sound Tory government.' Or, as Labour left-winger Tony Benn said in 2003, 'One of the reasons why the Conservative Party is in such a mess is because there is a much better Conservative Party in office.'

This was not wholly fair: there were 'old' Labour, social democratic aspects to the Blair governments' policies, such as the minimum wage; and there were liberal constitutional reforms such as the Human Rights Act; as well as

---

key term...

Democratic socialists Radical left-wing 'old' Labour advocates of extensive collective ownership, workers' democracy, welfare and equality of outcome.

key term...

Social democrats Moderate 'old' Labour advocates of a Keynesian mixed economy and moderate welfare.

key term...

'New' Labour A term used by Tony Blair for the first time at the 1994 Labour Party conference to describe the modernised, more right-wing Labour Party, repositioned to attract more middle-class voters.

Conservative policies on freezing income tax, privatising parts of the public services and pursuing increasingly illiberal law-and-order policies. 'New' Labour was not ideologically coherent but – perhaps for that very reason – it was electorally successful for over a decade.

Examples of 'old' Labour policies enacted by the post-1997 Labour governments:
- Amsterdam Treaty: opted into the EU Social Chapter, e.g. minimum wage.
- Record increases in spending on education and health.
- Goals to eradicate child and pensioner poverty.
- Railtrack 'deprivatised' in 2001.
- Nationalised Northern Rock bank in 2008 – but *very* reluctantly.
- Trade union funding of Labour rose from 30% in 2003 to 60% by 2010.

Examples of 'new' Labour policies enacted by the post-1997 Labour governments:
- 1997 cuts in lone parents' benefits and 1998 cuts in disabled people's benefits.
- Privatisation of air traffic control, the Tote, the London underground etc.
- Private Finance Initiatives (PFIs) in the NHS.
- Top-up university tuition fees.
- Crime and Disorder Act 1998: introduced Britain's first children's jail for 12- to 14-year-olds, curfews for under-10s, electronic tagging of 10-year-olds, etc. Draconian anti-terrorism laws; law on ID cards.
- Radical constitutional reforms: devolution, local government, House of Lords, Bill of Rights, Freedom of Information Act etc.
- Blairite Peter Mandelson's return to government under Gordon Brown in 2008. As he said, '"New" Labour is not dead . . . We have intervened in the banking crisis not to crush markets but to rescue them.'
- 2008 abolition of 10p income tax rate.

In 2007, Gordon Brown's supporters within the parliamentary Labour Party effectively forced Blair to stand down in mid-term and Brown took over – anointed, rather than elected by either the party or the public, and hence, in the eyes of his critics, lacking a personal mandate for leadership. Brown had a good first summer, dealing competently with terrorist car bombings, a foot-and-mouth outbreak and floods; but was undermined by his retreat on holding an early general election, and then by the collapse of the Northern Rock bank, the loss of HMRC computer discs, the 'dodgy donors' scandal, the credit crunch, the abolition of the 10p tax rate, rising fuel and food prices and Labour's disastrous results in the May 2008 local elections. Growing commentary on his leadership style – dour, awkward, private and uncharismatic, indecisive but also autocratic – and his plummeting poll rates damaged the party.

Labour lost badly in the 2010 general election and, after a brief and unsuccessful attempt to form an alliance with the Liberal Democrats in a hung Parliament, Brown resigned. Ed Miliband was elected as the new party leader, very narrowly beating his elder brother, David, after several rounds of preference voting (using the AV electoral system). In the early months he vowed to 'move beyond 'new' Labour'. It was expected that he would return the party slightly more to the left, but there were few clear policy specifics; Miliband himself said, 'We are starting with a blank page.'

Following the election of the Shadow Cabinet in 2010 (Labour MPs in opposition have elected the members of the Shadow Cabinet every two years since the 1950s), Miliband decided in 2011 to scrap these elections, so that in future he could appoint a Shadow Cabinet of his own choosing.

The Liberal Democrat Party

This party emerged out of the break-up of the Social Democratic Party–Liberal Alliance after the 1987 election and the merger of most of its members under the leadership of Paddy Ashdown. It is much the same, philosophically, as the old Liberal Party. It favours a largely private enterprise economy, but with state intervention to promote 'positive individual freedom' through, for example, the provision of welfare, and legislation to promote and safeguard freedoms such as the right to trial by jury and to non-violent protest. Historically, it was the party most enthusiastic about civil liberties and issues of constitutional reform – notably a written constitution and Bill of Rights, proportional representation, devolution or federalism and a democratically reformed second chamber. 'New' Labour stole many of the party's ideas (in limited form). However, the Liberal Democrats' ideas on constitutional reform go further than Labour's, to include proportional representation for Westminster and local authorities, an elected second chamber, elected regional assemblies for England and a Supreme Court able to veto legislation and to resolve disputes within a federal UK with a codified constitution. Of the three main parties, only the Liberal Democrat Party is fully committed to the development of a federal Europe.

By 2004, the Liberal Democrats seemed to be to the left of Labour on several issues: e.g. advocating a 50% tax rate on incomes over £100,000, separation of the church and monarchy, legalisation of cannabis for medical use and further devolution and House of Lords reforms. They did historically well in the 2005 election, winning 62 seats as the most distinctively different of the three main parties, with their tax-raising agenda and opposition to the invasion of Iraq and to compulsory national identity cards.

However, in 2008 Nick Clegg took over leadership of the Liberal Democrats. He was seen as being on the right of the party – more in favour of free market economics – and was clearly more comfortable in coalition with the Conservatives from 2010 than were many of his party colleagues. The voters' rejection of AV in the 2011 referendum was seen by some as a personal rebuff to Clegg.

The smaller parties

The Scottish and Welsh nationalists are now, or have recently been, in government in the Scottish and Welsh assemblies. The Greens celebrated their thirtieth anniversary in 2003, and by 2010 had representatives in the European Parliament, the Scottish Parliament and the London Assembly, as well as almost 100 local councillors and, for the first time in 2010, an MP at Westminster (Caroline Lucas).

The right-wing, anti-European UK Independence Party (UKIP) – with a membership of around 18,000 – won 13 seats in the European Parliament in June 2009. The far right British National Party, by 2011, had won a couple of European seats and a couple of local council seats. However,

Table 4.3   UK party membership (thousands)

Year	Conservative	Labour	Liberal Democrat	SNP	UKIP	Green	BNP
1951	2,900	876	110	n/a	n/a	n/a	n/a
1983	1,200	295	183 ★				
1987	1,000	289	138 ★				
1992	500	280	101				
1997	400	405	87				5
2001	311	272	73	9	10	6	3
2005	300	198	73	11	19	7	7
2008	250	166	60	15	15	8	12

★ SDP–Liberal Alliance

such small parties cannot do well under the first-past-the-post electoral system.

There has been a long-term fall in total UK party membership in recent decades, from over 4% of the electorate in the 1950s to less than 1% today.

Consensus politics and adversary politics

The term '**consensus politics**' applies to periods when the main political parties share similar ideological aims and values and hence compete to occupy a more centrist political position. The clearest example of this close accord was between the Labour and Conservative parties during the post-war economic boom of the 1950s and 1960s. When the economy is flourishing, voters do not seek radical political change, and so the main parties largely shared a Keynesian, social democratic centre ground in support of a mixed economy, full employment and a substantial welfare state.

This consensus evaporated with the economic recessions of the 1980s and the emergence of a much more right-wing Conservative government under Margaret Thatcher, who presided over a period of '**adversary politics**', with the main parties much more polarised on the right and left wings of politics.

In the late 1990s, with the emergence of 'new' Labour, a new, more right-wing phase of consensus politics emerged, with a commitment to the free market and an enabling welfare state. This, in turn, is likely to recede as the coalition government pursues an often painful and unpopular agenda of public spending and job cuts.

Organisation and financing of the major parties

The structure of the major parties used to reflect their different philosophies and principles. For example, traditional Conservative ideology stressed political hierarchy, 'natural governors' and loyalty to leadership; the Conservative leader was therefore responsible for policy making, party headquarters and internal appointments (e.g. the chairman and Shadow Cabinet). The conference was not a policy-making body, but a political rally intended to demonstrate unity and loyalty to the leader. Labour's philosophy, by contrast, demanded greater

key term...

Consensus politics A period of substantial ideological and policy agreement between the main parties.

key term...

Adversary politics A period of policy polarisation and sharp disagreements between the main parties.

internal party democracy: the Shadow Cabinet was elected by the Labour MPs; conference was a policy-making forum; and the Labour leader had much less formal power – until Tony Blair.

The positions were then almost reversed. As the Conservative Party became more internally democratic, Tony Blair centralised the Labour Party. The 'new' Labour leadership often simply ignored conference defeats on, for example, foundation hospitals in the NHS. There has also been a big decline in Labour Party membership since 1997, from 405,000 then to 166,000 in 2008 – the lowest for over 70 years. However, the party claims an increase in membership since 2010.

The Conservative Party is financed largely by private firms and individuals, whereas the Labour Party was previously financed largely by trade unions. However, this, too, has changed, with Labour looking increasingly to private donations – even setting up a 'Thousand Club' for wealthy individual donors like Bernie Ecclestone of Formula One. In 2002 Labour received a large and much-criticised donation from *Daily Express*/porn publisher Richmond Desmond. By 2003, trade union funding of Labour had declined from 90% to under 30%. However, it has since risen again to around 60%.

There were several scandals about party funding in the 1990s: e.g. the Conservatives took money from what their critics called 'foreign crooks', such as fugitive businessman Asil Nadir; and Labour had its 'Ecclestone affair', when the 1997 Labour government received a £1 million donation from Formula One boss Bernie Ecclestone – which coincided with an exemption for motor racing from a ban on tobacco sponsorship. The Labour government asked the Committee on Public Standards to establish clear rules about party funding. In 1999 the following rules were introduced:

- Foreign donations banned.
- Blind trusts abolished.
- All national donations of £5,000+ and local donations of £1,000+ to be made public.
- Anonymous donations of £50 or more banned. (N.B. How?!)
- £20 million ceiling on each party's national election campaign spending.
- Increased state funding for opposition parties.
- An Electoral Commission to oversee the rules, with the power to impose heavy fines.

Labour was also obliged to return Bernie Ecclestone's £1 million donation to him.

Table 4.4 Registered donations to some UK political parties in 2009

Party	Private donations	
	Value (£)	Number
Conservative	27,085,928	1,604
Labour	15,213,494	1,183
Liberal Democrat	3,886,634	1,020
UKIP	1,403,987	184
Co-operative Party	924,916	59
Green Party	352,163	143

Table 4.4 (continued)

Party	Private donations	
	Value (£)	Number
Christian Party	273,937	12
Scottish Nationalist Party	160,879	20
Plaid Cymru (Welsh)	142,656	27
Jury Team	50,000	3
BNP	45,332	14
Communist Party	10,084	2
Cornwall Party	9,411	4
Pirate Party	210	1

Source: Electoral Commission

Quiz

1. List five functions of a political party.
2. Distinguish between a 'dominant party system' and an 'elective dictatorship'.
3. Which of the three main parties is the most pro-European?
4. When was the Labour Party founded?
5. What was Clause Four?

MPs

Backbenchers are MPs in the House of Commons who are not, in addition, members of the government or of the shadow government – i.e. they are not members of Cabinet, junior government ministers or Opposition shadow ministers. The role of backbenchers (of any party) is to legislate, to scrutinise the executive and to represent their voters as elected representatives. This may involve them in: debates and votes on Bills in the House – and, occasionally, in backbench revolts; introducing their own private members' Bills; asking questions of the Prime Minister and ministers at Question Time; undertaking parliamentary committee work; and representing their **constituents** (local voters) both inside and outside of the House – for example, by holding regular 'surgeries' in their constituencies where they can meet their local voters and hear their political complaints.

> **key term...**
>
> **Backbenchers** MPs in the House of Commons who are not, in addition, members of the government or of the shadow government or major spokespersons for their party.

> **key term...**
>
> **Constituents** Residents of a local area represented by an MP.

Question...

4.1 How socially representative are MPs?

(10 marks)

Table 4.5   MPs' representation, 2010

Group	Representation
Female voters	52%
Female MPs	22%
Social class 3–5 voters	33%
Social class 3–5 MPs	4%
Private school-educated voters	7%
Private school-educated MPs	35%
University-educated voters	20%
University-educated MPs	90%
Ethnic minority voters	8%
Ethnic minority MPs	4%

analyse this...

British MPs must be British subjects, over 18 years of age (reduced from 21 in 2006). People disqualified from membership of the House of Commons include those disqualified from voting, plus: undischarged bankrupts, clergy of the established churches, judges, civil servants and other Crown officials, heads of nationalised industries and directors of the Bank of England, and those convicted of corrupt practices at elections.

Shared political ideology and natural party loyalty – together with ambition for higher public office and quite ruthless party discipline – usually combine to ensure that most backbenchers toe the party line and vote in support of their leadership. This usually means that the majority of MPs support the actions and policies of the government of the day.

Questions

a Why, do you think, are the categories of people listed above barred from membership of the House of Commons?

b Why do most MPs, most of the time, 'toe the party line'?

c What principled political arguments might there be (a) in defence of, and (b) against 'quite ruthless party discipline'?

Some exam questions ask about the diverse roles and conflicting loyalties of MPs; the key concepts of 'representation' and 'responsibility' should be addressed in exam answers. Who (or what) should MPs 'represent'? How feasible or valuable are different theories of representation? To whom should MPs be accountable or 'responsible'?

Diverse roles of an MP

Legislator

Westminster MPs are elected as law makers to a national legislative assembly. They debate and vote on parliamentary Bills in the House of Commons and in standing committees. They are constrained by party discipline from speaking or voting against the party line on a two- or three-line whip, on pain of suspension from the party. However, backbenchers may assert themselves by rebelling collectively against a Bill. This usually happens when MPs see the Bill as contrary to the basic principles or promises of their party. Backbenchers may also introduce their own legislation in the form of private members' Bills. However, there is usually little time set aside for private members' Bills and, in procedural terms, they are easily defeated, especially if the government of the day does not support them. Therefore few are passed (though good publicity may be won for the issue involved): on average, over 50 are introduced in each parliamentary session but only around half a dozen are passed.

talking point...

The term '**party whip**' was invented by Conservative MP Edmund Burke in the eighteenth century. He likened the disciplining of MPs on voting to the process of 'whipping in the hounds' during a fox hunt. Party whips are senior MPs in the House of Commons (or peers in the House of Lords) who have been selected by the leadership of their party to act as a channel of communication – i.e. information, guidance and party discipline – between the leadership and the party members in each House. The Chief Whip is the most important whip in each party – an MP of substantial power and authority.

The whips of each party issue an agenda of the week's business – a piece of paper also called the 'Whip' – to their members. They indicate how important each item is by underlining it once, twice or three times. If an item is underlined three times (a 'three-line whip') this shows that the party requires its MPs to be present and to vote as instructed.

PARTY WHIP

WEDNESDAY 26TH OCTOBER

Enterprise Bill   Consideration of Lords amendments
Important divisions will take place and your attendance at 3.30pm and until the business is concluded is <u>essential</u>.

key term...

Party whips Senior MPs in the House of Commons, or peers in the House of Lords, who have been selected by the leadership of their party to act as a channel of communication and party discipline between the leadership and the party members in each House.

THURSDAY 27TH OCTOBER

Tabling — To be announced

House meets at 11.30am for: **Trade and Industry Questions**

Agriculture Questions

At about 12.30pm for: **Business Questions**

Main business

Debate on **Defence in the UK on** a Motion for the Adjournment.

Your attendance is requested.

FRIDAY 28TH OCTOBER

The House will not be sitting.

The provisional business for the following week will include:

MONDAY 31ST OCTOBER

Adoption and Children Bill — Consideration of Lords amendments

Significant divisions will take place and your attendance at 3.30pm and until the business is concluded is required.

TUESDAY 1ST NOVEMBER

Nationality, Immigration and Asylum Bill

There will be a 3-Line Whip from 3.30pm and until the business is concluded.

It is potentially a serious matter for MPs to defy a three-line whip and therefore they do not do so lightly. It can lead to the whip being 'withdrawn' from an MP. Withdrawal of the whip means expulsion from the party (although this may be temporary). For example, Labour's George Galloway was expelled from the party in 2003 for the way in which he expressed his opposition to the invasion of Iraq. In 2005 he won election as a member of the new Respect Party. However, MPs cannot be sacked from Parliament by their parties, because liberal democratic theory suggests that only the voters should have the power to elect or reject an MP.

Controller of executive

According to the theory of parliamentary government, MPs – regardless of party – are supposed to scrutinise, check and publicise the activities of the government through, e.g. debates, votes on government Bills, Question Time, parliamentary committees and control of government finance as well as via the media etc. Some MPs have made their mark in this role: e.g. radical MPs such as Labour's Dennis Skinner have been a constant thorn in the flesh of their own party's leaders.

MPs are, however, constrained in this role by:

- The power of a majority government to push through Bills: e.g. in 2004, top-up university tuition fees were forced through despite a 72-strong revolt by Labour MPs; and in 2010, yet higher university tuition fees were forced through despite a 27-strong revolt by Coalition MPs.
- Lack of time available to backbenchers in the Commons.
- Lack of information granted to Parliament by the government in Britain's secretive system. e.g. in 2010, about anti-counterfeiting measures.
- Lack of office, research and secretarial facilities available to MPs (though a new building next to the Palace of Westminster, Portcullis House, has gone some way towards remedying this).
- MPs' own personal ambitions for promotion to the rank of minister – see the next point.

Trainee minister

All ministers should, by convention, be selected from either the Houses of Commons or the House of Lords. Parliamentary work – in debates, in committees, and in constituencies – may provide some useful training for future executive office. However, since ambitious MPs who see themselves as 'trainee ministers' may hesitate to offend their party leaders, they may do little to control or criticise their own governing party. The parliamentary system thus creates 'role conflict' for many backbenchers.

Representative

MPs are also, of course, elected to express the views or interests of their voters, individually or severally.

The diverse loyalties and responsibilities of an MP

MPs have wide-ranging and sometimes conflicting loyalties. To whom MPs are (or should be) loyal or accountable is a matter of debate; the answer depends on political ideology, party structure and personal inclination. The demands on an MP's loyalty include the following.

The parliamentary party

The nineteenth-century Conservative Prime Minister Benjamin Disraeli (1804–81) reportedly said, 'Damn your principles! Stick to your party.' The 'doctrine of the mandate' suggests that electors vote for a package of party policies as outlined in a manifesto, and therefore that MPs are most effectively representing the voters' wishes if they toe the party line. But what if the party breaks its manifesto promises?

Party conference

Whereas the annual Conservative Party conference is not a policy-making body but simply a jamboree, the Labour Party conference used to be a policy-making body. However, Labour conference attendees tend to vote for 'old' Labour policies, and therefore the conference was increasingly side-lined by the 'new' Labour leadership.

Constituency party

The local party selects its parliamentary candidate and provides the electoral campaign back-up; rank-and-file activists may also have a good understanding of constituency needs. The local party can also dese-lect its parliamentary candidate – that is, it may decide not to choose its MP as its party candidate at the next election. This usually terminates an MP's political career. Many MPs, therefore, pay special heed to the local party, even when this may jeopardise their standing with the national leadership.

Constituents

Total subservience to the party would negate the role of constituency MPs. Local voters' views and interests may conflict with party policy. However, it may also be difficult for MPs to serve diverse local interests – e.g. farmers versus farm workers; and it is hard for an MP to gauge the views of constituents as a whole.

talking point...

Did you know that you can contact your MP via the internet simply by going to the website below and typing in your post code?

www.writetothem.com

Interest groups

Many MPs have special personal interests (e.g. deaf Labour MP Jack Ashley campaigned on behalf of the handicapped). They are often sponsored or lobbied by pressure groups and private companies to act on their behalf. About one-third of Labour MPs are sponsored by trade unions (e.g. Dennis Skinner by the National Union of Mineworkers); here, the trade union pays some of the candidate's campaign costs in return for a voice in Parliament, where possible.

Many other MPs, especially Conservatives, are paid personal fees (ranging from £1,000 to £20,000 per year) as consultants or directors by pressure groups, private individuals and companies seeking to promote their own interests. This generated the 'cash for questions' scandal of the 1990s, in which two Conservative junior ministers, Neil Hamilton and Tim Smith, tabled parliamentary questions on behalf of Harrods' owner Mohamed Al Fayed in return for payment. Prime Minister John Major set up a Committee on Standards in Public Life under senior judge Lord Nolan. Lord Neill took over the chair of the committee in 1997. In 1996 the following rules were agreed:

- MPs must register all outside interests with a Parliamentary Commissioner for Standards.
- MPs must disclose the sources and amounts of outside earnings.
- MPs are forbidden from tabling questions on behalf of outside paying interests and must declare such interests when speaking in debates.
- A Commons Committee on Standards and Privileges was established to enforce the new rules.

Many MPs also receive fees for media and other public appearances.

National interest

Conservative politician Edmund Burke argued, in 1774, that an MP was a member of 'a deliberate assembly of one nation with one interest, that of the whole', and that MPs should pursue the 'general good' according to their personal judgement. The concept of a 'national interest' is central to the philosophy of traditional political conservatism, but is denied by liberals (who perceive diverse individual interests) and by socialists (who perceive conflicting class interests). However, all governments bring the concept into play when it suits their policy objectives.

Conscience

This is the second feature of Burke's theory of the role of an MP: 'Your representative owes you not his industry only, but his judgement; and he betrays instead of serving you, if he sacrifices it to your opinion.' For MPs, private conscience is given expression, in particular, in free votes in the Commons (e.g. on moral issues such as capital punishment, abortion and homosexuality laws), in private members' Bills and in backbench revolts. It may obviously conflict with party, constituency and other interests outlined above.

Recall of MPs

A system of '**recall**' would allow voters to remove an MP from office in mid-term, through a process of petition and election. There is currently no such provision in the UK, but the coalition government proposes to introduce recall arrangements for MPs guilty of serious misconduct. This is largely a response to the 2009 MPs' expenses scandal. However, much depends on what will be defined as 'serious misconduct' and how many petitioners will be required to trigger a ballot. There is also always the danger that a competent MP could be sacked by a well-organised group of voters who simply never wanted him or her to represent them in the first place.

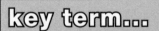

key term...

Recall A process by which MPs can be sacked by their voters in mid-term.

Questions...

4.2 How has the role of MPs changed in recent years? *(20 marks)*

4.3 Is this change undermining the representative nature of Parliament? *(20 marks)*

True or false?

1. There are ten parties in the House of Commons.
2. The Labour and Conservative parties do not stand candidates in Northern Ireland.
3. There are no independent MPs in the House of Commons.
4. Being an MP is a part time job.
5. The principle of the mandate ensures that the government's election promises will be carried out.

Answers to questions

Note: The following are notes for guidance only and are not intended to be taken as model answers.

Distinguish between two types of party system. *(5 marks)*

A party system implies political decision making and representation on the basis of formal, organised groups of (more or less) like-minded people who stand candidates for election on a common policy programme. A one-party system means that only one party is allowed to put up candidates for election; all other parties are banned. This is a non-liberal democratic system and it operated in, for example, Nazi Germany. A dominant party system, on the other hand, means that many parties exist and more than one party may have the chance of winning power, but one party is in power over long periods of time – e.g. the Conservatives in Britain for two-thirds of the twentieth century.

Quiz
1. Representation, participation, mandate; political recruitment, campaigning and financing for candidates; policy coherence, stability and accountability for government; a basis for choice, ideological identity and information on political issues for voters; a mechanism for political change.
2. In a 'dominant party system' one party is in power over exceptionally long periods of time – e.g. the Conservative Party in Britain for two-thirds of the twentieth century – regardless of the size of its majority. An 'elective dictatorship' occurs when the governing party has such a large majority in the Commons that it can overwhelmingly dominate it.

3. The Liberal Democrats.
4. 1900.
5. Clause Four was the most 'socialist' reference in the Labour Party's founding constitution, to 'common ownership' – hence its abolition in 1995.

4.1 *How socially representative are MPs?* *(10 marks)*

Despite significant improvements in recent general elections, parliamentary candidates and MPs are still by no means 'representative' of the electorate in terms of their social background; they are still predominantly white, male, middle-aged and middle class. This is partly because of discrimination in the process of selection of candidates; and partly because working-class people, young people, women and ethnic minorities are slower to come forward as candidates (because of pressures of work, financial constraints, or lack of political background, contacts or self-confidence). In the early 1990s, Labour adopted a policy of all-women short-lists in many constituencies, and a record number of female Labour MPs (101) were elected in 1997. Since the 1997 election, minor 'family friendly' reforms have been introduced in the Commons – such as fewer late-night sittings – which make it slightly easier for women, especially, to serve as MPs. Conservative leader David Cameron's 'A-list' of preferred party candidates sought – with some success – to bring more young, female and ethnic minority MPs into the party.

4.2 *How has the role of MPs changed in recent years?* *(20 marks)*

MPs are elected legislators in a national assembly with the additional task of scrutinising the executive in Britain's system of 'parliamentary government'. Thus, their essential roles – making laws, representing the people and controlling the executive – are unchanged. MPs today probably seek, increasingly, to represent their voters' views and not simply their voters' interests as the MPs themselves judge them (i.e. MPs are, increasingly, 'delegates' and not just trustees in the Burkean sense) – hence most hold regular 'surgeries' to meet their constituents and take up their grievances.

However, in recent years, MPs have tended to see themselves more as professional politicians pursuing a long-term career, often full time (rather than treating politics as a part-time hobby, as MPs in the nineteenth and even twentieth centuries tended to do). British MPs average 20 years in the Commons, far longer than in most comparable countries. They also have increasing links with outside bodies such as private businesses, charities and pressure groups, through paid consultancies and sponsorship.

4.3 *Is this change undermining the representative nature of Parliament?* *(20 marks)*

As MPs become increasingly careerist, they are more likely to heed their party leadership and toe the party line, since their jobs usually depend upon their party. Thus they may be less independent-minded, less likely to revolt and more likely to be 'lobby fodder' for the national and/or local party, which may mean that they represent voters' views or interests on controversial issues less well. Heavy lobbying of MPs by outside interests may distract MPs from focusing on their own constituents' interests. However, they have become more 'representative' of the voters in recent years in terms of social background – e.g. record numbers of female, black and Asian

MPs. In sum, the answer depends upon the interpretation of the key word 'representative'.

Note: Illustrative examples should be given for all points.

True or false?
1. True.
2. True.
3. False.
4. True.
5. False.

Sample questions

Short
- What is a political party?
- Define, with an example, consensus politics.
- Define the concept of the electoral mandate.

Medium
- Outline the role of minor parties in Britain's political system.
- How do political parties achieve their aims?
- What are the main policy areas that divide the Labour and Conservative parties?

Long
- To what extent has the Labour Party abandoned its traditional principles?
- Assess the nature of Britain's party system.
- How effective are political parties in promoting democracy in the UK?

References

Burke, E. (1774) Letter to Constituents in Bristol. In: *Edmund Burke: Selections from his Political Writings and Speeches*, T. Nelson and Sons, London.

Hailsham, Q. (1976) Elective Dictatorship. The Dimbleby Lecture. In: *The Listener*, 21 October.

Useful websites

www.bbc.co.uk/news
  An excellent, wide-ranging and impartial source for topical news items and archive articles.

news.bbc.co.uk/1/hi/uk_politics/8044401.stm
  A comprehensive list of the registered political parties in the UK.

**www.direct.gov.uk/en/Governmentcitizensandrights/UKgovernment/
Politicalpartiesandelections/DG_073226**
Directgov. A government website with a wide range of informative sections, including one on the UK party system.

www.parliament.uk/site-information/useful/politicalparties
The official website of Parliament, with links to all of the parties represented at Westminster.

www.pocketpolitics.co.uk
An independent comparison of the main parties' policies.

Public opinion and pressure groups

Aims of this chapter

- To examine the concept of 'public opinion'.
- To outline the diverse types of pressure group.
- To evaluate the role of trade unions.
- To outline diverse pressure group methods.
- To compare and contrast pressure groups and parties.
- To evaluate the contribution of pressure groups to democracy.

Public opinion

In a 'democracy' it is usually assumed that government should be responsive to **public opinion**; but this is a very difficult concept to define or measure. It is best defined as the majority view on a given issue at a given time; but if opinion is divided several ways there may be no 'majority' view; or the view of a vocal or powerful minority may dominate.

It is often assumed that the party system and the government of the day best represent public opinion. However, given that the 2005 'majority' Labour government had the support of only 22% of registered voters (that is, 35% of the votes cast on a turnout of just 61%), other factors come into play. Public opinion may be expressed or assessed through: elections for other bodies such as the devolved assemblies, local councils or the European Parliament; referenda (e.g. on remaining in the EU and on electoral reform for Westminster); television or radio chat shows, letters to the press or to MPs; the internet; opinion polls; or pressure group activity or direct action by individuals or groups.

Public opinion polls – surveys and questionnaires of representative samples of voters, carried out by professional pollsters – are paid a lot of attention by politicians and the media, and they can be quite reliable and informative indicators of people's views on key issues. For an example see the BBC news website poll tracker: www.bbc.co.uk/news/uk-politics-10963393.

However, a non-professional poll (as opposed to a poll by an official polling organisation such as Ipsos Mori or ComRes) may sometimes question an unrepresentative sample of people; it may offer limited options as answers; or it may shape the very responses it is trying to measure simply by posing questions about an issue which some people may have never before considered. Political parties often carry out their own polls; and they may publish misleading results in an effort to boost their own vote. It is sometimes suggested that even professional opinion polls should be banned in the days before an election, because they may influence the result of the election itself: for example, if one party seems very strong – or, indeed, very weak – its supporters may not bother to vote at all.

analyse this...

Opinion polls seek to determine the views of the general public by putting questions to relatively small groups of people – perhaps only one or two thousand in total. There are several ways in which such a group may be selected, but two main ways are to use a random sample or a quota sample. In the UK, for example, a random sample might consist of every thousandth name on the register of electors in various constituencies. A quota sample, on the other hand, seeks out specific groups, the composition of which is decided in advance – for example, specific numbers of males and females, working class and middle class, various age and ethnic groups and so on. By this method, questions are directed at a group of people who are perceived to be, on the whole, a cross-section of the public.

Opinion polls have potential flaws: for example, if certain sections of the public disproportionately refuse to answer questions, this may skew the results; if polls are conducted via the internet or even by telephone, poorer voters may be excluded; and if the answers on offer are too limited, again, the results will be distorted.

The belief that polling during election campaigns may actually influence voting behaviour has prompted some countries, such as France, to ban the publication of poll results in the run-up to the actual election.

Questions

a If you were conducting a political survey, would you opt for a random or a quota sample – and why?

b Should the publication of opinion poll results be banned in the run-up to a general election? Why or why not?

c Try to devise a short political survey and then put it to your fellow students. What insights and problems about polling have you gleaned from this exercise?

In voting and other forms of political activity, a distorted impression of public opinion may be conveyed, e.g. by tactical voting, abstentions and unequal degrees of political activism among different sections of the public (e.g. the middle classes tend to be more politically active and vocal than the working class); or, quite simply, by selective media reporting of such activities.

Even though public opinion is difficult to define or measure, it may influence Parliament or the government. An example is the so-called 'greening' of the Conservative and Labour governments from the late 1980s onwards, when they paid increasing attention to environmental issues, in response to growing public concern and pressure group activity.

However, it may be argued that politicians should *not* follow every whim of public opinion because it may be ill informed, selfish, fickle, emotional or irrational. Here, one example is capital punishment, which Parliament has consistently opposed since the 1960s – despite opinion polls suggesting that up to 60% of British voters favour it for the most serious crimes, such as murder and rape.

> ## talking point...
>
> Should the government simply do everything that majority public opinion appears to support? Why or why not? Bear in mind that this question is central to diverse interpretations of such key concepts as 'democracy' and 'representation'.

key term...

Pressure groups Organisations which do not stand candidates for election but seek to promote a cause or to protect a particular section of society by influencing government, Parliament or the public.

key term...

Promotional/cause/issue groups Pressure groups which seek to promote a specific cause external to their own membership.

key term...

Protective/sectional/interest groups Pressure groups which seek to protect the interests of their own members as a particular section of society.

Pressure groups

Pressure groups are organisations which seek to promote a cause or to protect a particular section of society, often by influencing government, Parliament or the public. Unlike parties, they do not stand candidates for election, and their aims and membership are often narrower; but they do often have close links with political parties. Pressure groups are usually centred upon promoting a single issue or upon representing a single group. Their aim is not to form the government but to influence it.

Two main types of pressure group are:

- **Promotional** or **cause** or **issue groups**, which seek to promote a specific cause, e.g. the Countryside Alliance (rural issues), Shelter (housing), Friends of the Earth (the environment).
- **Protective** or **sectional** or **interest groups**, which seek to protect the interests of their own members as a particular section of society, e.g. trade unions and professional associations such as the NUM (National Union of Mineworkers), the Law Society (solicitors), the CBI (Confederation of British Industry), etc.

According to the writer Wyn Grant, pressure groups may, alternatively, be

Question...

5.1 Do promotional or protective pressure groups tend to have more power, and why?

(5 marks)

subdivided into **insider** and **outsider groups**, depending on the closeness of their relationships with government, civil servants and other key policy makers. British farmers are often cited as an example of an insider group with close contacts with ministers and civil servants and with significant influence upon policy making – for example, upon the government's decision to approve genetically modified (GM) maize production in 2004, despite strong public disapproval. It is more common for sectional than for promotional groups to be insiders, but Action on Smoking and Health (ASH) is one example of a promotional insider group.

Outsider groups, by contrast, may have aims which are totally different from those of the government – for example, in the 1980s the Campaign for Nuclear Disarmament (CND) had no influence upon the Conservative governments of the day, despite its huge membership (over one million) and marches.

Similarly, the Stop the War group failed in its aim, despite a million-strong march against the invasion of Iraq in 2003. Outsider groups may also use methods which are deemed unacceptable by the government: for example, members of the Animal Liberation Front were found guilty in 2008 of conducting a hate campaign against an animal-testing research centre which included personal smears, criminal damage, bomb hoaxes and even the exhumation and theft of the body of a woman whose family farm supplied animals for experimentation.

Some outsider groups aim for insider status, either through a change in government or through a growth in their own influence or power. Other outsider groups aim to stay that way because they are ideologically opposed to the political system and to any governing party. The Anarchist Federation is one such example.

A third way of categorising pressure groups is to subdivide them into permanent and temporary groups. Temporary groups have limited and short-term goals and will disband if these are achieved – or, indeed, if they fail and the result cannot be reversed. The most common examples are groups seeking to prevent building work in their local area, such as an airport runway, a motorway or an asylum centre. (Their outlook is often described as the 'nimby' syndrome – the attitude of 'not in my back yard'.) Sometimes a particular event may lead to the formation of a pressure group: e.g. the Snowdrop group which campaigned for the banning of handguns following the 1996 massacre of schoolchildren at Dunblane, and which was dissolved when its aim was largely achieved.

Trade unions

A **trade union** is a protective organisation of workers which aims to protect its members' pay and working conditions. There are several types: industrial unions – e.g. the National Union of Mineworkers; white-collar unions – e.g. Unison (formed in 1993 by a merger of three big public sector unions); and general unions – e.g. the Transport and General Workers' Union. Generally, the more skilled and specialised its members, the more 'powerful' is the union.

In the 1960s and 1970s, during the period of 'consensus politics', trade unions were closely involved with governments – both Labour and Conservative – in shaping economic and industrial policy. Examples of trade unions' influence or power during this period included the 'Social Contract' of 1973–78, when the unions accepted pay restraints in return for promises of social benefits from

key term...

Insider groups Pressure groups which are regularly consulted by the ministers and civil servants who make policy decisions in the groups' special areas of interest and influence.

key term...

Outsider groups Pressure groups which are not consulted by policy makers because they have aims and/or methods which conflict with those of the government of the day.

key term...

Trade unions Organisations which represent groups of workers in negotiations with their employers.

key term...

Corporatism Tripartite (three-way) involvement and consultation of workers' and employers' groups with the government in economic policy making.

the government; and also the involvement of the trade unions in government-created bodies such as the Advisory, Conciliation and Arbitration Service (ACAS), which often mediated in disputes with employers.

This '**corporatist**' approach of three-way cooperation between employers, trade unions and government in economic planning and decision making was rejected by the Thatcher governments of the 1980s. Margaret Thatcher regarded trade unions as 'the enemy within'.

Legal curbs on trade unions since 1980
Successive laws passed during the Thatcher era have: prohibited sympathy and secondary action and mass picketing; required secret ballots of union members before industrial action, and for maintaining a political fund (i.e. union contributions to the Labour Party); allowed fines and 'sequestration', i.e. freezing and seizure of union funds by the courts; required union which ballot on industrial action in separate workplaces to win a majority vote in every workplace; and prohibited unions from disciplining strike breakers, even if a clear majority of members voted for strike action. Employers are still allowed to sack strikers, even after a ballot in favour of strike action.

The 'new' Labour governments reversed none of these constraints, and trade union membership has fallen markedly since the 1980s.

The defeat of the coal miners in 1985, after a year-long strike over pit closures, was seen by the government and trade unions alike as a watershed in the decline of the power and rights of trade unions.

Another turning-point in the fortune of trade unions was media tycoon Rupert Murdoch's 1986 'Wapping revolution', when he moved the production of his newspapers, such as *The Times* and *News of the World*, from Fleet Street to Wapping, where they were printed using new computer technology, thus eliminating the old crafts of the printers and excluding the unions. Some 5,500 workers were sacked overnight. There were mass union pickets and demonstrations at Wapping, and because these were illegal under the 1980 and 1982 Employment Acts, the trade union involved, SOGAT (the Society of Graphical and Allied Trades) had all of its funds sequestrated (confiscated). One 19-year-old picket was killed by a company lorry; although the inquest jury returned a verdict of unlawful killing, there was no prosecution. Eighteen police officers were prosecuted for excessive violence on the picket lines, but all of the charges were dropped after long delays in bringing the cases to court.

The most powerful 'trade unions' are now the professional associations such as the Bar (barristers), Law Society (solicitors) and British Medical Association (doctors), which have a legal monopoly on their own professional services, regulate entry to their own professions and often have the dual functions of protecting and disciplining their own members. Concern is sometimes expressed about these last aspects of their role and the possible conflicts of interest which may arise from them.

Although the 'new' Labour governments chose not to reverse the 1980s anti-union legislation, they introduced the minimum wage and legislated for trade union recognition in large workplaces if the majority of workers wanted it.

The case for the protection of individuals by trade unions:

- The weakness of individual workers versus employers.
- Historical role of unions in advancing working people's conditions of work, health, safety, pay, living standards and pensions. They also provide services for their members such as legal aid in tribunal cases and retirement homes for sick miners.
- The representative nature of unions: unlike most promotional groups, members elect their leaders, who are usually 'delegates' rather than mere 'representatives' (i.e. union leaders are very closely bound by the direct instructions of their members); and altogether they represent a larger sector of population than do any other pressure groups (currently seven million workers).
- **Direct action** by trade unions – e.g. strikes – may be seen as mass, direct 'people-power'.
- Visible union or workers' power – e.g. strikes – is a negative, uncertain and often counter-productive weapon of last resort, involving loss of pay and job security; it may thus be an indication of relative weakness, i.e. lack of alternative rights, powers and channels of influence for workers.
- Media coverage of unions and industrial action is often biased and hostile. For example, the majority of all strikes are 'wildcat' or unofficial, but are portrayed as if 'bully-boy' union leaders are calling out unwilling members; employers' figures on the 'costs' of strikes are usually presented uncritically, omitting company 'savings' in wages, raw materials, fuel etc.
- Thus, public hostility to trade unions and industrial action is greater, the *less* direct experience people have of them (and people therefore tend to say 'the unions are too powerful', but also 'my union is not strong enough on my behalf').
- Though workers' negative or disruptive power may be seen as significant and quite inconvenient by those members of the public affected by it, their power may be negligible when measured in terms of results – such as company closures, unemployment, redundancies, growing income inequalities and continuing imbalances of power between workers and employers in workplace decision-making.
- Contrary to popular myth, Britain was always well down the international league table on strike figures, even in the 1960s and 1970s, when trade unions' power was perceived to be at its height.

> ## key term...
>
> **Direct action** A form of political activism, in which participants act directly, ignoring established and representative political procedures; e.g. strikes, sit-ins, demonstrations.

Question...

5.2 What is meant by each of the following terms (all of which are related to the issue of trade unions)? *(20 marks)*

    a. Block vote.

    b. Closed shop.

    c. Corporatism.

    d. Functional representation.

    e. Sequestration.

Pressure group methods

Pressure groups seek pressure points, not only at Whitehall and Westminster but also beyond.

Insider groups – such as the National Farmers' Union (NFU) – have direct links with the executive in a relationship of mutual need, e.g. for information, expertise and influence. Such groups rarely need to resort to public lobbying or street demonstrations; the most powerful and influential groups are therefore often, paradoxically, the least visible. A few groups, such as the farmers, have the statutory right to be consulted on relevant legislation and policy initiatives. Examples of the farming lobby's influence include the huge extra subsidies given to beef farmers in the 1990s to compensate them for lost sales due to the BSE ('mad cow disease') crisis.

Many pressure groups work through Parliament, parties and MPs by:

- **Financing political parties:** the Labour Party, historically, has been funded largely by trade unions, while the Conservative Party has been funded mainly by business and industry.
- **Lobbying (influencing) MPs in Parliament** through letters, leaflets, petitions, gifts, dinners, trips, parties and personal 'consultancy fees' for MPs. Since the 'cash for questions' scandal of the 1990s, MPs are bound by stricter rules about financial links with pressure groups and other external interests.
- **Sponsoring MPs:** many trade unions pay some part of a local candidate's election campaign costs in return for support by an MP – e.g. veteran Labour MP Dennis Skinner (a former coal miner) is sponsored by the National Union of Mineworkers.
- **Drafting and promoting private members' Bills:** e.g. the (legalising) 1967 Abortion Act, introduced as a private member's Bill by Liberal MP David Steel, was largely drafted by the Abortion Law Reform Association, and later restraining Bills (by Conservative MPs such as Ann Widdecombe) were backed by anti-abortion groups such as the Society for the Protection of the Unborn Child (SPUC).
- **Seeking to influence government legislation:** e.g. the Lords' Day Observance Society successfully mobilised Conservative MPs into opposing Sunday shopping in 1986. Sunday shopping in the UK was introduced by the 1994 Sunday Trading Act.
- **Hiring professional lobbyists** (private public relations companies, such as Hill and Knowlton) to promote a cause among MPs, for which clients may pay around £30,000 per year.
- Many British pressure groups are increasingly **focusing their attention on the EU** rather than on domestic decision-making institutions – a reliable indicator of the shifting balance of power and influence towards Europe. For example, the Committee of Professional Agricultural Organisations (COPA) – comprising most of the national farmers' organisations, including Britain's NFU – is now based in Brussels.

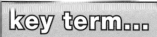

key term...

Lobbying Influencing politicians and policy makers.

key term...

Sponsored MPs MPs (usually Labour) whose campaign costs are aided by trade unions or other pressure groups.

Use of the courts

Pressure groups are increasingly using the courts in attempts to have government policies ruled illegal: for example, the Countryside Alliance repeatedly tried and failed to have the ban on hunting with dogs overturned by the courts. In 2010 some environmental groups (including Greenpeace and the Campaign for Rural England) successfully forced the Labour government to undertake a further review of the proposed third runway at Heathrow airport (the coalition government later dropped the proposal anyway). In 2011 the Poppy Project, a charity that provides support and accommodation to women who have been trafficked into exploitation, took the government to court over a 40% cut in its funding, but it lost its case.

Mobilisation of public opinion

Often a last resort for the least powerful but most visible cause groups is to seek to influence government indirectly through the public: e.g. the Child Poverty Action Group, Shelter and Greenpeace. The methods used include conducting or publicising opinion polls, petitions, pickets, leaflets and letters, media adverts, demonstrations and staged public events, such as Greenpeace's dumping of four tons of genetically modified soya beans outside the gates of Downing Street in 1999 in protest over Prime Minister Blair's backing for GM foods. Promotional groups have increasingly employed direct action to attract media and public attention: for example, the environmental group Plane Stupid, which campaigns against airport expansion, has staged sit-ins on runways, draped banners from the Palace of Westminster and showered paper planes on official political meetings. The 2010 demonstrations against the increases in university tuition fees, organised by the National Union of Students (NUS), involved damage to government buildings and to the car in which Prince Charles and the Duchess of Cornwall were travelling to the Royal Variety Performance. In the same year, the US charity Project Prevention offered to pay British drug users £200 if they agreed to be sterilised. Concern is sometimes expressed when pressure groups' publicity tactics are emotive, obstructive, illegal or violent.

Illegal methods

Pressure groups may use **civil disobedience** – non-violent but unlawful action as a form of political protest – in order to gain publicity for their cause: e.g. CND (anti-nuclear) protesters trespassing and cutting the perimeter wire at nuclear bases, refusing to pay taxes towards nuclear weapons and staging mass street 'die-ins' (obstruction); in 2004, one Fathers4Justice protester scaled Buckingham Palace dressed as Batman and another handcuffed himself to children's minister Margaret Hodge. These are examples of non-violent action.

Sometimes, however, pressure groups even resort to the threat or use of violence: e.g. from 2006 to 2010 the Animal Liberation Front planted bombs at the homes of research scientists who used animals in laboratory tests. Such groups would argue that it is fair to counter violence with violence; and such methods may also win more publicity and political response than legal, peaceful methods. This raises questions about the role and responsibility of the media in their coverage of public participation and protest.

> **key term...**
>
> **Civil disobedience** Non-violent but unlawful action as a form of political protest.

talking point...

What kind of May Day protester are you?

Anti-capitalism is a broad church. Are you a pacifist fluffy, pro-violence spiky or undercover investment banker?

You are exhausted after a long day of demonstrating. What do you do?

1. Head to the nearest Starbucks for a café latte.
2. Hang out with friends at a local pub, exchanging tales of how you shouted abuse at literally dozens of policemen.
3. Take off your white overalls, fire up your laptop and upload those protest pics onto a May Day protest website.
4. Phone your solicitor from a police cell.

What is your key May Day accessory?

1. A Louis Vuitton bag for storing your make up/hair gel.
2. A mobile phone so you can phone dad if you get in trouble.
3. A large foam battering ram.
4. A brick.

Which of these phrases are you most likely to say?

1. I am never going to reach the protests unless this M25 traffic eases up!
2. What time do you think the protest is going to finish, only I've got a dentist's appointment at 4.30?
3. Can anyone think of a comedy acronym for our anti-capitalism collective?
4. This is going to be bigger than Seattle!

You are walking down Oxford Street when a group of Balaclava-clad people start smashing windows. What do you do?

1. Call the police – that's daddy's firm they are breaking into.
2. Watch from a safe distance.
3. Beg them to stop – it is meant to be a party, not a riot.
4. Join in.

You count which of the following among your ideological influences?

1. Posh Spice, Naomi Campbell, Bill Gates.
2. Pre-mayoral Ken Livingstone, Chumbawamba, Happy Mondays.
3. Ya Basta!, Zapatistas, and the hippy movement.
4. Eta, Urban Alliance, Anarchist Federation.

What will be your greatest thrill on May Day?

1. Looting a darling pair of sunglasses from Harrods.
2. Getting home safely.
3. Getting arrested for lying down in front of rush-hour traffic.
4. Getting arrested for smashing up McDonald's.

You miss a day off work to attend the May Day protests. What do you tell your boss?

1. I've been on a management training course.
2. I've had 24-hour flu.
3. I've been fighting capitalist forces in London.
4. Nothing – being an anarchist is a full-time occupation.

Key to answers:

1. Undercover capitalist

Your motto: "I hope they smash up Gap – I need some new jeans."

You are about as committed to the anti-capitalist cause as George W. Bush is to the Kyoto protocol. You enjoy the thrill of dicing with the police, but you do not want to do anything that might jeopardise your graduate traineeship in merchant banking. You once belonged to the Young Conservatives but now it is cooler to be a May Day protester. Go home now, before mummy and daddy see you on TV and get worried.

2. Fair weather protester

Your motto: "It's started raining, let's go to Burger King instead."

You want to fight capitalism but can't quite bring yourself to go the whole hog. After all, those Nike trainers were gorgeous and a snip at only £80. You prefer to stay on the edge of the action and tend to flee at the first sign of trouble. Getting arrested is your biggest fear – after all, a criminal record could ruin your chances of getting onto that media studies course.

3. Fluffy

Your motto: "White Overall Movement Building Liberation Through Effective Struggle forever!"

You love sticking two fingers up at authority, and you plump for fun, non-violent tactics such as street parties and fire-breathing to make your point. You are likely to belong to Reclaim the Streets or the Mayday Collective, have not visited a hairdresser in the last five years and sport at least one penny whistle. You will probably end May Day at a friend's squat, regaling your mates with tales of guerrilla gardening.

4. Spiky

Your motto: "Anarchy in the UK!"

Brick in hand, balaclava on head, on May Day you'll sally forth to do battle with the evil capitalist forces of the world. You are likely to belong to the Anarchist Federation or the Urban Alliance, and be versed in the best ways to avoid police batons and smash windows. You will probably end up in court for your law-breaking activities, but what does that matter to a hard-core anarchist like you?

(Copyright Guardian News and Media Ltd, 2004)

Pressure groups and parties

Differences between pressure groups and parties

Strictly speaking, there are clear differences between pressure groups and parties. Above all, pressure groups do not stand candidates for election – they merely seek to influence those in political office. Also, the aims and membership of pressure groups are usually narrower than those of parties. For example, most promotional pressure groups support a single cause, such as saving a local library; whereas even small parties outside of Parliament, such as the British National Party, have a wide-ranging manifesto covering all major areas of political policy. Similarly, most protective groups seek to represent only one section of society – such as the National Union of Teachers, which seeks only to defend the interests of teachers; whereas even small parties seek much wider membership, support and representation. Political parties seek to bring together many interests and opinions into one single political group embracing a comprehensive ideology and capable of governing the country, whereas pressure groups can represent specialist interests and single issues – often in much more diverse, radical and popular ways.

Similarities between pressure groups and parties

As discussed in Chapter 4, many so-called 'parties' that take part in general elections are really pressure groups who put up candidates simply for publicity, not necessarily because they have any realistic hope of winning seats. Single-issue groups which stood candidates in 2010 included the Legalise Cannabis Alliance and Firefighters Against Cuts.

Also, many small parties, such as the Green Party, look and act much like promotional pressure groups such as Greenpeace. Indeed, some small parties – such as the United Kingdom Independence Party (UKIP) which really only seeks withdrawal from the European Union – are, in effect, single-issue groups.

Equally, many large pressure groups – such as the Confederation of British Industry (the umbrella body for many private employers) and the Trade Unions Congress (the umbrella body for most of the trade unions) – may have more real power, and closer links with Parliament through the main parties, than small parties such as the Natural Law Party. The Labour Party was, of course, founded by the trade unions, is still largely financed by them and has strong organisational links with them. The differences between parties and pressure groups are therefore often blurred.

Question...

5.3 To what extent have pressure groups become more important in recent years?

(25 marks)

Pressure groups and democracy

Arguments that pressure groups enhance democratic government

Pressure groups enhance pluralism, that is, competing centres of power, choice and representation; almost all shades of opinion are represented. This is especially true where 'pro' and 'anti' groups coexist – for example ASH (Action on Smoking and Health – anti-smoking) versus FOREST (the Freedom Organisation for the Enjoyment of Smoking Tobacco – pro-smoking).

Pressure groups 'fill the gaps' in the party system, e.g. by promoting causes which cut across party lines, especially on local issues or on 'moral' issues such as abortion and capital punishment. This is especially true where there are only two large parties which may be quite close together on the political spectrum.

Pressure groups provide channels of collective influence and power for the public where individual action (including voting) may be relatively weak or ineffectual. They provide channels of direct participation for the public, going beyond more indirect representation through Parliament; and channels of communication between the government and voters.

Pressure groups seek to represent deprived or inarticulate sections of society (e.g. Age UK, and the Child Poverty Action Group). Protective groups, especially, are usually internally democratic, in that their members elect their leaders. Trade unions, especially, are representative of large numbers of people (currently seven million in the UK); and their tactics of direct action – e.g. strikes – may be seen as mass, direct democracy or 'people-power'.

Pressure groups provide information, education and expertise for the public, Parliament and government (e.g. environmental groups), and therefore they are often consulted by MPs and the executive; and they may help to enhance open government by exposing significant events, information and issues – e.g. the Campaign for Freedom of Information.

Pressure groups channel new issues and concerns onto the political agenda – for example, the environmentalist and women's movements.

Pressure groups provide a check on 'parliamentary sovereignty' and 'elective dictatorship', especially where the electoral system is unrepresentative and parliamentary opposition is weak; hence they provide additional checks and balances in the UK's liberal democracy.

Pressure groups may promote continuity and stability of policy between successive governments.

Pressure groups may enhance political stability by providing a safety valve for more radical political grievances and demands.

Pressure groups may provide public services, e.g. legal aid and advice.

Arguments that pressure groups undermine democratic government

Pressure groups may by-pass or usurp the elected representatives in Parliament and government; MPs may be reduced to 'lobby-fodder'. (In the 1980s, Conservative Home Secretary Douglas Hurd likened them to sea-serpents, strangling ministers in their coils and distorting the constitutional relationship between government and electorate.)

Their lobbying tactics may amount to near-bribery and corruption of MPs.

Some international pressure groups, such as Greenpeace, control huge funds and have substantial influence in diverting investment and promoting campaigns which cut across national boundaries and government controls. 'When 122 countries agreed to stop using and selling land mines in 1997, the success was attributed not to the work of tireless government officials, but to the 1,000 or so non-governmental organisations (NGOs) in 60 countries which had lobbied ministers on the issue for years. At the signing ceremony in Ottawa, Jody Williams, the campaign's coordinator, remarked that NGOs had come into their own on the international stage. "Together," she said, "we are a superpower."' (Bond.)

This may be viewed positively or negatively.

Pressure groups may be small, sectional or unrepresentative but very influential or powerful, at the expense of majority or 'national' views or interests. For example, Mediawatch-UK (formerly, and famously, Mary Whitehouse's National Viewers' and Listeners' Association), campaigns against sex and violence in the media – but how far it really reflects wider public opinion is hard to gauge.

Insider pressure groups may have an excessively close and secretive relationship with the executive, excluding other views and interests – perhaps those of the majority.

The collective power of pressure groups may undermine individual rights and interests, contrary to 'liberal democratic' principles.

Promotional groups, especially, may be internally undemocratic – often with no election of leaders by members, leadership out of touch with its membership etc.; or they may claim to speak on behalf of others, but without any consultation or mandate to do so.

Pressure groups with constitutional aims may be internally dominated by people who seek to subvert liberal democracy itself: e.g. the Anti-Poll Tax Federation, the Stop the War Coalition and the 2010 student demonstrations contained many anarchists.

Pressure groups' methods may be illegal and/or coercive. In 2004, for example, the pressure group Fathers4Justice lobbed bags of purple flour from the public gallery of the House Commons at the Prime Minister during Question Time; they drew attention to their cause, but received very negative publicity and encouraged the security services to turn Parliament into a fortress. (But note that many pressure groups would defend such tactics in theory and in practice – see Chapter 8.)

Pressure group activities give powerless people a false sense of hope that they can have an impact and make a difference. It suits the ruling class or power elite that people channel their energies into narrow causes which do not question, challenge or threaten the fundamentals of the economic and political power systems. Meanwhile, only pressure groups which reflect and protect elite interests have much real chance of success.

Quiz

1. Suggest three possible criticisms of opinion polls.
2. Give two differences between promotional and protective pressure groups.
3. Which academic author devised the categorisation of pressure groups into 'insider' and 'outsider' groups?

4. Define 'insider' groups.
5. How many UK workers currently belong to trade unions?
6. List ten methods used by pressure groups.
7. What percentage of UK voters are members of any political party?
8. What is the main difference between parties and pressure groups?
9. What are 'extra-parliamentary parties'?
10. Give one example of a small party which looks and acts much like a single-issue pressure group.

Question...

5.4 Why are some pressure groups more successful than others? *(25 marks)*

Answers to questions

Note: The following are notes for guidance only and are not intended to be taken as model answers.

5.1 *Do promotional or protective pressure groups tend to have more power, and why?* *(5 marks)*

'Power' is the ability to act, or to make others act, as you wish, regardless of their consent. It is different from 'influence', which simply means persuasive effect. Protective (or sectional) groups tend to have more sanctions available to them – i.e. more real powers, such as withholding capital or labour. Private enterprise business groups can withhold finances, and trade unions can go on strike – for example, London underground workers can withdraw their labour and force commuters to walk to work. Promotional groups such as Shelter and the Child Poverty Action Group, on the other hand, tend to have only persuasive influence – they cannot make anyone do something against their will.

5.2 *What is meant by each of the following terms (all of which are related to the issue of trade unions)?* *(20 marks)*

a. **Block vote:** a method of union voting, e.g. at 'old' Labour conferences, where a majority union vote for a particular option resulted in 100% of that union's votes counting towards that option. This was phased out because of its disproportionality.
b. **Closed shop:** where an individual must belong to the appropriate union or association in order to work in a particular trade or profession. Largely prohibited by 1980s legislation, except for the professional associations.
c. **Corporatism:** tripartite (three-way) involvement and consultation of workers' and employers' groups with the government in economic policy making. A feature of the 1970s era of 'consensus politics'; Thatcherism in the 1980s was anti-corporatist.

d. **Functional representation:** consultation and/or decision making through occupational or industrial groups (rather than through parties). It was suggested as a democratic basis for a new second chamber by former Conservative Prime Minister Winston Churchill (1874–1965) in the 1930s.

e. **Sequestration:** freezing and/or seizure of some or all of a union's assets by the courts, as a penalty for contempt of court (introduced in 1984 by the Thatcher government, as an alternative to imprisoning union leaders, which tended to make them into political martyrs and to boost support for the union's cause).

5.3   *To what extent have pressure groups become more important in recent years?* *(25 marks)*

In the UK, the number of political parties is relatively small (around 150), whereas the number of pressure groups runs into thousands (the Directory of British Associations lists over 7,000). Political party membership in the UK is very low; less than 3% of British voters are members of any political party. This percentage has declined continuously since the 1960s (when it was about 10%). Over the same period, however, membership of and participation in pressure groups have increased markedly. (Famously, the Royal Society for the Protection of Birds, with 1.2 million members, is bigger than all of the main political parties combined.) Why might this be?

- Voters' disillusionment with political parties as self-serving, dishonest or simply boring.
- The stereotypical image of party politicians as unrepresentative 'grey men in grey suits'.
- The lack of clear ideological and policy differences – choice – between the main parties.
- The neglect of some key issues by the main parties.
- The lack of scope for active and productive voter participation in party politics.
- The scope for direct 'people power' and action in some pressure groups' methods.
- The focus upon a single, important issue or section of society by pressure groups.
- Growing public education, information and awareness about core political issues.
- The perception that pressure groups are more honest and altruistic than are political parties.
- New pressure groups being formed to oppose existing ones.
- The different membership of pressure groups – often younger and more diverse.
- The greater radicalism – even extremism – of some pressure groups.

On the other hand, however: parties, not pressure groups, still – and always will – form the bedrock of representative democracy in the UK. Pressure groups have no mandate from the voters (and promotional groups, especially, are often self-appointed, wholly unelected and quite unrepresentative). Pressure groups have, undoubtedly, become more important in recent years, but outright pressure group successes – in terms of aims achieved – are still not commonplace.

Quiz

1. Opinion polls may, sometimes, question an unrepresentative sample of people; they may offer limited options as answers; or they may shape the very responses that they are trying to measure.
2. Promotional groups pursue a cause external to their own membership, and are often internally undemocratic; whereas protective groups seek to protect their own, select membership and their leaders are elected by their members.
3. Wyn Grant.
4. Insider groups have close contacts with ministers and civil servants and significant influence upon policy making.
5. Seven million UK workers currently belong to trade unions.
6. Meeting with ministers, financing political parties, sponsoring MPs, drafting and promoting private members' Bills, striking, conducting or publicising opinion polls, petitions, pickets, leaflets and letters, media adverts, demonstrations and staged public events.
7. Three per cent of UK voters are members of any political party.
8. Pressure groups do not stand candidates for election – they merely seek to influence those in political office.
9. Extra-parliamentary parties are parties with no seats in Parliament – that is, most of them.
10. The Green Party looks and acts much like the pressure group Greenpeace.

5.4   *Why are some pressure groups more successful than others?*   (25 marks)

Pressure groups vary enormously in power and influence, depending on their type, size, membership, financial resources, links with parties, methods, media coverage and current trends in government policy. Even a single event – such as the BSE crisis, an epidemic of foot-and-mouth disease or an explosion at a nuclear power station – may suddenly boost the influence of an environmental pressure group. Large groups are not necessarily the most powerful. Protective groups tend to have more sanctions available to them than promotional groups, and hence more power – for example, the members of a key economic interest group may withdraw their labour or capital. Promotional groups may have considerable influence on public opinion or on government policy: for example, the NUS campaign against increases in tuition fees mobilised substantial support; but even the largest promotional groups – such as the Stop the War Coalition (against the invasion of Iraq) – usually lack the power to change government policy.

In sum, the factors which may affect pressure groups' success include:
- Whether they are insider or outsider pressure groups.
- Whether their aims or causes coincide with the ideological stance of the government of the day.
- Whether they are protective or promotional pressure groups.
- The size of the pressure group: for example, in 2010 Help the Aged and Age Concern merged to form Age UK, thereby increasing not only their numbers but their resources and contacts.
- The resources at their disposal – especially finances.
- Their supportive contacts and influence with the major political parties.
- Their supportive contacts and influence with the media.

- The character of their membership – for example (for promotional groups) middle-class, vocal, literate and active members; or (for protective groups) specialised, skilled and irreplaceable workers. For example, in 2011 the coalition government did a hasty U-turn over plans to privatise UK forests in the face of well-organised and vocal opposition from 'middle England' groups such as Save England's Forests.
- Whether they have the support of many, or most, voters.
- Presence/absence of influential opposition; for example, groups which help poor pensioners and children meet with little organised opposition.
- Celebrity support and involvement: for example, in 2009 the actress Joanna Lumley led a successful campaign to grant members of the Gurkha regiment residence rights in the UK.
- EU focus and access, e.g. Friends of the Earth Europe, and the European Small Business Alliance.
- Similarly, in response to devolution, many pressure groups in relevant policy areas such as education, health and transport have increasingly targeted Edinburgh, Cardiff and Belfast.
- Whether their cause coincides with a significant political occurrence such as a natural disaster or a war (reminding us of Prime Minister Harold Macmillan's comment that the most significant influences upon his tenure were 'Events, dear boy, events'). For example, the severe damage caused to the Fukushima nuclear power plant in Japan by a tsunami in 2011, and the resulting concern about radiation leakage, boosted support for anti-nuclear groups around the world.
- The Human Rights Act 1998 and Freedom of Information Act 2000 have given many pressure groups new opportunities for legal challenges to government policies and for gaining more access to official information.
- Pressure group methods – whether legal or illegal, peaceful or violent, serious or fun. If they are sufficiently eye catching, they may have influence. Disruptive tactics, such as strikes, exert power. Illegal or violent tactics may actually be counter-productive and create negative publicity for the pressure group and its cause. Activities which entertain as well as inform and mobilise – such as charity concerts – often have greater success.

Sample questions

Short
- What is a public opinion poll?
- What is a pressure group?
- Distinguish between 'insider' and 'outsider' pressure groups.

Medium
- What are the main types of pressure group?
- Outline the main differences between political parties and pressure groups.
- What methods do pressure groups employ to influence the political process?

Long
- Examine the view that pressure groups assert minority interests over those of the majority and that they are therefore a hindrance in a liberal democracy.
- To what extent have pressure groups become more important in recent years?
- Why are some pressure groups more powerful than others?

References

Bond, M. (2000) The Backlash against NGOs. In: *Prospect*, April.

Grant, W. (1989) *Pressure Groups, Politics and Democracy in Britain*, Philip Allan, London.

Useful websites

www.bbc.co.uk/news
   An excellent, wide-ranging and impartial source for topical news items and archive articles.

www.bbc.co.uk/learningzone/clips/pressure-groups/5620.html
   A BBC Schools Learning Zone website with short video clips on a range of useful topics, including pressure groups.

www.modernstudies.org.uk/press.htm
   A study and revision website with bullet-point summaries of a range of topics, including pressure groups.

www.historylearningsite.co.uk/pressure_groups.htm
   A study website with very useful summary notes on a range of topics in History and Politics.

www.google.co.uk
   Hundreds of thought-provoking images are also available by performing a Google image search on the topic of 'pressure groups'.

Parliament

Aims of this chapter

- To outline the history and functions of Parliament.
- To outline the changing composition and powers of the House of Lords.
- To evaluate the issues surrounding reform of the House of Lords.
- To outline and evaluate the diverse functions of the House of Commons.
- To outline recent reforms of the House of Commons.

History and functions of Parliament

> **key term...**
>
> **A bicameral legislature** A legislature with two chambers (or 'houses').

The UK Parliament at Westminster was created in the thirteenth century. It is now **bicameral**, that is, it has two 'chambers', or Houses – the House of Commons and the House of Lords – and is headed by the monarch. Every new parliamentary **Bill** (draft law) has to go through all three parts of Parliament before it can become a **statute law**, that is, an Act of Parliament.

Parliament is said to be the sovereign body in the UK political system – that is, it has law–making supremacy.

> **key term...**
>
> **Bill** Draft law going through Parliament.

> **talking point...**
>
> There is a very strong convention that no modern monarch will refuse 'royal assent' to a Bill, because it would be undemocratic for a non-elected monarch to challenge the will of the elected House of Commons. The last time a monarch refused royal assent for a Bill was in 1707, when Queen Anne tried to block the Scottish Militia Bill.

> **key term...**
>
> **Statute** Act of Parliament – a law passed by the Commons, Lords and Crown.

Functions of Parliament

1. Making the law.
2. Controlling the executive.
3. Representing the people.

Subsidiary functions
a. Debate and deliberation.
b. Controlling government finance.
c. Channel of communication between government and electorate.

The above list of the roles of Parliament could provide a useful framework for longer and more analytical AS level exam questions such as 'How effective is Parliament in performing its various functions?' Such broad questions on the roles of Parliament also cover the electoral system, the party system, the theory and practice of 'parliamentary government', the roles of MPs and peers and the impact of the EU and devolution – all of which, critics say, combine to limit Parliament's effectiveness in carrying out its functions today. Answers to such exam questions should be very broad ranging, concise and topical.

The House of Lords

Composition of the House of Lords

The House of Lords is a wholly unelected chamber. Until the 1950s, it was made up entirely of **hereditary peers** whose right to sit and vote in the chamber derived purely from a title inherited within the family. In 1958, **life peers** were established: members appointed by the Prime Minister of the day, for their lifetime only, whose titles are not hereditary. This gave the moribund chamber a new lease of life, with conscientious members appointed to do a proper job of work. Nevertheless, for most of the twentieth century, hereditary peers still made up two-thirds of the House of Lords – almost 800 of a potentially huge chamber of 1,200 peers. However, many of them rarely attended – a further source of criticism.

Also entitled to sit and vote in the House of Lords are the 26 senior bishops of the Church of England (including the Archbishops) – the Lords Spiritual. Until 2009, the most senior judges in the country – the **Law Lords** – were also legislators in the House of Lords, but they have been separated out to a new Supreme Court, in a significant constitutional reform which enhanced the separation of powers and hence the UK's claim to be a liberal democracy. The Law Lords are also now chosen by an independent Judicial Appointments Commission, rather than by senior politicians. Previously, the Law Lords were appointed and headed by the Lord Chancellor. The office of Lord Chancellor was an ancient and constitutionally unique office whose incumbent was simultaneously the Speaker of the House of Lords, a Cabinet minister with departmental responsibilities and the head of the judiciary in England and Wales. Thus, the office of Lord Chancellor had legislative, executive and judicial roles – a major breach of the principle of separation of powers. The Labour Government effectively abolished the office of Lord Chancellor in 2005. The title is still held by the Secretary of State for Justice (not, currently, a peer), but the House of Lords now has an elected Speaker and the top judges are independently appointed.

Most peers are members of the main parties. However, there are around 200 **cross-benchers** (so called because of the chamber's seating arrangements), who are independent peers without any party affiliation. They provide a relatively independent element which is absent from the House of Commons.

As long ago as 1909 (during his Budget speech), the then Liberal Chancellor of the Exchequer, David Lloyd George, criticised the hereditary peers in the following terms: 'They do not even need a medical certificate. They need not be sound in either body or mind. They only require a certificate of birth – just to prove that they were the first of the litter. You would not choose a spaniel on those principles.'

key term...

Hereditary peers Peers whose right to sit and vote in the chamber derives purely from a title inherited within the family.

key term...

Life peers Members of the House of Lords appointed by the Prime Minister of the day, for their lifetime only, and whose titles are not hereditary.

key term...

Law Lords The most senior judges in the UK.

key term...

Cross-benchers Independent peers without any party affiliation.

The 1997 Labour government came to power with a manifesto commitment to end the right of hereditary peers to sit and vote in the House of Lords, saying 'This will be the first stage in a process of reform to make the House of Lords more democratic and representative.' Most of the hereditary peers were excluded from the chamber in 1999. Lord Cranborne, then leader of the Conservatives in the House of Lords, did a secret deal with the Labour government to keep 92 hereditary peers, in return for the smooth passage of government legislation. (Much to the irritation of successive governments, however, the Lords have been more obstructive ever since, asserting a new degree of legitimacy since reform.)

There was traditionally a large majority of Conservative peers in the House of Lords, but this is no longer the case since the exclusion of most of the hereditary peers. Currently no party has an absolute majority in the House. There is no fixed limit to the number of peers in the Lords, as there is for MPs in the Commons.

Also in 1999, Prime Minister Blair voluntarily gave up his prerogative power to veto the names of Conservative and Liberal Democrat nominees for life peerages, and he announced a new appointments commission to nominate cross-bench peers; but the Prime Minister currently retains control of the *numbers* of new peers from each party, which is clearly the more significant power. Meanwhile, within his first three years in office, Blair created more new life peers (over 200) than Margaret Thatcher did in her entire 11 years as Prime Minister. Critics labelled many of these 'Tony's cronies' – such as his former flatmate Charlie, now Lord Falconer of Thoroton. As Conservative leader Michael Howard said in 2003, 'What of the pledge in the 1997 Labour manifesto to "make the House of Lords more democratic"? Well, we now know exactly what the Prime Minister means by democracy. One flatmate, one vote.'

It was widely expected that 'second stage' reform of the House of Lords would include a substantial elected element. In 2003, MPs were given seven free votes on options ranging from 0% to 100% elected members of the second chamber; this confused them so much that they voted against *all* of the options, leaving the UK with a wholly unelected second chamber – an option explicitly favoured by Prime Minister Blair. In 2007, MPs voted for a wholly elected second chamber, but the Lords again voted for a wholly appointed chamber, resulting in stalemate.

The 2010 coalition government proposed the following reforms:
- A small Senate of 300 members.
- 80% elected by PR, to serve 15-year, non-renewable terms.
- 20% independently appointed life peers.
- No changes to current powers.

Obvious problems with these proposals include:
- How to retire existing peers.
- How to ensure that a more democratic second chamber does not challenge the primacy and authority of the House of Commons.
- How to hold elected members accountable if their tenure is non-renewable, i.e. if voters cannot re-elect or sack them.

Meanwhile, Conservative Prime Minister David Cameron created 117 new life peers during his first year in office, making the total number of peers 792 by April 2011. Facilities in the House of Lords, such as bars, dining rooms and libraries, became quite overcrowded.

Powers of the House of Lords

The powers of the House of Lords, as a wholly non-elected chamber, are much more limited than those of the Commons. The Lords can play a useful role in amending and revising legislation, but they cannot touch **money Bills**, i.e. Bills which are largely about the raising and spending of government money. They have the power to delay other Bills for a maximum of one year, after which the Commons can invoke the Parliament Act 1949 and simply override the Lords. The only kind of Bill which the Lords can block entirely is any Bill seeking to extend the life of Parliament beyond its five-year maximum legal term – in effect, any Bill which seeks to postpone or cancel a general election. The Lords have never, yet, had to use this power.

If amendments by the House of Lords are not accepted by the Commons, usually the Lords will back down – but not always. They have become more obstructive in recent years, claiming a new legitimacy since the 1999 reforms. The average number of successful government defeats in the Lords per year under the Conservative governments of 1979–97 was 13; but the average number per year of Labour government defeats by the Lords 1997–2010 was 43. For example, they repeatedly blocked curbs on the right to jury trial. However, the Blair governments were determined to overturn most of the Lords' changes – further examples of 'elective dictatorship'. For example, Blair governments invoked the rarely used Parliament Act to override the House of Lords and push through the introduction of closed lists for European Parliament elections (1999), the lowering of the gay age of consent to 16 years (2000) and the ban on fox hunting (2004).

In 2010, the House of Lords defeated the coalition government by restricting its power to abolish quangos (ironically, by a Liberal Democrat amendment). In 2011 it rejected the government's plans for future five-year, fixed-term Parliaments, and for elected police commissioners – again ironically, thanks to a Liberal Democrat rebellion. Most government defeats in the House of Lords are, however, temporary.

Defence of the House of Lords

One possible argument in defence of an unelected chamber is that its members gain knowledge and experience over their many years of service, and that they add stability and continuity to the law-making process. Since the members have total job security (short of outright abolition of their right to sit in the chamber), they are less beholden to their parties and to the government than are MPs, and so peers may be more independent-minded and less vulnerable to party pressure.

People who have distinguished themselves in wider public life, such as in industry, the trades unions, education, science, the arts and local government, are often brought into the House of Lords. 'Expertise' is also, therefore, often cited as a merit of the Lords; examples include former Prime Ministers such as Thatcher and Callaghan; former foreign secretaries such as Hurd and Carrington; Law Lords such as Nolan and Neill; businessmen such as the banker Lord Williams of Elvel; and media people such as Lord Melvyn Bragg. Lord Hives was an expert on beekeeping, and contributed usefully to the Bees Act

key term...

Money Bills Government Bills concerned mainly with the raising or spending of public money.

1980! Following a positive report by the prestigious House of Lords' Science and Technology Committee, medical trials of cannabis began late in 1999. (Of course, the House of Commons also contains experts in many diverse fields, i.e. election does not preclude expertise – though it may render the presence of expertise in the chamber less permanent.)

Although it is unrepresentative in electoral terms, the House of Lords is, in many ways, as socially representative (or unrepresentative) as the Commons: for example, in 2010 21% of peers were women and 4% were from ethnic minorities, very much like the membership of the House of Commons.

Criticisms of the House of Lords

However, it is hard to defend a wholly non-elected legislative chamber in a twenty-first-century liberal democracy – particularly one that still contains hereditary members.

In 2010, three peers were suspended for abuses over second homes allowances.

Following the Constitutional Reform and Governance Act 2010, which required peers and MPs to be domiciled in the UK for taxation purposes, some peers gave up their non-domiciled status. Others, such as architect Lord Foster, gave up their seats in the House of Lords so as to remain non-domiciled – that is, to live abroad and avoid paying UK taxes.

Peers' attendance allowance of £300 per day does not require them to do any useful work, merely to sign in and out.

The main problem holding back further reform of the House of Lords is the lack of consensus among the main parties and politicians.

---

analyse this...

Past proposals for reform of the House of Lords include:

- Complete abolition (in the radical 'old' Labour manifesto of 1983).
- 'Functional representation' based upon pressure and interest groups, rather than upon a party system (suggested by Winston Churchill in the 1930s).
- Indirect election of representatives from regional bodies (in the Liberal–SDP Alliance manifesto of 1987).
- A directly elected second chamber based on proportional representation (suggested by Conservative Lord Hailsham in his 1976 lecture 'Elective Dictatorship').

Question

AS level exam questions often ask what reforms of the Lords *you* would recommend, and why.

Consider the following points:

- The first issue to consider is what roles and powers the second chamber should have – that is, how strong it should be as a check upon the first chamber. For example, should its delaying power be extended? Should it be allowed to amend government money Bills? If you want a substantially stronger and more effective second chamber than the present House of Lords, then it should be democratised to ensure that its powers are legitimate.

- How many members should there be in the second chamber?
- Should they all be elected or should some be appointed?
- Who should appoint the appointed members?
- By what system should the elected members be elected?
- What term of office should the elected members have?
- Should the upper chamber be elected on different constituencies from the House of Commons?
- Should the term of office coincide with that of the House of Commons or, like the US system, overlap?
- Should any such changes require a referendum?

The House of Commons

This section attempts to describe and assess the role of the House of Commons, under the headings of the three main functions of Parliament, listed at the beginning of this chapter:

- Making the law.
- Controlling the executive.
- Representing the people.

Making the law

Parliamentary sovereignty

The Westminster Parliament is the supreme – ultimate – law-making body within the UK. It can pass, amend or repeal any law without challenge from any other UK institution. Parliament cannot be ruled illegal, nor can it be bound by any laws of any previous Parliament. Thus no Parliament can bind its successors. All other rules of the constitution (e.g. conventions) can be overridden by Parliament, which can also take back, by law, any power given away to any other bodies – e.g. the European Union or the devolved assemblies. Also, Parliament is not always bound by its own laws (statutes), but instead by a special body of law known as **parliamentary privilege**. (This exempts MPs from some ordinary law; for example, they cannot be sued for slander for words spoken in Parliament.) The Westminster Parliament is subject only to the political sovereignty of the people at a general election (as long as Parliament chooses not to ban elections).

There are two broad types of parliamentary Bills:

1. **Public Bills** – concern the general public interest:
   a. Government Bills.
   b. Money Bills: a special type of government Bill, which cannot be amended by the House of Lords.
   c. **Private members' Bills**: introduced by a backbench MP rather than by the government. These are usually public Bills. These rarely succeed because of lack of time or lack of government support; only seven were

key term...

Parliamentary privilege The exemption of MPs from some ordinary laws under the special laws and customs of Parliament.

key term...

Public Bills Laws which concern the general public interest.

key term...

Private members' Bills Bills introduced by backbench MPs of any party rather than by the government.

key term...

Private Bills Laws which concern individual or group interests.

successful in the 2009–10 session. One such was the Autism Act 2009, which sought to improve provisions for adults with autism.

2. **Private Bills** – concern specific individual or group interests: these breach the 'rule of law' and the principle of legal equality; they are therefore subject to special procedures and scrutiny.

Box 6.1   Example of a private Bill

Allhallows Staining Church Act 2010

2010 CHAPTER v

An act to remove certain restrictions relating to the use of land comprising the former church of Allhallows Staining, its churchyard, and other adjoining land in the City of London; to make provision for the removal of any human remains from the land and to enable its use for other purposes; and for connected purposes.

---

key term...

Green Paper A consultation paper preceding a Bill.

key term...

White Paper The draft document of a Bill.

key term...

Standing committees House of Commons committees of backbench MPs from all parties in the Commons, which scrutinise proposed legislation.

The stages of parliamentary legislation are usually quite lengthy and complicated:

- **Preparation and consultation:** government Bills are drafted by lawyers and civil servants, and may be preceded by a consultation paper (**Green Paper**) and/or a draft proposal (**White Paper**) – so called simply because of the colour of paper upon which they are printed.
- **First reading:** a purely formal reading of the Bill's title to alert the MPs, groups and interests concerned (a necessary process before the invention of printing, and it has lived on by tradition).
- **Second reading:** this is the really important stage of the Bill, when it is outlined by the relevant minister and debated in detail and voted upon in the Commons chamber.
- **Committee stage:** the Bill goes to a **standing committee** of backbench MPs (the composition of which reflects the parties' numerical strength in the House of Commons) which scrutinises and amends the details of the Bill, clause by clause. The party whips have substantial control over the composition of the committees; thus, on average, only 5% of committee amendments have not been previously agreed with the government and, of these, only 1% succeed.
- **Report stage:** the amended Bill is reported back to the whole House of Commons.
- **Third reading:** only minor amendments to grammar and wording can be made at this stage, and the whole Bill is then either passed or rejected by the House of Commons.

---

talking point...

When a Bill has been passed by the House of Commons, it goes to 'another place' – the Commons' quaint name for the House of Lords because, traditionally, the two Houses cannot name each other!

The Bill now goes through similar stages in the House of Lords, where it may be amended.

Then it is returned to the Commons, where the Lords' amendments are debated and either accepted or rejected. A controversial Bill may go back and forth between the two Houses several times (so-called 'parliamentary ping-pong') until one backs down. For example, the Parliamentary Voting System and Constituencies Bill (paving the way for the AV referendum and boundary changes) spent several weeks in dispute between the Lords and the Commons in early 2011, including a rare all-night sitting in the Lords and the highest turnout since the vote on reform of the House of Lords itself. In the end, the House of Commons overturned every significant Lords' amendment.

- **Royal assent**: nowadays a formality.

Although the parliamentary law-making process is usually slow and cumbersome, occasionally it may move very fast: for example, draconian new anti-terrorism laws were passed through Parliament in a single day in 1998 – the Criminal Justice (Terrorism and Conspiracy) Act 1998 – despite a significant backbench revolt; and, in 2010, the Loans to Ireland Bill was rushed through, despite Conservative MPs' protests.

Question...

6.1 Distinguish between the roles and powers of the House of Commons and the House of Lords.

(10 marks)

Challenges to Parliament's law-making role

The European Union

A major challenge to Parliament's law-making function has come from the UK's membership of the European Union, whose legislation takes precedence over the laws of member states. The assent of Parliament is not required. This effectively negates parliamentary sovereignty; although, technically, Parliament could legislate to withdraw from the EU at any time, in practice this is unlikely. The more policy areas that are transferred to the decision making of the EU – for example, by the Single European Act 1986 and the Maastricht Treaty 1993 – the less law-making power rests with Westminster.

Devolution

Devolution means the delegating – passing down – of some legislative or executive powers from central to regional bodies. This included, in 1999, the creation of a fairly powerful Scottish Parliament, which has also considerably lightened the load of Westminster and may ultimately – in practice, if not in theory – threaten its national sovereignty. In 2011, following a referendum, the powers of the National Assembly for Wales were increased to give it primary law-making powers.

key term...

Devolution The delegation of some legislative or executive powers from central to regional bodies.

key term...

Delegated legislation Laws made by bodies other than Parliament – e.g. ministers or local authorities – under powers passed to them by Parliament.

Delegated legislation

Delegated legislation is also known as 'indirect' or 'secondary' legislation because it allows ministers, local authorities and others to make detailed regulations under powers delegated by Parliament in a parent Act. It can thus turn ministers into law makers, breaching the principle of 'separation of powers'. Alternative titles are 'statutory instruments' and 'Orders in Council'. There are thousands each year, compared with just a few dozen primary Acts of Parliament.

Box 6.2   Example of a statutory instrument

Statutory Instrument

2011 No. 981

ANIMALS, ENGLAND AND WALES

The Aquatic Animal Health (England and Wales) (Amendment) Regulations 2011

Question...

6.2   What are the limits on the sovereignty of Parliament?   *(10 marks)*

Controlling the executive

This is the most controversial issue of all. In 'parliamentary government', the executive (government) is appointed from among the members of the legislature (Parliament) and is, in theory, subordinate and accountable – responsible – to the legislature. Parliament is therefore supposed to examine, debate, criticise and check the activities of the government, to publicise executive actions, to convey public opinion to the government and to authorise the raising and spending of money by government – through, e.g. debates, votes on government Bills, Question Time and committees. The ultimate form of control is a vote of no confidence in the government by the House of Commons, which would oblige the government to resign.

Her Majesty's Opposition (HMO) (comprising the second-largest party in the Commons) is a formal element of the constitution: the leader and whips are paid a special salary and HMO is given special time and opportunities in House of Commons' procedures which are unavailable to other parties. The Leader of the Opposition is traditionally consulted on bipartisan matters (e.g. the invasion of Iraq), and is given a chauffeur-driven car. Twenty Opposition Days are set aside in the Commons' yearly timetable for debate and criticism of government, with the topics chosen by the Opposition. Nevertheless, the Opposition is clearly weak against a majority government.

Occasionally the House of Commons does persuade the government to back down on an issue – e.g. cutting the provision of free school books in 2011 – but invariably this is under pressure from the government's own backbenchers. The Opposition alone cannot 'control' a majority executive; its main function is to present itself to the electorate as 'the alternative government'.

Scrutiny and control of government finance should be the House of Commons' most significant check on the executive, but debate on 'estimates' of how much money is required by each government department are given only three days of parliamentary time each year, and no Budget item has been defeated since 1910. The Commons Public Accounts Committee (PAC) and National Audit Office (NAO) scrutinise £700 billion per year of public money to ensure that it has been lawfully spent. However, the Public Accounts Committee has itself said that the Commons' control of government finance – 'Parliament's key constitutional function' – is 'largely a formality', because the estimates and accounts provided by Whitehall are both too vague about key financial categories and objectives, and too complex on minor details. The PAC can only criticise *after* the event, to little effect; for example, its 2011 report on health inequalities in the UK stated that 'The current government emphasis on individual responsibility, "nudge", and fairness does not address the inequitable structure of society. The decision to scrap the socioeconomic duty of the Equality Act is especially problematic . . .'. The budgets of the security and intelligence services – an estimated £2 billion per year – are not subject to parliamentary scrutiny at all. The PAC also often accuses apathetic MPs of simply ignoring its many critical reports about government waste and mismanagement.

Question Time – the noisiest and most publicised part of the House of Commons' day – epitomises government's accountability to Parliament; but many query the usefulness of the whole exercise, and it has been described as 'ritualised combat' and 'a Punch and Judy show'. Prime Minister's Question Time (PMQT) occupies a half-hour slot every Wednesday. Other ministers answer questions only about once a month under a rota system. Confident ministers, well briefed by their officials and advisers, can usually deal easily with oral questions by giving combative or evasive answers. Sycophantic questions planted by the whips and asked by docile backbenchers make the process even easier for ministers. As former MP Tony Benn said in 2001, 'Question Time now has so many planted questions, it might as well be called gardeners' question time.'

Nevertheless, a genuine 'rottweiler' – especially from the minister's own party – highlights Question Time as a pure form of ministerial accountability, under the media spotlight, which can occasionally make or break ministerial careers.

Select committees

Departmental select committees, comprising backbench MPs from all of the parties, scrutinise each government department's policies, activities and spending. In a typical parliamentary week, about two dozen inquiries are being conducted by the select committees. They generally scrutinise specific departmental issues and publish reports, to which the government must respond. 'Establishment of Select Committees [in 1979] is routinely cited as one of the most important reforms in the House of Commons' recent history, and one of the few occasions when a reform unequivocally strengthened Parliament against

key term...

Departmental select committees
House of Commons committees of backbench MPs from all of the parties, which scrutinise each government department's policies, activities and spending.

the executive' (UCL Constitution Unit). They also sometimes give external witnesses – such as oil company and bank bosses – a highly publicised rough ride.

Departmental select committees 2010
  Business, Innovation and Skills
  Communities and Local Government
  Culture, Olympics, Media and Sport
  Defence
  Education
  Energy and Climate Change
  Environment, Food and Rural Affairs
  Foreign Affairs
  Health
  Home Affairs
  International Development
  Justice
  Northern Ireland Affairs
  Science and Technology
  Scottish Affairs
  Transport
  Treasury
  Welsh Affairs
  Work and Pensions

The select committees do attract growing media attention – e.g. the Energy Committee's highly critical report in 2011 on the government's energy policy as 'incoherent and misleading' was much publicised; absenteeism is low; they are quite independent minded – e.g. in 2011 the Conservative-dominated Public Administration Committee was highly critical of the coalition government's 'botched' efforts to save money by cutting quangos, and the Public Accounts Committee strongly criticised a £36 billion 'black hole' in defence spending. The government has sometimes acted on select committees' recommendations: e.g. in 2002, Prime Minister Blair agreed that he would henceforth appear twice yearly before a special Liaison Committee made up of all of the chairpersons of the select committees, and Prime Ministers Brown and Cameron continued this exercise in accountability. In 2006, the Home Affairs committee rejected the government's call for 90-day detention without charge for foreign terror suspects and instead recommended 28 days – a proposal ultimately supported by the House of Commons and accepted by the government. In 2010, the Culture, Media and Sports committee opposed the introduction of new privacy laws – again, accepted by the House of Commons and the government.

Importantly, since 2010, committee chairs and members are elected by fellow MPs through secret ballot rather than being hand-picked by the whips, which has produced more independent-minded and balanced committees.

However, the select committees still lack the time, resources, staff, expertise, power and, perhaps above all, even the will, to be more than an irritant to the government. Often the government simply ignores the recommendations of the committees – e.g. the Health Committee's early criticisms of the 2011

Health and Social Care Bill; and they have been criticised for headline-grabbing by interviewing celebrities (e.g. the Home Affairs Committee and Joanna Lumley). Most committee reports, it is said, end up on the dusty shelves of Whitehall.

In sum, most commentators agree that the select committees have done little to shift the real balance of *power* between executive and legislature, though they do have *influence* and provide information, detailed scrutiny and public criticism of government. Reformers say that they need bigger budgets, stronger powers and more capacity to conduct research, initiate debates and interrogate ministers and civil servants more rigorously. Such solutions lie largely in the committees' own hands.

The Ombudsman

The **Ombudsman** This is a parliamentary bureaucrat whose job is to investigate public complaints about government maladministration – but who (again) lacks power and resources. The current Ombudsman – Ann Abraham – has threatened to resign because the government is still too secretive and has banned her investigations of ministerial conflicts of interest, e.g. former Prime Minister Blair's private gifts from foreign leaders.

key term...

Ombudsman A parliamentary bureaucrat whose job is to investigate public complaints about government maladministration.

Factors that contribute towards 'elective dictatorship'

In summary, some commentators argue that the task of Parliament is simply to scrutinise and sustain the government rather than to 'control' it. However, most say that Parliament should control the government but usually cannot, for the following reasons:

- Majority governments.
- Party discipline.
- Government control of parliamentary time.
- Government secrecy and obfuscation, especially on finance.
- Government control of civil service personnel and information.
- The growth of delegated legislation.
- The lack of power of parliamentary committees and the Ombudsman.
- Lack of resources and facilities for MPs.
- The weakness of the non-elected House of Lords.
- The growing influence on government of extra-parliamentary bodies such as the EU, business, pressure groups and the media.

For all of these reasons – but, above all, because of the power of a majority government in control of a sovereign Parliament with a flexible constitution – Lord Hailsham's phrase 'elective dictatorship' is often used to describe the British system of government.

One rare exception to this concerns the stringent Anti-terrorism, Crime and Security Act 2001, which replaced 14-day detention of foreign terror suspects with internment – indefinite detention without charge (far less, trial or conviction). Some individuals were held at Belmarsh prison for years under this draconian provision. However:

- In 2004, the Law Lords ruled internment illegal because it discriminated against foreign nationals.
- In 2005, the government's attempt to replace internment with 90-day detention without charge was defeated by the House of Commons.

- In 2008, the government's attempt to replace internment with 42-day detention without charge was defeated by the Lords; 28-day detention was accepted by Parliament.
- In 2011, the 28-day detention rule was allowed to lapse and detention reverted to the original 14-day rule.

> ## talking point...
>
> The Anti-terrorism, Crime and Security Act is a useful example of the main checks and balances upon the executive:
> - 2004: the courts ruled internment illegal.
> - 2005: the House of Commons defeated 90-day detention.
> - 2008: the House of Lords defeated 42-day detention.

MPs are not as supine as they are sometimes portrayed. The 2001–5 and 2005–10 Parliaments witnessed the greatest number of backbench revolts since the Second World War, with rebellions in 21% and 28% of divisions, respectively. Notable examples were:

- 2003: Iraq (139 Labour rebels – the largest revolt in modern UK politics, but unsuccessful because the Conservative opposition backed the government).
- 2005: top-up tuition fees (72 Labour rebels – unsuccessful).
- 2005: Blair's Labour government was defeated in its attempt to introduce 90-day detention without charge for foreign terror suspects.
- 2006: Blair's Labour government needed Conservative support to win the votes on education reform and Trident nuclear weapons.
- 2009: Brown's Labour government was defeated in its attempt to refuse members of the Gurkha regiment the right to live in the UK.

The 2010 coalition government has made some significant policy U-turns in the face of political, pressure group, public and press opposition – for example, on funding for school sports, free school books and school milk, and the privatisation of UK forests. In 2011 it announced a 'pause' in the controversial Health and Social Care Bill to allow for consultation. In sum, elective dictatorship is not a permanent feature of UK politics; it depends, crucially, upon the size of a government's majority.

Representing the people

The extent to which Parliament represents the British people depends, first, upon what is meant by the concept of a 'representative' – e.g. reflecting the views, interests and/or social backgrounds of the voters. The pros and cons of Westminster's first-past-the-post electoral system (already discussed in Chapter 3) are obviously central to this issue. So is the question of 'elective dictatorship', when the government can usually use its majority to dominate the Commons.

Another issue which has reared its ugly head is 'sleaze' – immoral or dishonest behaviour by politicians – notably and most recently with the revelations (thanks to the Freedom of Information Act) in 2009 about the abuse of MPs' expenses. By 2011, four MPs – Derek Chaytor, Jim Devine, Eric Illsley and Elliott Morley – had been jailed for up to 18 months for expenses abuses.

Parliamentary privilege is the exemption of MPs from some ordinary laws under the special laws and customs of Parliament. It is therefore a special category of constitutional law, which breaches 'the rule of law' and principle of legal equality. It was originally a defence against the power of the Crown, and is now justified on the grounds that MPs can better represent the people if, for example, they have complete freedom of speech. Thus they are immune from slander or libel actions for words spoken in Parliament. This may be used to expose wrongdoing: e.g. Labour MP Stuart Bell used parliamentary privilege to expose the scandal of 'cash for questions' in the 1990s; and in 2011 Liberal Democrat MP John Hemming used it to expose former banker Fred Goodwin's 'super-injunction', i.e. prohibition on media reporting. However, this privilege may be abused by MPs: in 1999, Unionist MP Ian Paisley named and accused a man of being an IRA killer although the police said that the man was an innocent farmer. Several MPs accused of expenses abuses sought, in 2010, to escape court trial on grounds of parliamentary privilege, but failed.

Reforms of the House of Commons

The 1997–2010 Labour government made a few small and piecemeal reforms to the House of Commons (apart from devolution, which was a major constitutional change):

- Modernisation Committee: This was set up to consider reforms to the Commons. It recommended, for example, changes to the Commons timetable, so that its proceedings start and finish earlier in the day. This was done to reduce the number of late-night and all-night sittings and to make the place more 'family friendly', especially for its women members.
- A new building – Portcullis House, next door to the Palace of Westminster – has given MPs added office space.
- Prime Minister Tony Blair changed Prime Minister's Question Time from two 15-minute slots per week to one 30-minute slot at noon on Wednesdays. Successive Prime Ministers have continued this.
- Prime Ministers have answered questions from the Commons' Liaison Committee (of select committee chairpersons) twice a year, since 2002.
- Pre-legislative scrutiny: more parliamentary scrutiny of draft Bills prior to formal legislation was introduced.
- Carry-over of legislation: Bills that fail to pass in one parliamentary year can be carried over into the next.
- Westminster Hall debates consider uncontroversial issues and select committee reports.
- The 2010 coalition government proposed a referendum on reform for Westminster elections, reduction of the number of MPs to 600, fixed-term Parliaments, recall of MPs and reform of the House of Lords. The referendum (in May 2011) failed. At the time of writing, other reforms were still in process.

Quiz

1. When did a monarch last refuse assent to a Bill?
2. What is a White Paper?
3. Who is responsible for drafting government Bills?
4. List the stages of legislation for public Bills.
5. What is a joint committee?
6. What is Hansard?
7. Once elected by the Commons, does the Speaker cease to be an MP?
8. List three functions of the Speaker.
9. Who is the present Speaker of the Commons?
10. What are Standing Orders?
11. What is a 'simple closure'?
12. What are 'the usual channels'?
13. List three functions of the whips.
14. What is 'pairing'?
15. What is meant by 'withdrawing the whip' from an MP?
16. Why might an MP seek a written rather than oral answer at Question Time?
17. What is the function of the Ombudsman?
18. What is the Consolidated Fund?
19. When was a government last defeated in the Commons on a vote of no confidence?
20. What are (a) the PLP and (b) the 1922 Committee?

Answers to questions

Note: The following are notes for guidance only and are not intended to be taken as model answers.

6.1 *Distinguish between the roles and powers of the House of Commons and the House of Lords.* *(10 marks)*

In theory, the UK Parliament – Commons and Lords together – has legal sovereignty: i.e. it can pass, amend or repeal any law and no other UK body can override its laws. The Commons and Lords share the same roles of making the law, scrutinising and controlling the executive and representing the people. These functions include debate and deliberation, and acting as a channel of communication between the government and the electorate.

'Power' is the ability to do, or make others do, something regardless of their consent, based on the capacity to coerce, i.e. to reward or punish. Parliament's power is supposed to be based on authority – derived from elections for the House of Commons and from tradition for the House of Lords. However, since the House of Lords is wholly unelected, it has much more limited powers (laid down by the Parliament Acts of 1911 and 1949) than does the House of Commons. The Lords cannot touch money Bills. They have the power to delay other Bills for a maximum of one year, after which the Commons can 'invoke the Parliament Act' and simply override the Lords, e.g. the 2004 ban on hunting with dogs. The only kind of Bill which the Lords can block entirely is any Bill seeking to extend the life of Parliament beyond its five-year maximum term.

Given that the House of Commons is elected and the House of Lords is not, and given their different legal powers, the two chambers perform their roles in different ways. For example, the Commons has more legitimate authority in scrutinising the executive, and especially in representing the British people.

6.2   *What are the limits on the sovereignty of Parliament?*   *(10 marks)*

External limits:
- The European Union
- Economic power bodies – domestic and transnational
- USA
- Other international institutions – UN, NATO, IMF etc.
- Devolved bodies, such as the Scottish Parliament
- Pressure groups
- Media
- Referenda
- Ultimately: the political sovereignty of the electorate

Internal limits:
- Government from within Parliament

Conclusion: In theory, there are no absolute, *formal* limits to the sovereignty of the Westminster Parliament. In practice, however, there are significant constraints.

Note: as always, credit will be given in exams for topical examples of each point made.

Quiz
1. 1707 – Queen Anne, the Scotch Militia Bill.
2. A draft outline of proposed legislation, before publication of a Bill.
3. The Parliamentary Counsel of 30 lawyers – part of government, not Parliament.
4. First reading, second reading, committee stage, report stage, third reading, amendments in the Upper House, royal assent.
5. A committee of MPs and peers combined.
6. The official record of proceedings in the House of Commons.
7. No – but s/he must become impartial.
8. a.   Decides allocation of Commons time to parties and MPs.
   b.   Exercises casting vote on a Bill where votes are tied; by convention, arranges for vote to be taken again.
   c. Selects chairmen for, and allocates Bills to, standing committees.
9. John Bercow.
10. Written rules on the conduct of Commons business.
11. A time limit on debate in the Commons; the Speaker decides whether to allow a vote on it, and 100+ MPs must win a majority vote for the motion to be carried.

12. The Government and Opposition chief whips, who between them arrange special debates etc.
13. a. Circulate weekly notice of Commons business to their party MPs.
    b. Arrange pairing, ensure that MPs vote as required, and count the votes.
    c. Convey backbench opinion and make recommendations for promotion to the party leadership.
14. Government and Opposition backbenchers arrange permanent 'pairs' at the beginning of each Parliament; they can then be mutually absent on important votes (with the permission of the whips).
15. Suspending or expelling the MP from the party (not from Parliament).
16. For more detailed information, rather than mere publicity.
17. To investigate citizens' complaints of maladministration by government departments.
18. The government's account at the Bank of England.
19. 1979 – a *minority* Labour government.
20. a. The Parliamentary Labour Party – all Labour front and backbenchers in the Commons.
    b. All Conservative backbenchers; not frontbenchers.

Sample questions

Short
- Describe the membership of the House of Lords.
- Describe the functions of Parliament.
- Outline two features of a presidential system of government.

Medium
- Outline the role of the whips in maintaining party unity in the House of Commons.
- What are the features of parliamentary sovereignty?
- In what ways is Parliament representative?

Long
- To what extent are there limits on the sovereignty of Parliament?
- Discuss the view that MPs should always support their party in Parliament.
- Should the House of Lords be further reformed and, if so, how?

References

Hailsham, Q. (1976) Elective Dictatorship. The Dimbleby Lecture. In: *The Listener*, 21 October.

House of Commons Public Accounts Committee (2011) *Report on Health Inequalities in the UK.*

UCL Constitution Unit (2011) *The Impact of House of Commons Select Committees, April 2010–January 2011.*

Useful websites

www.bbc.co.uk/news
An excellent, wide-ranging and impartial source for topical news items and archive articles.

www.parliament.uk
The official website of the UK Parliament.

www.parliament.uk/visiting
Helpful details about visiting Parliament.

www.parliamentlive.tv/Main/Home.aspx
Live Parliamentary webcasts.

http://news.bbc.co.uk/1/hi/programmes/the_westminster_hour/default.htm
The Westminster Hour. The website of a long-running and informative weekly Radio 4 programme.

The executive

Aims of this chapter

- To outline and evaluate the role of the monarchy.
- To outline the diverse functions of the Cabinet.
- To outline and evaluate the doctrines of ministerial responsibility.
- To outline and evaluate the powers of the Prime Minister.
- To assess the leadership styles of recent Prime Ministers.
- To explain the role of the civil service.

What is the executive?

The executive consists of the Crown; the political policy makers: the Prime Minister, a Cabinet of the 20 or so most senior ministers, and other, junior ministers (around 100 altogether); and the administrators: the civil servants, a hierarchy of non-elected, permanent, impartial and professional 'bureaucrats' (around 500,000 altogether) who administer the policies and machinery of government. The work of the government is divided into around 20 policy departments – defence, foreign affairs, employment, education, etc. – and the ministerial heads of the major departments are members of the Cabinet.

Box 7.1 Example of a government department and its ministers

The Foreign and Commonwealth Office 2010

Rt Hon William Hague MP

Secretary of State for Foreign and Commonwealth Affairs with overall responsibility for the work of the FCO.

David Lidington MP

Minister of State responsible for European issues and NATO.

Jeremy Browne MP

Minister of State responsible for South East Asia/Far East, Caribbean, Central/South America, Australasia and Pacific, human rights, consular, migration, drugs and international crime, public diplomacy and the Olympics.

Alistair Burt MP

Parliamentary Under-Secretary of State responsible for Afghanistan/South Asia, counter terrorism/proliferation, North America, Middle East and North Africa, FCO finance and human resources.

Henry Bellingham MP

Parliamentary Under Secretary responsible for Africa, United Nations, economic issues, conflict resolution, and climate change.

Rt Hon Lord Howell of Guildford

Minister of State responsible for all of FCO Business in the House of Lords, the Commonwealth, and International Energy Policy.

> **key term...**
> **Crown** The permanent, abstract institution which embodies the supreme power of the state in the UK, culminating in the monarchy.

In the British system of 'parliamentary government', ministers are appointed from within Parliament and are accountable to Parliament, and thus (indirectly) to the electorate, for the policies of the government and the actions of government departments.

> **key term...**
> **Monarchy** The institution of hereditary rule by a royal family.

Question...

7.1 What steps might citizens take if they felt that they had been unfairly treated by a government department? *(20 marks)*

The monarchy

The **Crown** is the permanent, abstract institution which embodies the supreme power of the state. It is the formal head of all three branches of government – legislature, executive and judiciary – and all acts of state are done in the name of the Crown. The **monarchy** is the institution of hereditary, royal rule (as opposed to a republic, which is usually headed by an elected president). The sovereign or the **monarch** is the individual person upon whom the Crown is conferred. In Britain, succession to the throne is determined by the Act of Settlement 1701; this states, for example, that male heirs take precedence over females, and that the monarch is not allowed to be, nor to marry, a Roman Catholic – outdated and offensive rules, according to some critics.

The **royal prerogative** is the term given to the formal powers of the Crown. They are part of common law, and *de jure* are substantial. They include: the appointment and dismissal of the Prime Minister; other powers of patronage; the opening and dissolving of Parliament; approval of statute law; the declaration of war and signing of treaties. However, Britain no longer has an **absolute monarchy**, but a **constitutional monarchy**: an impartial (non-party political), largely symbolic head of state whose powers are exercised by, and on the advice of, ministers, in theory subordinate to the will of Parliament, the people and the rules of the constitution. Most of the powers listed above have either passed

> **key term...**
> **Monarch** The individual person upon whom the Crown is conferred.

> **key term...**
> **Royal prerogative** The formal powers of the Crown.

> **key term...**
> **Absolute monarchy** Rule by a hereditary head of state with total political power.

> **key term...**
> **Constitutional monarchy** Rule by an impartial (non-party political), largely symbolic, hereditary head of state.

to the Prime Minister and other ministers or are governed by strict convention. The monarch, therefore, has very little personal power. This is meant to 'democratise' the powers of the Crown and to keep the monarch out of political controversy. In the nineteenth century, therefore, constitutional writer Walter Bagehot classed the monarchy as a 'dignified' rather than 'efficient' part of the constitution, with much symbolic and ceremonial authority but little real power. Except in times of constitutional crisis, he said, 'The Queen reigns, but does not rule'.

- **Crown immunity:** The monarch, in her private capacity, is above the law. The legal immunity conferred by the royal prerogative may also extend to institutions and servants of the Crown such as ministers and intelligence agents. Since this puts them, too, above the law, it is sometimes controversial.

analyse this...

The royal prerogative

The conventional view of the royal prerogative is that, following the Glorious Revolution of 1688, it was made subject to parliamentary control; and the British constitution, based on parliamentary government under the rule of law, dates from that time.

The fact is that the royal prerogative is alive and well, and living, for the most part, in 10 Downing Street. Prime ministerial (and ministerial) use of the royal prerogative allows ministers to bypass parliamentary, and often judicial, control – especially where 'national security' is invoked. Examples have included: ministers trying to withhold information in the court case about 'arms to Iraq' in 1995; MI5 officers being allowed to 'bug and burgle' without fear of prosecution; the government forbidding some civil servants to be members of trades unions; and the Home Office supplying the police with plastic bullets and CS gas.

Questions

a Suggest why the powers of the Crown have not been *formally or legally* transferred to the Prime Minister and other ministers.

b Suggest three exceptional circumstances in which the monarch may exercise real power.

c Since the monarch usually has little real personal power, give reasons why the royal prerogative – the power of the Crown – is still controversial.

key term...

Cabinet Combined heads of executive policy departments and team of senior policy makers.

The Cabinet

The 20 or so most senior government ministers form the **Cabinet**, which grew out of the body of policy advisers to the monarch in the eighteenth century. According to current constitutional theory (since Bagehot), we have **Cabinet**

government: collective policy making by a united team of senior ministers, with the Prime Minister *primus inter pares* (first among equals). All Cabinet ministers are MPs or peers drawn from Parliament, and most are appointed as heads of major government departments such as the Foreign Office and Treasury. The Prime Minister decides on the size and composition of the Cabinet and allocates portfolios, i.e. departmental responsibilities.

The 2010 coalition cabinet contained 23 ministers, five of them Liberal Democrats. The more junior ministerial posts were allocated in roughly the same proportion. There were 119 ministers in all.

key term...

Cabinet government Collective policy making by a united team of senior ministers, with the Prime Minister *primus inter pares* (first among equals).

Functions of Cabinet

In theory, Cabinet is the collective policy-making body within the government, with the Prime Minister simply first among equals. So said Bagehot in the 1860s. In practice, however, it is not possible for a committee of around two dozen people, meeting for perhaps one hour per week, to make all of the key policy decisions. Ministers' diaries since the 1960s reveal that Cabinet meets less frequently and makes fewer decisions nowadays.

In reality, therefore, the modern Cabinet performs the following roles:

- Endorsing – sometimes merely rubber-stamping – policy decisions made elsewhere, such as in Cabinet committees.
- Shaping presentation of policy decisions.
- Reviewing the on-going successes and failures of previous policy decisions.
- Coordinating and arbitrating on policy disputes and decisions across diverse departments – seeking to ensure 'joined-up' government.
- Discussing and intervening in political and policy crises.
- Negotiating the process of government business in Parliament.

Prime Ministers often hold meetings with small and select groups of senior ministers, officials and advisers to discuss and decide specific policies. This practice is dubbed a 'kitchen cabinet'. Examples of its use include decision making over the Falklands conflict (1982), sterling's exit from the ERM (1992), military action in Kosovo (1999) and Iraq (2003). Kitchen cabinets have long been criticised as undemocratic and unaccountable.

Functions of ministers

Note: An exam question on the 'functions of ministers' includes both Cabinet ministers and junior ministers, but does not include the collective functions of Cabinet, nor the legislative or constituency functions of MPs.

- Policy making.
- Political responsibility for a whole department or for a policy subsection of a department.
- Managing a department or a subsection of it.
- Defending the interests of a department, for example in receiving government funds from the Treasury, in media statements and in international forums such as the EU Council of Ministers.
- Steering departmental Bills through Parliament.
- Answering to Parliament for the decisions of their department, for example in question times and select committees.

Question...

7.2 What factors affect the appointment of ministers? *(10 marks)*

key term...

Collective ministerial responsibility The convention that ministers make policy decisions collectively and that if ministers disagree so strongly with a policy that they cannot defend it in public, they should resign.

key term...

Individual ministerial responsibility The convention that ministers should be publicly accountable for all of the actions of their departments and themselves, and should resign in the event of serious departmental or personal error.

The Ministers of the Crown Act 1937 gives ministers (together with the Leader of the Opposition and Chief Whip) a special salary, and the Ministerial and Other Salaries Act 1975 sets an upper limit of 22 paid Cabinet members; but the Cabinet's composition, functions and powers are otherwise governed largely by conventions. The two most important of these are the doctrines of **collective** and **individual ministerial responsibility**.

Collective ministerial responsibility

This doctrine rests on the assumption that ministers make policy decisions collectively and that they should, therefore, publicly support and defend all government policies and should be accountable for them to Parliament and, thus, to the electorate – e.g. through Question Time and votes of censure (no confidence) in the House of Commons. If ministers disagree so strongly with a policy that they cannot defend it in public, they should resign, as did Cabinet minister Robin Cook in 2003 over the invasion of Iraq. In 2010, the Labour Secretary of State for Work and Pensions, James Purnell, resigned in protest against Gordon Brown's leadership. He hoped by doing this to incite a collective rebellion, but failed to do so.

Following a change of government in 2010, three minor parliamentary aides – two Liberal Democrats (e.g. Jenny Willott) and one Conservative – resigned in protest against the increase in student tuition fees. However, not one minister voted against the policy.

A united front – even if it is sometimes a façade – increases public confidence in the government and gives it strength and stability. More importantly, collective responsibility is central to the principle of the democratic accountability of the whole government to Parliament and, thus, to the voters.

In recent years this convention has been weakening. Because of the rise of prime ministerial power, 'adversary politics' in the 1980s and internal party divisions in the 1990s, ministers have often disagreed publicly with government policy but have not resigned over it. For example, in 2004, Cabinet ministers such as Jack Straw made public their opposition to government plans for compulsory national identity cards – but no one resigned.

The convention is particularly weak within a coalition government. Within the first year of the 2010 coalition government, Liberal Democrat Business Secretary Vince Cable repeatedly and publicly disagreed with his own government's policies (for example, with Prime Minister Cameron on immigration targets), telling journalists that he could resign and 'bring the government down' if 'pushed too far' by Conservative ministers. He was to have been responsible for making a 'quasi-judicial' decision on whether media mogul Rupert Murdoch could buy up the remaining 61% of BSkyB but, after telling undercover journalists posing as constituents that 'I have declared war on Mr Murdoch', he was removed from decision making on media policy – but not sacked from office. In 2011, Liberal Democrat minister Chris Huhne criticised education cuts in his constituency, and survived. The Labour Opposition was, naturally, critical; but some right-wing Conservative MPs also perceived one rule for Conservative dissidents and another for Liberal Democrats, who were essential to the survival of the coalition government. However, by 2011 some Conservative ministers were also in open revolt: Cabinet minister Iain Duncan Smith actually joined a cross-party protest on the steps of Number 10 against closures at a local hospital – again, he survived unscathed.

Table 7.1 Examples of ministerial resignations over collective responsibility

Date	Minister	Post	Reason for resignation
2011	Lord Oakeshott	Treasury minister	Banking policy
2010	Jenny Willott	Ministerial aide	Tuition fees
2009	James Purnell	Secretary of State for Work and Pensions	Against Prime Minister Brown
2003	Clare Short	Secretary of State for International Development	Iraq
2003	Robin Cook	Leader of the Commons	Iraq
1995	John Redwood	Welsh Secretary	Against Prime Minister Major
1990	Geoffrey Howe	Leader of the Commons	Against Prime Minister Thatcher

Collective responsibility should also apply to the Opposition but, in its early months in 2010, the leadership of the Labour Opposition was divided with Shadow Home Secretary Alan Johnson publicly disagreeing with leader Ed Miliband on the issue of tuition fees, but surviving in office.

Note: The resignation of the whole government after a no confidence vote in the House Commons (e.g. 1979) or a general election defeat is also an example of collective responsibility in action.

Individual ministerial responsibility

This doctrine rests on the assumption that ministerial heads of department are the chosen representatives of the people, while the non–elected civil servants who administer policy within each department are impartial, anonymous bureaucrats merely carrying out political orders. Ministers, not civil servants, should therefore be publicly accountable for all of the actions of their departments, and should resign in the event of serious error.

For example, in 2010, Scottish transport minister Stewart Stevenson resigned over the handling of the winter snow crisis. In 2004, immigration minister Beverley Hughes resigned over policy errors within her department. Education Secretary Estelle Morris resigned in 2002 over her personal failure to meet key policy targets.

However, this convention is also weakening. In the 1990s, Conservative Home Secretary Michael Howard made a novel distinction between 'policy' and 'operational' responsibilities and sacked top civil servant Derek Lewis, rather than resigning himself over a series of prison crises. Other ministers have, since, copied his example: e.g. Labour Leader of the Commons Peter Hain blamed police operations rather than policy decisions for the breach of Palace of Westminster security by Greenpeace protesters who scaled the Big Ben clock tower in 2004. Ministerial resignations over departmental errors are now conspicuously rare, mainly because ministers can pin the blame on their civil servants. This may undermine the democratic accountability of government ministers and openly embroil civil servants in controversial political matters.

Individual ministerial responsibility also covers *personal* impropriety – often sexual or financial scandals. For example, Labour's Welsh Secretary Ron Davies resigned in 1998 over sexual impropriety on Clapham Common; and at the end of that year, Peter Mandelson and Geoffrey Robinson both resigned over a large, undeclared loan from Robinson to Mandelson at a time when Mandelson's Department for Trade and Industry was investigating fellow minister Robinson's personal financial affairs. Trade and Industry Secretary Stephen Byers had to resign in 2002 after forcing his senior civil servant Martin Sixsmith's sacking over a row with his (Byers') personal spin doctor Jo Moore (who, infamously, had e-mailed the department on 11September 2001 that 'This is a good day to bury bad news'). In 2004, Home Secretary David Blunkett resigned over the fast-tracking of a visa for his lover's nanny. In 2010, barely a fortnight after the general election, Liberal Democrat Chief Secretary to the Treasury David Laws was the first minister in the new government to resign, over a personal scandal about his expenses.

Most of these ministers went reluctantly, under sustained pressure from the media, party and public opinion.

It is significant that ministers resign far more frequently over personal indiscretion (since there is no one else to blame) than over departmental error; although the latter seems, constitutionally, to be more important.

Table 7.2 Examples of ministerial resignations over individual responsibility

Date	Minister	Post	Reason for resignation
2010	David Laws	Chief Secretary to the Treasury	Expenses (personal)
2008	Peter Hain	Work and Pensions minister and Welsh Secretary	Donations (personal)
2005	David Blunkett	Secretary of State for Work and Pensions	Private job (personal)
2004	David Blunkett	Home Secretary	Private life (personal)
2002	Estelle Morris	Secretary of State for Education	Policy failure (departmental)

Table 7.2 (continued)

Date	Minister	Post	Reason for resignation
2002	Stephen Byers	Secretary of State for Transport	Conflict between civil servant and spin doctor (departmental)
2001	Peter Mandelson	Northern Ireland Secretary	Abuse of office (personal)
1998	Peter Mandelson	Secretary of State for Trade and Industry	Private finances (personal)

Very occasionally, ministers resign for purely private (usually family) reasons, as did Shadow Chancellor Alan Johnson in 2011. These resignations have no great constitutional import.

Note: The conventions of collective and individual responsibility apply only to frontbench ministers, not to ordinary backbench MPs, who can rebel or commit personal indiscretions without being expected to resign.

The Prime Minister

Table 7.3 UK Prime Ministers, 1945–2010

Period of office	Prime minister	Comments
1945–51	Clement Attlee (Lab.)	
1951–55	Sir Winston Churchill (Cons.)	Resigned 1955; new Prime Minister Eden called and won election.
1955–57	Sir Anthony Eden (Cons.)	Resigned over ill-health and Suez crisis.
1957–63	Harold Macmillan (Cons.)	Resigned 1963. No general election.
1963–64	Sir Alec Douglas-Home (Cons.)	
1964–70	Harold Wilson (Lab.)	Majority of four. Re-elected 1966.
1970–74	Edward Heath (Cons.)	
1974–76	Harold Wilson (Lab.)	Feb. 1974 election: minority government. Oct. 1974 election: majority of three. Resigned 1976. No general election.
1976–79	James Callaghan (Lab.)	1977–79 minority government. Informal 'Lib-Lab Pact'. Defeated on vote of censure in House of Commons.
1979–90	Margaret Thatcher (Cons.)	Resigned 1990. No general election.

Table 7.3   (continued)

Period of office	Prime minister	Comments
1990–97	John Major (Cons.)	Lost his majority by 1997.
1997–2001	Tony Blair (Lab.)	1997 election: record 179 majority. 2001 election: 167 majority. 2005 election: 66 majority. Resigned 2007. No general election.
2007–10	Gordon Brown (Lab.)	
2010–	David Cameron (Cons.)	Conservative–Liberal Democrat coalition.

Of the last ten prime ministers, only four were removed by the voters; three resigned for personal reasons (Eden, Macmillan and Wilson), two were (formally or *de facto*) forced out by their parties (Thatcher and Blair), and one was forced out by Parliament (Callaghan). This highlights the limits to prime ministerial power.

By convention, the monarch chooses as Prime Minister the leader of the majority party in the House of Commons. The first Prime Minister in the modern sense is usually said to be Sir Robert Peel, who held office after the 1832 Reform Act, which established the principle of executive accountability, through Parliament, to the electorate.

talking point...

UK voters do not elect the Prime Minister. In a general election, voters elect individual constituency MPs (usually on the basis of a party label) to Westminster, and if one party has over 50% of Commons' seats, its leader – by convention – is appointed as Prime Minister by the monarch. This fact becomes clear on the rare occasions when there is no majority party – in which case, the monarch may have some real degree of choice of Prime Minister, since there is no convention to guide her (for example, in February 1974 and in 2010); and also when the governing party chooses to sack its own leader – and hence also the country's Prime Minister – in mid-term, as the Conservatives did with Margaret Thatcher in 1990, and as Labour also effectively did with Tony Blair in 2007.

The powers of the Prime Minister derive from the royal prerogative and rest entirely on convention, not law. They include:

- Huge powers of patronage, including the appointment and dismissal of all ministers and the allocation of departmental responsibilities; appointing top civil servants and clergy; awarding peerages, honours and titles.
- Deciding the structure of government – e.g. creating, merging or splitting departments.
- Deciding the agenda for Cabinet meetings, chairing Cabinet meetings, and summing up decisions reached in Cabinet (without a vote).
- Deciding the number, composition and terms of reference of Cabinet committees; and the Prime Minister may chair important Cabinet committees personally.
- Coordinating government policy.
- Political head of the civil service, ultimately responsible for the number, duties and conditions of work of civil servants.
- Representing the government and country at international summits.
- Deciding the date of the general election within the five-year term.
- Deciding the timetable of government legislation in the House of Commons – a function usually delegated to the Leader of the House, a senior Cabinet minister.
- Leader of the party (this role differs somewhat within different parties).
- Communicating government policy and advice to the monarch through weekly meetings.

According to the theory of collective Cabinet government, the Prime Minister is simply *primus inter pares* ('first among equals') – but a leader who can hire and fire all other ministers is clearly more than this. The conventional list of the Prime Minister's powers is extensive and, since the 1960s, many commentators have perceived a trend towards prime ministerial rather than Cabinet government in Britain. However, the real *powers* of a Prime Minister vary considerably according to circumstance; above all, they depend on *authority*.

Cabinet or prime ministerial government?

Former Labour minister Richard Crossman, in the 1960s, was among the first to assert that 'The post-war epoch has seen the final transformation of Cabinet government into prime ministerial government'. He borrowed Bagehot's 1860s phraseology to argue that the Cabinet had joined the monarchy in 'dignified impotence'. It is often difficult to assess the real balance of power within the executive because of the exceptional secrecy which shrouds the whole machinery of UK government and policy making. For example, only after the 2010 general election did the civil service release a 'secret' letter from the former Labour Attorney General (government lawyer) to then Labour Prime Minister Tony Blair, dated January 2003, stating that 'the existing UN resolution does not authorise the use of force in Iraq'.

Factors enhancing prime ministerial power

- Party discipline.
- Prime Minister's Office: the increasingly powerful group of political advisers and press officers (or 'spin doctors') and civil servants at 10 Downing Street.
- Prime minister's control of the wider civil service bureaucracy throughout government.

key term...

Prime ministerial government
Policy making dominated by the Prime Minister rather than by Cabinet.

- Media: the growing influence of the modern mass media and their increasing focus upon the Prime Minister.
- The EU: the Prime Minister is national leader and policy maker at the European Council and EU summit meetings.
- Consensus politics: when the policies of the two main parties are quite similar, the media and voters focus, instead, upon the personalities and images of the party leaders.
- Time: the Prime Minister has no departmental responsibilities.
- Control of **Cabinet committees**, which have existed since the 1920s and which are established by the Prime Minister to enable the Cabinet to deal more efficiently with policy making. All Cabinet committees are chaired by a senior Cabinet minister chosen by the Prime Minister – if not by the Prime Minister personally – and have a number of Cabinet ministers, and perhaps civil servants, as members. There are currently around a dozen Cabinet committees in total, but their numbers, personnel and powers are decided solely by the Prime Minister. Some are permanent committees, while others are set up to deal with particular issues as they arise. Cabinet committees carry out the bulk of Cabinet policy-making work. These (according to writer Peter Hennessy) are the real 'engine room' of British government. The Prime Minister also decides whether the committees merely make recommendations to the full Cabinet or actually make key policy decisions.

> **key term...**
>
> **Cabinet committees** Small subgroups of ministers, chosen by the Prime Minister, to aid policy making.

CABINET COMMITTEE SYSTEM

1. Cabinet and Cabinet committees are groups of ministers that can take collective decisions that are binding across government. The Cabinet is the supreme decision-making body in government, dealing with the big issues of the day and the government's overall strategy. Cabinet committees reduce the burden on Cabinet by enabling collective decisions to be taken by a smaller group of ministers. The composition and terms of reference of Coalition Cabinet committees are a matter for the Prime Minister, in consultation with the Deputy Prime Minister.

2. The Coalition Committee is a formal committee of Cabinet which meets to consider issues relating to the operation of the Coalition. It is co-chaired by the Prime Minister and the Deputy Prime Minister.

3. Under the Coalition Government, each committee has a chair from one party and a deputy chair from the other party. The chair and deputy chair have the right to remit an issue to the Coalition Committee if it affects the operation of the Coalition and cannot be resolved by the originating committee. The use of this right will be kept to a minimum.

Table 7.4   Cabinet committees, 2010

Cabinet committee	Members	Chair
Coalition Committee	10	Prime Minister and Deputy Prime Minister
National Security Council (NSC)	11	Prime Minister
NSC (Threats, Hazards, Resilience and Contingencies)	18	Prime Minister

Table 7.4   (continued)

Cabinet committee	Members	Chair
NSC (Nuclear Deterrence and Security) (restricted attendance)	7	Prime Minister
European Affairs Committee	14	Foreign Secretary
Social Justice Committee	10	Secretary of State for Work and Pensions
Home Affairs Committee	19	Deputy Prime Minister
Economic Affairs Committee	13	Chancellor of the Exchequer
Banking Reform Committee	7	Chancellor of the Exchequer
Parliamentary Business and Legislation Committee	13	Leader of the House of Commons

Source: Cabinet Office.

Prime Ministers have other, informal sources of policy advice such as sympathetic pressure groups (e.g. for Thatcher, the Adam Smith Institute; and, for Blair, Demos). Critics of prime ministerial power fear that these bodies do not simply advise on policy but help to make policy decisions. Since they are non-elected, and bypass cabinet government, this may be seen as 'unconstitutional'.

Many key policy decisions since the Second World War are said to have been made by the Prime Minister (usually with the advice and agreement of a few senior ministers, civil servants, policy advisers, etc.) rather than by the Cabinet as a whole.

Key examples of 'prime ministerial policies' are said to include: the Budget, nuclear weapons, and intelligence and security, which have never been matters for Cabinet government.

- **Thatcher (1979–90):** the Falklands conflict (1982); abolition of the Greater London and metropolitan councils (1985); the bombing of Libya by US planes from British bases (1986); the 'Spycatcher' affair (1986–88); the poll tax (1988).
- **Major (1990–97):** the Gulf 'War Cabinet' (1991).
- **Blair (1997–2007):** Formula One tobacco advertising exemption; the Millennium Dome; Amsterdam Treaty; personal veto of Chancellor Brown's plan to increase the top rate of income tax in 1998; appointment of friend and Scottish media owner Gus McDonald as Scottish industry minister from *outside* Parliament, contrary to powerful convention; Blair, personally and strongly, backed US President George W. Bush on the 'war on terror' and invasion of Iraq – despite clear Cabinet divisions on the issue.
- **Brown (2007–10):** intervened decisively in 2008 to prop up the ailing banking system, and was widely supported internationally for this as well as for his leadership on world poverty and climate change; but he was, by nature, an autocratic leader who quickly alienated many senior colleagues and who was blamed by opponents and punished by the electorate for presiding over economic recession.
- **Cameron (2010–):** demonstrates the personal capacity for effective leadership, but will find dominance difficult in a coalition government with dissidents in both parties at all levels.

Suggested reforms to curb the powers of modern Prime Ministers include:
- A 'constitutional premiership' – outlining and limiting the powers of the Prime Minister (and perhaps also the Cabinet) in law.
- Election of the Cabinet by the parliamentary party.
- Transferring the Prime Minister's powers of patronage to committees, the House of Commons or the Speaker.
- More political advisers for ministers.
- Ministers choosing their own senior departmental civil servants.
- Less power and authority for the Prime Minister's spin doctors.

However, the case for prime ministerial government in the UK should not be overstated. All Prime Ministers face real constraints.

Constraints on 'prime ministerial government'

Authority is the essential precondition of prime ministerial power. It derives from the electorate, the House of Commons, the Crown and, above all, the party. Unlike an US President, a British Prime Minister depends upon party support and loyalty (e.g. Thatcher, who was ousted by her party in 1990, despite having a safe majority in the Commons). The authority of a coalition Prime Minister such as Cameron is undermined by government membership of party opponents, and by the fact that his party did not win the general election outright.

Every prime ministerial power is also a responsibility; if it is misused, the Prime Minister may lose authority, and even risk losing office: e.g. Thatcher over Europe and the poll tax; Major over his failure to control party divisions and 'sleaze'; and Blair over Iraq.

There are constraints upon the Prime Minister's appointment and dismissal of ministers: they should come from Parliament, should represent all regions of the country, should reflect the range of political feeling in the party and retain party support, and they should, preferably, be honest and competent. Such constraints in a parliamentary system contrast with the unlimited patronage powers of a US President, which may generate a 'spoils system'. A Prime Minister also must 'be a good butcher' (i.e. be willing to sack incompetent or dishonest ministers when necessary); on the other hand, too many reshuffles suggest prime ministerial misjudgement – after all, s/he appointed them in the first place.
- Cabinet revolts are rare, but significant: e.g. against Blair's proposed compulsory national ID cards (2004).
- Backbench revolts: e.g. against 90-day detention of terrorism suspects in 2005. Also, Prime Minister Blair wanted to support a licensing system for fox hunting, but was defeated.
- The Lords: e.g. defeats in 2011 of the government's plans for future fixed-term Parliaments.
- Pressure groups may be a key constraint: e.g. the Communication Workers Union prevented the part-privatisation of Royal Mail in 2008, during Gordon Brown's tenure.
- The EU is a growing constraint on the policy-making power of any Prime Minister (e.g. the world-wide ban of the export of British beef, imposed by the EU in 1996 to prevent the spread of 'mad cow disease' and lifted only in 2006) and may also affect his or her authority if relations are clumsy (e.g. Thatcher).

The media and civil service may be a hindrance as well as a help, but a Prime Minister's effective power at any time depends on a wide variety of circumstances: personality and charisma, health and energy, size of majority, length of time in office and the proximity of a general election, the state of the economy, international events (e.g. war), the popularity and competence of the Opposition (especially its leader) etc. When former Prime Minister Harold Macmillan was asked what was his biggest challenge, he famously replied, 'Events, dear boy, events'. For example, Blair unexpectedly had to delay the 2001 general election because of an epidemic of foot-and-mouth disease; Brown presided over a credit crunch and economic recession, which were not of his making; and Cameron had to respond to popular uprisings across North Africa, notably in Libya.

To quote former Liberal Prime Minister Herbert Asquith (1852–1928): 'The office of the Prime Minister is what its holder chooses and is able to make of it.' This stresses the flexibility of prime ministerial power, but also its limitations.

In sum, to expect to assume either cabinet government or prime ministerial government, in any literal sense, may be too simplistic. The tasks of modern government are too many for a group of 20 or so busy (and more or less temporary) ministers – never mind one person. Policy making is a pluralist process, dispersed throughout what writer Peter Madgwick calls 'the central executive territory' – though the diverse groups of ministers, civil servants, advisers and experts involved may often be directed or even dominated by the Prime Minister. The key problems arising from this process are:

- The secrecy surrounding the policy-making process.
- The fear that PM-dominated policy making may produce unbalanced or ill-judged policies, unchecked by Cabinet or the House of Commons (given the strength of party discipline).
- The fear that policy decisions are made by non-elected, unaccountable groups and individuals.
- The perceived decline in ministerial accountability to Parliament and to the voters.

A UK presidency

The growing emphasis in British politics and in the media on party leaders' individual personalities, styles and images has led some (e.g. Michael Foley) to suggest that British government is becoming 'presidential'.

However, a formal presidential system is based on separation between the executive and legislature; for example, in the USA, the President is separately elected by the people, and neither he nor his appointed executive team (also called the Cabinet) are allowed to be members of Congress (the US equivalent of Parliament). The President may therefore lack a majority in Congress, and may thus be weaker than a British Prime Minister – e.g. Obama's failure to close Guantanamo Bay prison. An outright 'presidential system' therefore has additional checks and balances which are lacking in the British system of 'parliamentary government'.

In the looser sense, however, recent prime ministers, such as Tony Blair, undoubtedly displayed a more **'presidential'** *style* of leadership than most: i.e. a carefully cultivated and exceptionally personal, populist, 'hands on' style and image, in touch with the public and distanced from both his Cabinet and his

key term...

UK 'presidentialism' A style and image of prime ministerial leadership which is exceptionally personal, populist and 'hands on', distanced from Parliament, Cabinet and party.

party ('spatial leadership' or 'leadership stretch'). Blair's style of leadership was dubbed 'sofa government' – informal, private meetings which neglected Cabinet government. It was strongly criticised in a 2004 report by the former Cabinet Secretary Lord Butler; given Butler's status as a former top UK civil servant, the BBC's Andrew Marr called this report 'a red card from God'. Examples of Blair's presidential style included: his claiming of a personal mandate for the creation and success of 'new' Labour; his walkabout with wife Cherie upon his victory in 1997 (and Cherie herself personifying the 'first lady' syndrome, e.g. her attendance at the 1999 music Brit Awards); his 'call me Tony' relationship with ministers and officials; his 'people's Princess' speech after the death of Diana, Princess of Wales; his personal intervention in the Northern Ireland and Middle East peace talks; and personal slogans such as the 'third way' etc. A leaked memo from Blair in 2000 said, 'We need eye-catching initiatives . . . and I should be personally associated with as much of this as possible'. Blair visited 22 countries in the three months following the 11 September 2001 attacks on America. In 2002 he launched monthly, live TV press briefings. The decision on the 2003 invasion of Iraq was a supremely presidential act

Gordon Brown, by contrast, was criticised for his apparent personal discomfort in media appearances, his 'fake' smiles and his public gaffes (e.g. about his meeting with 'bigoted woman' Gillian Duffy during the 2010 election campaign).

The 2010 election was highly personalised and the televised leadership debates were conspicuously presidential. David Cameron's heavily airbrushed 2010 election billboard was ridiculed for glamorising him, and he was criticised for side-lining his senior colleagues. His 'Big Society' project was a clear echo of US President Lyndon Johnson's 'great society'. His foreign visits – e.g. to India and Egypt – were notably self-referential. Even Larry the cat, who arrived at 10 Downing Street in 2011 (to kill the rats), was widely presented as the latest in presidential pets.

Modern Prime Ministers, emulating the White House model, have a powerful team of party-political advisers in Number 10 (each with their own staff), including a Chief of Staff, Principal Private Secretary, Director of Communications, Director of Events, Director of Policy Operations, Head of Policy Directorate and Chief Adviser on Strategy.

After the 2010 general election, Prime Minister David Cameron put his personal photographer and film maker on the public payroll, but quickly had to return them to the party payroll after widespread protest – highlighting, again, limits on the role of the Prime Minister and contrasts with the American presidential model.

The civil service

Civil servants are non-elected administrators and officials of the government. There are around 500,000 of them, and they form a hierarchy within each government department. At the top are the higher civil service – the Permanent Secretaries and other 'mandarins' (as they are often called, after the Chinese bureaucrats of old). Their functions include: giving information and policy advice to ministers, preparing policy papers and speeches, keeping the ministers' official diaries and dealing with correspondence, organising and

key term...

Civil servants Permanent, impartial, non-elected career administrators and officials of the government.

minuting meetings, anticipating parliamentary questions and preparing answers for ministers, consulting with outside interest groups and running the departments. Further down the ladder are the administrative and clerical officials who administer the departments and policies of government in Whitehall and around the country.

As permanent, non-elected career officials who serve under successive governments of any party, civil servants are required to be **neutral**, i.e. they should not let political or personal bias influence their work. Civil servants are also not supposed to have policy-making power, although their advice may legitimately influence ministers' decisions. Therefore, civil servants are also meant to be **anonymous**, i.e. not publicly accountable for the work of their department; the minister in charge is answerable to Parliament and the public for government policy and administration, according to the convention of individual ministerial responsibility.

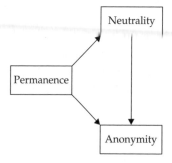

Figure 7.1   Civil service conventions

The New Right Conservative government under Thatcher sought to 'roll back the frontiers of state' and 'cut the bureaucracy', in accordance with its *laissez-faire* economic philosophy and its wish to cut public spending. Civil service numbers were reduced in the 1980s by over 100,000. They now total around 500,000, and are falling still further with the post-2010 programme of cuts in public spending and jobs.

Also under Thatcher's government, politically sympathetic businessmen and industrialists were brought in to devise ways of making the civil service more efficient and management minded. Criticisms of these proposals centred mainly upon fears of loss of political (ministerial) accountability for policy administration.

There has, indeed, been some blurring of the question of political responsibility. One prime example is of the former Conservative Home Secretary Michael Howard, who sacked the chief executive of the prison service, Derek Lewis, in 1995 over a series of prison crises, rather than resigning himself, by asserting a novel constitutional distinction between 'policy' and 'operational' decisions. Many other ministers have since followed his example: under Blair's government, Lord Falconer passed the blame for financial problems incurred by the Millennium Dome project to civil servant Jennie Page; Defence Secretary Geoff Hoon blamed his officials for not telling him about reports of prisoner abuse in Iraq; and Leader of the Commons Peter Hain blamed police operations rather than policy decisions for the breach of Palace of Westminster security when Greenpeace protesters scaled the tower of Big Ben in 2004. All of these ministers, thus, successfully resisted pressures to resign. This is, arguably, unconstitutional.

> **key term...**
>
> **Civil service neutrality** As permanent, non-elected career officials who serve under successive governments of any party, civil servants should not let political or personal bias influence their work (though they are allowed to vote).

> **key term...**
>
> **Civil service anonymity** Civil servants should not be publicly accountable for the work of the department; the minister in charge is answerable to Parliament and the public for government policy and administration, according to the convention of individual ministerial responsibility.

> **key term...**
>
> **Executive agencies** Organisations of civil servants, structurally separate from the departments and headed by a chief executive but still, *de jure*, subject to ministerial responsibility.

True or false?

1. Parliament can abolish the monarchy at any time.
2. The monarch, in her personal capacity, is above the law.
3. The modern monarch has no political power.
4. There are approximately 100 members of the government.
5. Some ministers are wholly unelected.
6. The Cabinet has been described as 'the real engine room' of British government.
7. The Prime Minister is not elected as such.
8. The monarch's choice of Prime Minister is based on convention, not law.
9. Assertions of 'prime ministerial government' began in the 1980s with Thatcher.
10. Civil servants should be neutral and therefore cannot vote.

Civil service power and influence

As non-elected officials, civil servants may influence ministers' policy decisions but they should not, in theory, have power themselves.

However, critics, such as writer Peter Kellner, argue that civil servants derive power from many sources, such as:

- Their large numbers, compared with ministers.
- Their permanence, compared with ministers.
- Their experience and expertise.
- Their network of inter-departmental committees, which parallels the Cabinet committee network.
- Their effective control of the administrative processes.
- Their close involvement in national security and intelligence matters.
- Their extensive powers of patronage over thousands of titles and appointments which are nominally the responsibility of the Prime Minister.
- British membership of the EU, which has necessitated much more preparation and coordination of policies by officials.

Quiz

Briefly answer the following questions

1. List three significant prime ministerial powers.
2. Define 'Cabinet government'.
3. Which constitutional writer asserted that the UK has Cabinet government?
4. Who said that Cabinet has joined the monarch in 'dignified impotence'?
5. List five (policy) examples of prime ministerial government.
6. List five constraints on a Prime Minister.
7. List five factors which may affect the relationship between the Prime Minister and the Cabinet.
8. Suggest three reasons why a Prime Minister might reshuffle his/her ministerial team.
9. Explain Foley's concept of 'a uniquely British presidency'.
10. In what sense is Britain *not* presidential?

11. To whom is the executive accountable?
12. List the three key conventions which govern the role of civil servants.
13. Why are civil servants required to be neutral?
14. Why are civil servants required to be anonymous?
15. Suggest three reasons why civil service permanence may be declining.

Answers to questions

Note: The following are notes for guidance only and are not intended to be taken as model answers.

7.1 *What steps might citizens take if they felt that they had been unfairly treated by a government department?* *(20 marks)*

* Contacting the relevant government department.
* Contacting their local MP (who should pass on and pursue the complaint).
* Asking their MP to contact the parliamentary Ombudsman.
* Going to an administrative tribunal.
* Going to the UK courts for a legal hearing.
* Going to the European Court of Human Rights or European Court of Justice.
* Using the media.
* Using the internet – even setting up a specific website.
* Mobilising or setting up a relevant pressure group.
* Working through a useful political party.
* Taking individual direct action (legal or illegal).

7.2 *What factors affect the appointment of ministers?* *(10 marks)*

* Seniority within the party.
* Popularity within the party.
* Political and personal loyalty to the Prime Minister.
* Policy-making experience and expertise.
* Policy successes and failures.
* Managerial and administrative competence as head of department.
* Media competence and popularity.
* Ideological balance across the party.
* Geographical balance across the country.
* Rewarding backbench effort, loyalty and competence.
* Bringing political challengers 'under the thumb' of collective responsibility.
* Size of the parliamentary pool.
* (For Labour, especially): political correctness – e.g. women, gays and ethnic minorities.
* Involuntary reshuffles, due to, e.g. forced ministerial resignations.

Note: as always, credit will be given in exams for topical examples for every point.

True or false?
1. True.
2. True.
3. False.
4. True.
5. True.
6. False.
7. True.
8. True.
9. False.
10. False.

Quiz
1. Patronage, declarations of war, signing treaties.
2. Collective policy making by the team of senior ministers, with the Prime Minister first among equals.
3. Walter Bagehot (1867)
4. Richard Crossman (1963).
5. Formula One tobacco advertising exemption; the Millennium Dome; Amsterdam Treaty; invasion of Iraq; referendum on a new EU constitution.
6. Party, Parliament, EU, media, pressure groups.
7. Prime Minister's character, style of leadership and experience; degree of party unity and policy consensus; state of economy, policy successes and failures; popularity of government; proximity of election.
8. To reward ministerial successes and punish failures, to reward loyalty and punish disloyalty, to introduce new blood and fresh ideas.
9. A carefully cultivated and exceptionally personal, populist, 'hands on' style and image, distanced from both the Cabinet and the party.
10. Britain has a system of parliamentary government, i.e. fusion, not separation, of the legislature and the executive.
11. Parliament.
12. Permanence, neutrality and anonymity.
13. Civil servants are permanent, non-elected career bureaucrats who must serve under successive governments of any party.
14. Civil servants, in theory, have no policy making power, and therefore – unlike ministers – should not be publicly accountable for the actions of their departments.
15. Job cuts; civil servants being blamed and sacked for policy errors (contrary to convention); civil servants being sacked for being politically incompatible with their political masters (contrary to convention).

Sample questions

Short
- Outline the role of the Cabinet in the government of the UK.
- Define collective ministerial responsibility.
- Outline the traditional features of the British civil service.

Medium
- What are the main sources of prime ministerial power?
- What factors affect the appointment of ministers?
- In what circumstances do ministers resign?

Long
- Discuss the view that Cabinet is no longer an important part of the executive in the UK.
- To what extent does Britain now have 'presidential politics'?
- Evaluate the merits and demerits of coalition governments.

References

Lord Oxford and Asquith, H. (1926) *Fifty Years in Parliament*, Cassell, London.

Bagehot, W. (1867) *The English Constitution*, Fontana, London.

Crossman, R. (1963) Introduction in W. Bagehot, *The English Constitution*, Fontana, London.

Foley, M. (1993) *The Rise of the British Presidency*, Manchester University Press, Manchester.

Hennessy, P. (1990) *Whitehall*, Fontana, London.

Madgwick, P. (1986) 'Prime Ministerial Power Revisited' in *Social Studies Review*, May.

Useful websites

www.bbc.co.uk/news
An excellent, wide-ranging and impartial source for topical news items and archive articles.

www.number10.gov.uk
10 Downing Street. The official website of the UK Prime Minister's Office (take an interactive tour of Number 10).

www.cabinetoffice.gov.uk/content/executive
The official website of the Cabinet Office.

http://news.bbc.co.uk/1/hi/uk_politics/8675705.stm
A BBC News website with a clickable guide to who's who in the government.

www.direct.gov.uk/en/index.htm
Directgov. An official government website with directory and detail of public services.

Rights and liberties

Aims of this chapter

- To outline and evaluate the doctrine of 'the rule of law'.
- To outline the structures and roles of the UK and European courts.
- To explain the functions and roles of the judges.
- To assess the principles of judicial independence and impartiality.
- To assess the provision of civil rights and freedoms in the UK.
- To assess judicial protection of civil liberties.
- To examine the UK Human Rights Act 1998.

Law, justice and morality

Laws are the rules of state which (unlike conventions) are enforceable in the courts. There are many different types of law, including: EU law, statute law, common law, case law and delegated legislation.

Broadly, all of these types of law fall under one or other of two headings:

- **Civil law** concerns disputes between individuals or groups in society. The aggrieved individual (or company etc.) decides whether to take proceedings, and the aim is compensation.
- **Criminal law** concerns offences against society or the state, and the aim of proceedings is punishment. The offence may be the same as in a civil dispute (e.g. assault) but under criminal law the Crown Prosecution Service (CPS) may take action even if the victim does not desire it. The legal processes are different and are often in different types of courts: e.g. county courts and the High Court for civil cases, and magistrates' courts and Crown courts for criminal cases.

The rule of law

The phrase 'the rule of law' was coined by the constitutional writer A.V. Dicey (1885). The concept, which seeks to equate law and justice, is said to be central to any constitutional democracy. However, it is best seen as a statement of an ideal (or as a list of ideal principles), to which many legal systems may aspire; but, in Britain and other countries, all of its key principles are often breached in practice.

Principles and breaches of 'the rule of law'

Legal equality: everyone, including government, should be equally subject to the same laws.

	Exceptions: parliamentary sovereignty; and hence the capacity of any UK government, through Parliament, to rewrite the law and even to legalise its own, previously illegal, actions; the legal immunities of the monarch, diplomats, MPs etc.; the cost of litigation – 'The law, like the Ritz Hotel, is open to all' (Lord Justice Darling); legal immunity orders (for government and MI5, for example).
Legal certainty:	there should be a clear statement of people's rights and duties under the law.
	Exceptions: the sheer quantity and complexity of law; retrospective (backdated) law, e.g. a retrospective increase in the penalty for terrorist hoaxes from six months to seven years (2001) and the retrospective abolition of the double jeopardy rule (2003).
Just law:	justice should be an end in itself, with no arbitrary law or government. There should be fair, consistent and open court procedures.
	Exceptions: inconsistent sentencing, e.g. former director of public prosecutions Lord Macdonald, and others, complained about inconsistent sentencing of individuals charged following the summer 2011 riots in England; alleged police bias, e.g. in racially motivated cases such as the murder of Stephen Lawrence in 1993.
Innocent until proved guilty:	no one should be subject to legal penalty unless s/he has broken the law.
	Exceptions: remand before trial; effective removal of the right to silence in the Criminal Justice Act 1994.
There should be an independent and impartial judiciary:	Exceptions: alleged judicial bias – e.g. the serious miscarriages of justice in the 'numbers cases' of the 1980s where the 'Guildford Four' and 'Birmingham Six' were wrongly imprisoned for up to 17 years; and Lord Hutton's 2004 inquiry into the death of Iraq weapons inspector Dr. Kelly which, said critics, 'whitewashed' the government's role in the affair.

Something is 'legal' if it is in accordance with the law of the land; whereas something is 'just' if it is deemed fair and equitable. The idea of the 'rule of law' seeks to equate law and justice, but sometimes the law may be regarded as unjust: e.g. the poll tax, the legal immunity of diplomats, legal tax avoidance, retrospective (backdated) law, the high costs of litigation, etc. Conversely, an action may be seen as 'just', though illegal: e.g. personal retribution – 'an eye for an eye'; breaking the law to prevent a greater crime; the Robin Hood principle (stealing from the rich to give to the poor); illegal political protest, e.g. cannabis 'smoke-ins' in Hyde Park; 'just' violence against an 'unjust' state (one man's 'terrorist' is another man's 'freedom fighter'), etc.

Similarly, an action that is deemed 'moral' (ethically right and proper) may be illegal; anti-nuclear protests such as trespassing in nuclear bases; euthanasia ('mercy killing'), etc. Or an 'immoral' action may be legal: e.g. suicide, adultery, divorce or abortion.

analyse this...

All three concepts – law, justice and morality – are subjective; even whether an action is legal or illegal is often a matter of debate between senior judges, as the divisions among the Law Lords over the model Naomi Campbell's privacy claims (2004) demonstrated.

However, perceived conflicts between law, justice and morality are sometimes used to justify **civil disobedience**: deliberate, peaceful law-breaking as an act of public, political protest. Some examples are: public refusals to pay the poll tax and council tax; cannabis 'smoke-ins' in Hyde Park; the obstruction by the pressure group Greenpeace of nuclear waste discharges into the North Sea, its occupation of the Brent Spar oil platform and its 2004 protest on Big Ben against the invasion of Iraq; the freeing of animals from research laboratories by the Animal Liberation Front; and the peaceful occupation of luxury store Fortnum and Mason in 2011 by pressure group UK Uncut in protest against tax avoidance by big businesses.

Questions

a Find (in the media) further recent examples of civil disobedience by pressure groups or individuals.

b What arguments were used to justify the action in each case?

c List three general arguments for, and three arguments against, civil disobedience.

key term...

Civil disobedience Deliberate, peaceful law-breaking as an act of public, political protest.

The courts

The civil and criminal courts in England and Wales are summarised in Figure 8.1.

Besides the British courts, Britain is a member of two separate European courts:

- **The European Court of Justice (ECJ) in Luxembourg:** this enforces European Union law, e.g. on the world-wide ban on the sale of UK beef during the BSE crisis in the 1990s; the 48-hour maximum working week; against Britain's discriminatory motor insurance premiums for men and women (2011); pollution of British beaches, etc.
- **The European Court of Human Rights (ECHR) at Strasbourg:** this has *nothing* to do with the EU. It was established in 1959 and enforces the 1950 European Convention for the Protection of Human Rights, ratified by 47 countries including the UK. However, its rulings are not formally binding in the way that EU law is: for example, in 2005, the ECHR ruled

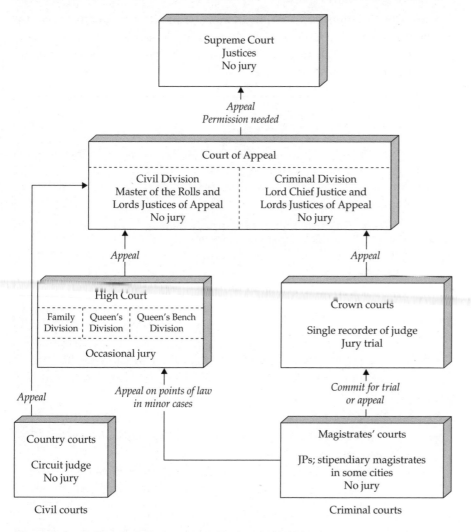

Figure 8.1 Civil and criminal courts in England and Wales

against the UK's blanket ban on votes for UK prisoners. Parliament finally debated the issue in 2011, and voted overwhelmingly not to give voting rights to any prisoners.

The ECHR has ruled against British governments on issues such as phone tapping by government agencies, corporal punishment in state schools, the ban against gays in the armed forces, torture of prisoners in Northern Ireland, press censorship, discrimination against women, gays and ethnic minorities, and many other matters. In 2008, it ruled illegal the indefinite retention of DNA samples of innocent English citizens. In 2010, the government stopped random police stop and search and restored the need for 'reasonable suspicion', in response to an ECHR ruling.

British governments have lost more cases at Strasbourg than have any other governments, largely because, until 2000, Britain had no domestic Bill of Rights and did not enforce the European Convention in its own courts; and also because much UK government action is still based simply on convention rather than on law. However, the Labour government enshrined the European Convention in UK law as the Human Rights Act 1998, and it took effect in the year 2000. This has reduced the number of UK cases which go all the way to the ECHR.

Rights under the European Convention on Human Rights

Rights under the European Convention on Human Rights are covered in the following conventions and protocols.

Conventions

Article 2: Right to life

Article 3: Freedom from torture or inhuman or degrading treatment or punishment

Article 4: Freedom from slavery or forced labour

Article 5: Right to liberty and security of person

Article 6: Right to a fair trial by an impartial tribunal

Article 7: Freedom from retroactive criminal laws

Article 8: Right to respect for private and family life, home and correspondence

Article 9: Freedom of thought, conscience and religion

Article 10: Freedom of expression

Article 11: Freedom of peaceful assembly and association, including the right to join a trade union

Article 12: Right to marry and found a family

Article 13: Right to an effective remedy before a national authority

Article 14: Freedom from discrimination

Protocol 1

Article 1: Right to a peaceful enjoyment of possessions

Article 2: Right to education, and to education in conformity with religious and philosophical convictions

Article 3: Right to take part in free elections by secret ballot

Protocol 2

Article 1: Freedom from imprisonment for debt

Article 2: Freedom of movement of persons

Article 3: Right to enter and stay in one's country

Article 4: Freedom from collective expulsion

The courts and Parliament

Parliament is sovereign; the British courts therefore cannot challenge or veto the law of Parliament; they can only interpret and enforce statute law as it is written.

EU law takes precedence over UK law and, where the two conflict, the British courts are required to enforce EU law. This was established by the *Factortame* case of 1990 (about the rights of Spanish trawlers to fish in British waters, contrary to the UK Merchant Shipping Act 1988). Parliament remains technically sovereign in that it could pass a law expressly overriding European law or, indeed, it could withdraw from the EU altogether – but this is unlikely in practice.

Parliament's law may be unclear or ambiguous; in a test case, the judges must interpret the law precisely, which can allow for a very 'creative' judicial role amounting effectively to 'law making' by the judges. This is called **case law**. In 2004, for example, the UK courts gave some protection to the model Naomi Campbell's right to privacy, and to the right to anonymity of Maxine Carr

> **key term...**
>
> **Case law** Judicial interpretation of the law in test cases which sets a precedent for future, similar cases.

(former girlfriend of Soham murderer Ian Huntley). The courts and Parliament may clash when the courts interpret a statute in a way which Parliament did not intend. Parliament may then, of course, rewrite the law; it can thus 'legalise illegality' or set aside court decisions.

The UK Human Rights Act has undoubtedly extended the role of the UK judges; but it expressly maintains the principle of parliamentary sovereignty and says that the judges cannot set aside parliamentary statutes when they conflict with the Human Rights Act; the judges can only point out such conflicts and leave it to Parliament to resolve them or not. In other words, the UK Human Rights Act has no superior status – it is not entrenched in the way that the US Bill of Rights is.

The courts and the executive

Administrative law is the whole package of laws which apply to government and other public bodies. There is no distinct body of administrative law, nor administrative courts in Britain (unlike in, e.g. France). However, the ordinary courts may hear civil or criminal actions against members or departments of central or local government. They may declare the orders or actions of a minister or department to be *ultra vires*, i.e. beyond their legal powers, either because of what was done or because of the way in which it was done.

Court hearings against governments – the process of '**judicial review**' – have risen in the UK from under 1,000 per year in the 1980s to over 7,000 per year now. Examples:

- In a major constitutional ruling in 2004, the Law Lords ruled that the internment (indefinite detention without charge or trial) of foreign terror suspects was contrary to both the UK and the European human rights laws.
- In 2008, the government was ruled to have acted illegally in freezing the assets of terror suspects because Treasury orders had by-passed Parliament. It was also ruled to have acted illegally in denying members of the Gurkha regiment the right to stay in the UK.

Some more recent examples include:

- 2010: the Supreme Court ruled that two gay men from Iran should not be deported from the UK with the advice to 'be discreet' in order to avoid prison, torture or death. Also, the government's request to hold some of the inquest into the 7/7 bombings in secret was ruled unlawful; and a temporary cap on immigration was ruled procedurally unlawful.
- 2011: the government's cuts to the schools buildings programme were ruled procedurally unlawful. Also, the Department of Health lost a court battle to keep secret some abortion statistics.

However, any central government usually has a majority in a sovereign Parliament. Therefore, if it is ruled illegal by the courts, it may use Parliament to rewrite the law and so legalise itself. The government may even backdate the rewritten law so that the government was never technically illegal – so-called '**retrospective law**'.

Retrospective law may also apply to ordinary citizens. After 11 September 2001, the government hastily imposed a retrospective increase in the penalty for terrorist hoaxes from six months to seven years. The abolition of the double jeopardy rule is also retrospective in its effect.

key term...

Administrative law The law as applied to executive and administrative bodies, especially government.

key term...

Judicial review The process of court hearings on government policies and actions.

key term...

Retrospective law Backdated law: the sovereign UK Parliament can decree that a law takes effect before it was written.

talking point...

The retrospective abolition of the double jeopardy rule means that:

Whereas, before, no one could be tried twice for the same offence, now a person can be tried repeatedly for the same offence which was, perhaps, committed even *before* this Act of Parliament was passed.

For example, in 2011 it was announced that two men would be tried for the racially motivated murder of black teenager Stephen Lawrence in 1993, one of whom had been tried and acquitted of the same offence in 1996.

What do you think were the merits of the double jeopardy rule; and what are the merits and demerits of the backdated abolition of this rule?

The courts' control of central government is therefore limited, and is bound up with the issue of parliamentary sovereignty. It is also debatable how far non-elected and, arguably, unrepresentative judges *should* control 'democratic' public bodies.

Nevertheless, cases of judicial review continue to rise: perhaps because the judges are less 'executive-minded' nowadays; or because citizens are increasingly aware of their legal rights against government; or perhaps because governments are increasingly careless about obeying the letter of the law.

The coalition government has been increasingly vocal in criticising judicial rulings: for example, in 2011, Prime Minister Cameron said that he would do only the 'minimum necessary' to uphold a UK Supreme Court ruling that sex offenders should have the right of review of mandatory life-long registration with the police; and also that it made him 'feel physically ill' to contemplate upholding an ECHR ruling against the total ban on voting for all UK prisoners. Such executive criticism arguably undermines judicial independence (see below).

Question...

8.1 What are the main features of judicial review in the UK, and how effective is the process?

(20 marks)

The judges

There is a hierarchy of judges in the British courts, from magistrates or Justices of the Peace (JPs) who are laypeople rather than trained lawyers, through recorders (part-time judges) and judges in the Crown courts, up to the most senior Justices of the Supreme Court (formerly Law Lords in the House of Lords).

The independence and impartiality of the judiciary

According to the 'rule of law', justice should be an end in itself, and judges should not be subject to political pressure from the legislature or executive, nor should they be partial or prejudiced in their interpretation or enforcement of the law.

> **key term...**
>
> **Judicial independence** The freedom of judges from the influence of the executive or legislative branches of the state.

> **key term...**
>
> **Judicial neutrality** The absence of political or personal bias amongst judges in law enforcement.

Question...

8.2 Explain the difference between judicial independence and judicial neutrality.

(5 marks)

To these ends, there are certain rules and principles in the British legal system:

- The judiciary should be separate from the other branches of government, in accordance with Montesquieu's principle of the 'separation of powers'.
- Judicial appointments should be based on merit, not on political patronage.
- Senior judges have security of tenure: under the Act of Settlement 1701, they can be removed from their jobs only by a vote in both Houses of Parliament (which has never yet happened).
- Judges receive salaries which are fixed by a formula and are not subject to political debate in Parliament.
- Judges' decisions should not be questioned in Parliament or criticised by politicians.
- Judges' remarks in court (like those of lawyers, witnesses and jury members) are not liable to legal actions for damages.

However, many commentators, such as John Griffith, question how far judges are, or can be, 'non-political'. This concept has at least four dimensions: separation of powers; freedom from external political pressure; lack of personal or political prejudice; and lack of involvement in any political role.

Overlaps between the judiciary, legislature and executive have been much reduced by constitutional reforms introduced by 'new' Labour, including:

- The effective abolition of the office of Lord Chancellor, which, for centuries, had a central and very senior role in all three branches of the state. (The government's Justice Secretary retains the additional title of Lord Chancellor but is no longer a Lord or a judge.)
- The creation in 2005 of an independent appointments process for senior judges, who had previously been appointed by the Lord Chancellor's office (although the Justice Secretary must still approve appointments).

- Separation of the Law Lords (top judges) from the House of Lords into a new Supreme Court (2009).

These reforms have significantly enhanced judicial independence. However, external political pressure on the judges, in the form of parliamentary and executive criticism, has increased over recent years. Examples have been given above.

Moreover, the other side of the coin of judicial 'independence' is judicial unaccountability. Election of judges, either by the general public or by an electoral college of lawyers, is therefore sometimes suggested. Note, however, that this would very likely make judges more, rather than less, political. Appointment by a genuinely independent commission is, perhaps, preferable.

On the thorny question of impartiality, judges' personal and political views may be skewed by their unrepresentative social background: over 80% of the top judges are public school and Oxbridge educated, and the judiciary is still over-whelmingly white and male. Their above-average age, and the nature of their legal training (still steeped in nineteenth-century Victorian values), may combine to foster a conservative, if not Conservative (i.e. party political), outlook. Judges' comments, especially on class, race and gender have often caused controversy. Even in 2005, when Otis Ferry and seven other pro-hunt protesters were found guilty for storming the House of Commons, they were given conditional discharges and personally praised by Judge Timothy Workman. On the other hand, of course, just because they are largely drawn from a narrow social elite does not necessarily mean that all judges will think the same way, nor that they will let their personal opinions impinge upon their judicial work.

Nevertheless, 'Judges are part of the machinery of authority within the state and as such cannot avoid the making of political decisions' (Griffith). Also as 'part of the state', judges may have a particular view of the 'national interest'; in cases of dispute between state and citizen, they may 'show themselves more executive-minded than the executive' (Lord Atkin) – especially on issues of national security and official secrecy, such as the banning of trade union membership for some civil servants in the 1980s, and also in key industrial disputes, such as the 1984–85 miners' strike. Marxists, such as Ralph Miliband, go further, to argue that the whole legal system in a capitalist country like Britain is necessarily class based and that judges are – unavoidably – part of the political 'super-structure' which protects private property and profits for a minority bourgeois (capitalist) ruling class.

Judges are also, inevitably, embroiled in day-to-day politics. They must review executive actions under administrative law – an unavoidably 'political' role, whichever way they rule, as, for example the Labour government being ruled illegal, in 2004, over the internment of terrorists. The Supreme Court Justices have also been given the politically fraught task of ruling on any conflicts between the Scottish and Westminster Parliaments. Commissions of inquiry are appointed by the Prime Minister and usually headed by senior judges (e.g. the Scott Inquiry into arms to Iraq, the Macpherson Inquiry into the Stephen Lawrence affair, the Hutton Inquiry into the death of Dr Kelly) etc. Whatever their findings, these will be perceived as political. Finally, judges must enforce parliamentary statutes which sometimes seem overtly party political: e.g. the anti-trades union laws of the 1980s and 1990s, the legislation on council tax capping etc.

Civil rights and freedoms

Rights are entitlements, e.g. to some kind of freedom or equality. **Natural rights** are those to which, according to some philosophers, everyone is entitled simply by being human; **civil rights** are those granted to citizens in law, by a particular state or government, and they may differ widely from one society to another.

Different political ideologies adopt different views on rights and freedoms. Liberals tend to stress positive individual rights and freedoms which should be enhanced by state action if necessary, e.g. the right to own private property; and freedom from sexual or racial discrimination, protected by law. Socialists tend to stress collective rights (e.g. the freedom of assembly; or of industrial action, for trade unions) and economic, political or social equalities (such as the right to employment, housing and a decent standard of living); and socialists are (more or less) opposed to private property.

Freedom and equality may conflict; for example, the freedom to choose between private or public health and education (a liberal tenet) may conflict with the goal of equal access to healthcare and equal educational opportunities (a socialist tenet). Similarly, progressive taxation in pursuit of greater economic equality or welfare (which means that wealthy people pay more income tax than poor people) may conflict with the freedom of individuals to spend their own money as they wish.

Conflict may also arise between individual and collective freedoms: for example, the collective right to strike, as against the individual's right to strike-break, was a source of acute conflict within mining families and communities during the bitter 1984–85 coal dispute.

The European Convention on Human Rights and the UK Human Rights Act enshrine conflicting rights, notably between the right to respect for family and private life (Article 8) and the freedom of expression (Article 10). This has generated controversy over the courts' granting of injunctions (media gags) – for example, to celebrities against revelations about their extra-marital affairs. This prompted Prime Minister David Cameron in 2011 to express concern about 'the judges using the European Convention on Human Rights to create a privacy law without Parliament saying so'. In fact, judges are fulfilling their proper constitutional role of interpreting and enforcing conflicting priorities within (a single) existing UK parliamentary statute.

Law, by its nature, may both enhance and constrain freedom: for example, it may protect the individual against violence, theft or discrimination, but it also limits individual freedom of action in those spheres. Is discrimination – sexual, religious, racial, ageist or fattist – an individual right or a social wrong?

Some laws in Britain are often seen as excessive constraints on individual or collective freedoms, and this view is sometimes used to justify civil disobedience. For example, the Police Act 1997 gave the police extensive powers to enter private premises, plant bugs, inspect files etc. with no external authorisation; and the Terrorism, Crime and Security Act 2001 allowed some foreign nationals to be detained indefinitely without any charge or trial, until the courts outlawed this in 2004. The UK was the only country to have opted out of part of the European Convention on Human Rights in order to introduce this measure. Also, over 100,000 people were stopped and searched under the

key term...

Rights Entitlements – e.g. to some kind of freedom or equality or security.

key term...

Natural rights Those rights to which, according to some philosophers, everyone is entitled simply by being human.

key term...

Civil rights Those rights granted to citizens in law, by a particular state.

anti-terror laws in 2010 (a 60% fall on the previous year), yet none was charged with any terror offence.

---

analyse this...

Consider the following list of rights and freedoms:

The right to life
The right to death
Freedom of assembly
Freedom of movement
The right to strike
Freedom of speech
Freedom of information
Freedom of the media
The right to privacy
Freedom of religious conscience
Freedom from arbitrary arrest or imprisonment
Freedom from discrimination
Legal equality
Political equality
Equal educational opportunities
The right to work
The right to housing

Note: Consider, for example, the law or practice on:
Murder; abortion; euthanasia; treason and sedition; libel and slander; official secrets; obscenity and pornography; control orders; remand; the 'sus' (suspicion) laws; the costs of litigation; race relations and religious, sexual and age discrimination; immigration and asylum; political and religious 'extremism'; personal privacy; personal morality; the electoral deposit; a minimum wage; conditions of work; trade union membership; picketing; state and public schooling; corporal punishment; unemployment; homelessness; poverty and welfare.

Questions

a For each of the rights and freedoms listed above, can you list some of the limits which currently exist in British law and practice?

b What limits, if any, do you think there *should* be on each, and why?

c Do some rights conflict with others?

Judicial protection of civil liberties

Some well-known court cases have significantly constrained civil liberties over the last few decades. Examples:

- 'Numbers cases' prior to prisoners' release by Court of Appeal (1970s and 1980s).
- Ban on trade unions at GCHQ (1984).
- Miners' strike cases (1984–85).
- Government secrecy upheld by judges in Tisdall and Ponting cases (1985).

- Eight men imprisoned for private and consensual acts of sado-masochism (1991).
- In 1999 an elderly, arthritic cannabis smoker (Eric Mann) was jailed for a year, despite the introduction of medical trials for the use of cannabis in the same year.
- In 2003 the courts ruled that evidence obtained through torture in other countries may be admissible in court.
- In 2011, London Mayor Boris Johnson finally won his court case to evict lone peace protester Brian Haw from Parliament Square (in case he proved an eyesore to a royal wedding procession).

However, in other cases, the judges have protected civil liberties. Examples:

- In 2004, the UK courts gave some protection to the model Naomi Campbell's right to privacy.
- Also in 2004, the Law Lords ruled that internment without trial was illegal.
- The coalition government has been ruled illegal since 2010 on, for example, its cuts to the schools buildings programme and to the provision of free school books.
- In 2011 the Roma Support Group successfully challenged the cutting of a £10 million council grant to voluntary and community groups across London.

Note: these and many other cases may raise complex and *conflicting* civil liberties issues for all of those involved.

Timeline on anti-terror law

- 2001 Terrorism, Crime and Security Act replaced 14-day detention before charge for foreign terror suspects with indefinite internment. Several men were imprisoned for over three years without charge or trial.
- 2004: the Law Lords ruled against internment. The government then sought to legalise 90-day detention without charge.
- 2005: the House of Commons defeated 90-day detention without charge. The government then sought to legalise 42-day detention without charge.
- 2008: the House of Lords defeated 42-day detention without charge; 28-day detention was accepted by Parliament.
- 2011: the 28-day detention rule was allowed to lapse and reverted to the original (pre-2001) 14 days' maximum detention without charge.

Several more anti-terror laws were passed by 'new' Labour governments, which were conspicuously authoritarian on law and order. They passed 19 Criminal Justice Acts between 1997 and 2010. Examples:

- Reducing the age of criminal liability and extending abolition of the right to silence to 10-year-olds.
- Curfews for under-10s and electronic tagging of 10-year-olds.
- The first prison for 12- to 14-year-olds was opened in Kent in 1998.
- The retrospective abolition of the double jeopardy rule.
- The UK now has more CCTV cameras per head of the population than any other country in the world.
- By 2010, the prison population was a record 85,000, and numbers of female prisoners had increased by 175% since the 1990s.

Such trends in parliamentary legislation are bound to shape the role of the judges in protecting or restricting civil liberties, since (according to the doctrine of parliamentary sovereignty) they can only interpret and enforce, but not challenge, the laws of Parliament.

The UK Human Rights Act 1998

In Britain, until the passing of the Human Rights Act, few rights were guaranteed in law; such rights as citizens had tended to be negative, i.e. they were allowed to do something if there was no law against it. The Human Rights Act 1998 (HRA) incorporated the European Convention on Human Rights into UK law and it came into force in 2000 after British judges had undergone relevant training. However, in cases of conflict between the HRA and other parliamentary statutes, the judges (to maintain the concept of parliamentary sovereignty) can only point out any such conflicts to Parliament for possible action. The HRA also contains sweeping exemptions 'In accordance with the law and the necessity for public safety, prevention of disorder or crime, protection of public health or morale or rights and the freedoms of others'. It is therefore much weaker than, for example, the US Bill of Rights – but it has prompted more 'rights awareness' in the drafting of laws, in judicial interpretation of those laws and, increasingly, amongst the general public – and even amongst politicians.

Question...

8.3 Argue for and against the incorporation of the Human Rights Act into British law.

(20 marks)

talking point...

Contrary to the assumptions of some UK Eurosceptics, it was former UK Conservative Prime Minister Winston Churchill who inspired and drafted the European Convention on Human Rights, which was signed by the UK in 1951.

Question...

8.4 To what extent are civil liberties protected in the UK?

(25 marks)

talking point...

'Corporal punishment' refers to the beating of students (which is, incidentally, still allowed in some UK private schools, although the ECHR has banned it from all state schools since the 1980s). 'Capital punishment' means the death sentence. Students often confuse these terms in exam answers!

Parliament may protect civil liberties through legislation such as the right to vote, the Freedom of Information Act and the Human Rights Act.

Pressure groups can also protect civil liberties. For instance, the Snowdrop campaign helped to ensure the ban on most handguns, thus protecting the right to life.

Media campaigns may also highlight certain issues, especially the freedom of information and expression: for example, the exposure of MPs' expenses abuses in 2009.

However, civil liberties in the UK are not fully protected.

Parliamentary sovereignty is potentially the biggest hindrance to civil liberties. A majority government in control of a sovereign Parliament with a flexible, unwritten constitution has a lot of power. For example, the Regulation of Investigatory Powers Act 2000 has allowed increasingly extensive investigation and surveillance of citizens' private electronic communications by public bodies. More recent statutes have endorsed internment, retrospective law and control orders (stringent house arrest).

Since UK courts and judges must enforce the laws of the UK's sovereign Parliament, they, too, may constrain civil liberties: by, for example, electronic tagging; the interception of letters, e-mails and phone calls; and control orders for terrorist suspects who have not been found guilty, including the power of house arrest.

One person's civil liberty may be another's constraint. For example, Naomi Campbell's successful court battle for a privacy ruling undermined wider public freedom of information and media freedom of expression.

The police sometimes hinder civil liberties through their curbs on peaceful protests, such as the mass arrests of peaceful campaigners during the 2011 anti-cuts demonstration. Also in 2011, the trial of six green campaigners for conspiring to shut down a power station, collapsed after undercover police officer Mark Kennedy was exposed and even offered to give evidence on their behalf.

Therefore, despite many safeguards, civil liberties are far from fully protected in the UK. An entrenched Bill of Rights would improve safeguards.

True or false?

1. The UK courts can rule Parliament illegal.
2. The UK courts can rule the government illegal.

3. Parliament can backdate the enforcement of a new law to take effect before it was actually passed.
4. Parliamentary sovereignty is, itself, merely a convention.
5. Parliamentary privilege means that MPs have certain legal immunities.
6. The European Court of Human Rights is the court of the European Union.
7. A government minister appoints the top judges.
8. Attempting suicide is illegal.
9. The prosecution always opens a court case.
10. A unanimous decision by the jury is necessary for a guilty verdict.

Quiz

1. Define 'laws'.
2. What is the main principle of 'the rule of law'?
3. Give one exception to the principle of legal equality in the UK.
4. Give an example of the breach of the principle of an impartial judiciary.
5. Define 'civil disobedience', and give one example.
6. When did the UK Human Rights Act come into effect?
7. Give three ECHR rulings against UK governments.
8. Give one example where the 2010 coalition government has been ruled illegal.
9. What is meant by 'internment'?
10. When was internment ruled illegal in the UK?

Answers to questions

Note: The following are notes for guidance only and are not intended to be taken as model answers.

8.1 *What are the main features of judicial review in the UK, and how effective is the process?* *(20 marks)*

- Judicial review means that the UK courts and judges have the power to decide whether the policies and actions of central and local governments are legal or illegal.
- When asked, UK courts and judges can decide that, for example, ministers have exceeded their powers, or have not taken an action which they should have done, or have simply done something wrongly, according to the law.
- There is no general right to judicial review – a review will be granted by the High Court, if there is an arguable case.
- UK judges do not have the power to challenge the sheer merit, efficiency or justice of an executive decision; they can only challenge a decision that is actually illegal.
- UK judges do not have the power to challenge a law of Parliament – unless it conflicts with EU law. They can usually only interpret and enforce statute law as it is written.

Effectiveness:
- The effectiveness of judicial review has increased in recent years, in the sense that the sheer number of cases brought against the government has greatly increased.
- This has been a growing check against 'elective dictatorship'.
- This has also been a growing protection of individual rights and liberties.
- The UK Human Rights Act has increased the effectiveness of judicial review.

However:
- Much depends on the public's access to, and the time and the cost of, legal action.
- UK judges have been accused of being 'executive-minded' – that is, too sympathetic to the views and interests of the government and state, as against the rights and liberties of UK citizens.
- Above all, a majority government in effective control of a sovereign Parliament can overturn court decisions simply by passing new legislation.

Conclusion: not sufficiently effective.

Note: Examiners will, as always, credit students who can use topical examples throughout and who can suggest appropriate reforms at the end of their answers.

8.2 *Explain the difference between judicial independence and judicial neutrality.* (5 marks)

Judicial independence refers to the judges' separation and autonomy from the other parts of the state. Thus they should be structurally separate from the legislature and executive, and should not be subject to any form of pressure or influence from the politicians. UK judges, for example, are not appointed or trained by the government, and 'separation of powers' has been enhanced by the creation in 2009 of the UK Supreme Court. Whereas judicial independence is a matter of external arrangements, judicial neutrality is an internal state of mind: judges should not let their personal or political opinions affect their professional conduct in any way. They should uphold the rule of law and protect individual rights and liberties in a fair and impartial way, regardless of either external political pressures or their own personal views.

8.3 *Argue for and against the incorporation of the Human Rights Act into British law.* (20 marks)

Case for the Human Rights Act:
UK residents can now use the UK courts for human rights issues, whereas before 2000 they usually had to go all the way to the European Court of Human Rights – often involving considerable time and expense (though this option is, of course, still available even though Britain now has its own statute law).

According to some observers (e.g. pressure groups such as Liberty and Charter 88), basic civil liberties in Britain are always under threat, with a majority government in a sovereign Parliament in effective control of a flexible, unwritten constitution. They point to the draconian 'anti-terrorism' laws passed through Parliament in a single day in 1998, which were extended to cover environmentalists and animal rights activists. The 2001 anti-terrorism law, which reintroduced internment, was particularly harsh. They also say that the growing political emphasis on law and order (e.g. the introduction of child jails for 12- to 14-year-olds in 1998), together with growing police powers, state surveillance and a quite conservative judiciary, have all added to the threat.

The conflict situation in Northern Ireland – where rights of political activity and legal equality, residence, movement, privacy, jury trial, freedom from arbitrary detention and from 'cruel and inhuman punishment' etc. were long curtailed – demonstrated the fragility of basic liberties in the UK.

The 'rule of law' demands a clear statement of citizens' rights and duties, which has long been lacking in Britain.

The Human Rights Act has imposed more legal limits on governments' actions, which are often guided only by convention and are therefore effectively above or beyond the law.

Since Britain was already a signatory of the European Convention on Human Rights, it was simple and logical to incorporate it into domestic law.

Case against the Human Rights Act:
Which rights should be entrenched? How general or specific should they be? There is still not political or party consensus on these questions.

How entrenched should the UK Human Rights Act be? Some critics feared excessive rigidity, but the fact that ordinary (and sometimes very illiberal) parliamentary statute laws may take precedence over the provisions of the UK Human Rights Act is now, perhaps, causing greater concern.

Many existing UK laws conflict with the Human Rights Act – e.g. the Police Act, Prevention of Terrorism Acts, Criminal Justice Acts etc. (though this is precisely why defenders of civil rights wanted more legal protection for human rights in the UK). There are also conflicting entitlements within the HRA itself. The issues of state security versus citizens' liberties, and privacy versus freedom of information and expression, are especially fraught.

All governments are reluctant to increase constraints against themselves and against the state. The UK Human Rights Act is, therefore, relatively weak.

It is hard to reconcile majority and minority rights, or collective versus individual rights, or freedom versus equality.

Left-wingers are suspicious of statutory rights which may entrench 'liberal' principles such as individual property rights and undermine 'socialist' principles such as collective trades union and workers' rights.

Many (such as Griffith) do not trust the judges to interpret and enforce a Human Rights Act in a liberal-minded and progressive way, because they see British judges as unrepresentative, conservative and 'executive-minded'. The HRA has inevitably transferred some power from elected MPs to non-elected, unaccountable judges, and it has also made the judges more overtly 'political'.

Every Bill of Rights has some qualifying clauses allowing for the restriction of rights e.g. 'in the national interest', and some are scarcely worth the paper on which they are written.

Rights in Britain were said by some (especially Conservatives) to be adequately protected already through Parliament and the Ombudsman, the 'rule of law', the courts (including the European Courts), administrative tribunals, pressure groups and the media, etc.

Note: By 2011, many students still seemed to be unaware that the Human Rights Act – and, indeed, the ECHR – have nothing to do with the EU. To repeat, the European Convention and Court of Human Rights, and the UK Human Rights Act, have no connection at all with the European Union! Students need not, therefore, even mention the EU in answers to questions about the Human Rights Act. Nor were any of these legal arrangements 'imposed' upon the UK; they have all been entirely voluntary.

8.4 *To what extent are civil liberties protected in the UK?*   *(25 marks)*

In many ways, civil liberties in the UK are protected. Judges should enforce the laws in an independent and neutral way, now including the UK Human Rights Act, which has given judges more scope for protecting the civil liberties of citizens: for example, privacy rights (especially for celebrities, such as Naomi Campbell and Ryan Giggs).

Also, the use of judicial review safeguards individuals against illegal central and local government action. For example, the courts have ruled against the government's secret extension of GM crop research and, in 2011, against councils' cutting of charity grants. There has been a significant growth in the use of judicial review in the last 20 years, perhaps because citizens are becoming more aware of their civil rights, or perhaps because judges may be becoming less 'executive-minded' (i.e. pro-government).

Judges also conduct inquiries into controversial political issues, such as the Saville Inquiry (1998–2010) into the 'unjustified' killing of 14 unarmed civil rights demonstrators in Northern Ireland on 'Bloody Sunday' in 1972.

Also, judges now speak more openly about their views on government policy and civil liberties, e.g. against internment and cuts in jury trials. On balance, UK judges have become more liberal and less pro-state in their rulings over the last two decades. There has been growing, and often open, conflict between governments and judges for this reason.

The European Court of Justice enforces EU law and helps to protect the civil liberties of UK citizens: for example, it ruled against discriminatory retirement ages for men and women in the UK. The European Court of Human Rights has had an even longer history of protecting our civil liberties: for example, it has ruled against the ban on gays in the army, torture in UK prisons and corporal punishment in state schools.

Pressure groups can also protect civil liberties. For instance, in recent years, public sector trade unions have staged large protests against cuts in their members' numbers, pay and pensions. Media campaigns may also highlight certain issues, especially the freedom of expression – e.g. over the 2012 phone hacking scandal.

However, civil liberties are not fully protected.

Many (such as Griffith) argue that UK judges are not sufficiently impartial, given their narrow socio-economic background (overwhelmingly white, male, public school and Oxbridge educated). For example, in 2012, High Court judge Sir Paul Coleridge criticised the government's support for gay marriage, and was accused by critics of being partisan and political.

Outsider pressure groups such as Exit (pro-euthanasia) and UK Uncut (against public spending cuts) are rarely successful in their attempts to defend entitlements such as the right to die or the right to gainful employment.

Also, one person's civil liberty may be another person's constraint. For example, in 2012 the Attorney General blocked the publication of Prince Charles' many letters to government departments (the so-called 'black spider memos'). This protected his privacy but undermined wider public freedom of information and media freedom of expression.

The police also sometimes hinder civil liberties – for example, by cover-ups (e.g. the 1989 Hillsborough tragedy), corruption (e.g. 2011 phone hacking bribery), criminal violence and sheer incompetence (e.g. in 2012 they tasered a blind man whose white stick was mistaken for a samurai sword).

Parliamentary sovereignty is potentially the biggest hindrance to civil liberties. A majority government in control of a sovereign Parliament with a flexible, unwritten constitution has a lot of power. For example, the 2012 Communications Data Bill proposes to allow the government to monitor all of the phone calls, emails, texts and website views of everyone in the UK. Despite widespread opposition, there was little that could defeat this bill.

Parliament may also pass retrospective law, such as the backdated abolition of the double jeopardy rule.

Therefore, despite many safeguards, civil liberties are far from fully protected in the UK.

True or false?

1. False.
2. True.
3. True.
4. True.
5. True.
6. False.
7. True.
8. False.
9. True.
10. False.

Quiz

1. Laws are rules of state, enforceable by the courts.
2. Legal equality.
3. Parliamentary sovereignty, and the costs of litigation.
4. The 'numbers cases'.
5. Peaceful, illegal political protest – for example, cannabis 'smoke-ins' in Hyde Park.
6. 2000.
7. Phone tapping by government agencies, corporal punishment in state schools, the ban against gays in the armed forces and torture of prisoners in Northern Ireland.
8. The government's cuts to the schools buildings programme were ruled procedurally unlawful.
9. 'Internment' means indefinite imprisonment without charge or trial.
10. 2004.

Sample questions

Short
- Outline *two* functions of judges.
- Describe the main features of judicial review in the United Kingdom.
- Define the principle of the rule of law.

Medium
- Explain the difference between judicial independence and judicial neutrality.
- Describe and explain the significance of case law in the UK.
- In what ways can judges protect civil liberties?

Long
- Discuss the view that having an independent judiciary is the best method of protecting the rights and liberties of UK citizens.
- 'Without a codified constitution and entrenched bill of rights there can be no proper defence of liberties.' Discuss.
- Discuss the view that judicial review in the United Kingdom is ineffective.

References

Atkin, J. (1942) *House of Lords Judicial Committee*, Liversidge v Anderson.
Dicey, A.V. (1885) *Law of the Constitution*, Macmillan, London.
Griffith, J. (1991) *The Politics of the Judiciary*, Fontana, London.
Miliband, R. (1983) *The State in Capitalist Society*, Verso, London.
Montesquieu, C.-L. (1748) *The Spirit of Laws*, Free Press, Illinois.

Useful websites

www.bbc.co.uk/news
An excellent, wide-ranging and impartial source for topical news items and archive articles.

www.amnesty.org.uk
The website of international human rights pressure group Amnesty.

www.liberty-human-rights.org.uk/index.php
The website of UK civil rights pressure group Liberty.

www.bbc.co.uk/search/news/human_rights_watch
A BBC page with links to hundreds of current human rights stories and articles.

www.guardian.co.uk/law/uk-civil-liberties
A Guardian newspaper site with links and updates to stories about civil liberties in the UK.

9 Local government and devolution

Aims of this chapter

- To outline the structure, functions and financing of local government in the UK.
- To explain the checks and controls on local government.
- To evaluate the advantages and disadvantages of local government.
- To outline the history and development of devolution in the UK.
- To explain the roles and powers of the devolved assemblies.
- To outline the main parties' views on devolution.

Local government

Local government entails the election of local people to run local services such as education, housing, rubbish collection, social services, planning, transport, leisure and recreation, police etc. The structure of local government in the UK is somewhat complicated and, at the same time, local councils do not have very much real power in Britain's centralised system. These two points help to explain why voter turnout for local elections is usually low.

Since the 1970s local government structures have been reorganised frequently by central governments through parliamentary statutes – partly in a search for greater efficiency and accountability, but also sometimes from the less laudable motives of party interest and political control.

The structures and major functions of local government

There are almost 500 local councils or 'authorities' in the UK, which have two main structures: single-tier and two-tier systems. This situation is further confused because of the wide range of names that these councils can have.

The single-tier system

The single-tier system exists in all of Scotland, Wales, Northern Ireland and parts of England. It means that one all-purpose council has responsibility for all local authority functions. It includes unitary councils, such as Bristol City

Council, and metropolitan councils, such as Birmingham City Council, and the 33 London boroughs, such as the London Borough of Lewisham.

Single-tier, or 'unitary', councils can be given different names such, as county borough council, county council or city council, but they are all the same thing.

The two-tier system

The rest of England, covering mostly rural areas, has a two-tier system with responsibilities divided between large county and smaller district councils. There are 34 large county councils, such as Buckinghamshire County Council, and 238 smaller district councils, such as Aylesbury Vale District Council.

Again, county and district councils can have different names. Some district councils, for example, are called city councils. Small wonder that voters get confused!

Parish and community councils

In addition to unitary, county and district councils, local areas are also represented by parish and community councils. These cover very small areas and do not have much formal political power, but they can be quite influential at a very local level.

Below is a list of the main areas of responsibility for each type of council. Some of the responsibilities may overlap, with housing being under a county council in one area and a district council in another.

Unitary (single-tier) councils
Social services
Education
Housing
Libraries
Transport (except London boroughs)
Planning applications and development
Leisure, recreation and the arts
Environmental health
Highways
Waste collection
Revenue collection

Two-tier councils
  County councils
  Social services
  Education
  Libraries
  Transport (public and planning)
  Leisure, recreation and the arts
  Highways
  Fire and emergency services
  Refuse disposal

  District councils
  Housing
  Planning applications and development
  Leisure, recreation and the arts

Environmental health
Waste collection
Revenue collection
Parish, community and town councils
Community centres
Allotments
Cemeteries and churchyards
Clocks
Commons, open spaces and playing fields
Street lighting
Litter
Parking places
Public lavatories
Road verges
Seats, shelters and signs

Police and fire services are run separately – but they do have local councillors on their governing bodies and their civilian employees are often employed by one of the nearby local councils.

The Greater London Authority (created in 2000) is responsible for London-wide strategic issues such as transport, but day-to-day services are still run by the local borough councils.

talking point...

Why go to your local council?

Councils are responsible for a wide range of services covering many areas of local life, from education and housing to local planning. So for lots of problems and issues, your council is the place to go for help.

You should contact your council or your councillor if you want to:

- Influence council decisions.
- Try to reverse decisions that have already been made.
- Access services.
- Complain about services.
- Seek council support or permission for an event.

Ways to get in touch . . .

Write to your councillor

This is the most common way of contacting councillors. Research your councillors and see if you can take advantage of any special interests they may have. You can send a letter to them by addressing it care of the council headquarters, you can send it to their home address, or you can contact them via e-mail or the council's website.

Councillor's surgeries

All councillors have a duty to represent the people who live in their local areas or 'wards'. Many hold 'surgeries' on a regular basis, when people can come to discuss local issues. Again, you will be able to get details of surgeries from your council, and probably from its website.

Council meetings

All council meetings are open to the public unless they are classed as 'exceptional'. All council Cabinet meetings where important decisions are due to be made must be held in public. You may be able to speak at some of these meetings and you should consult your council about which meetings are open to the public and which you can speak at. Quite often this information is available on council websites, or you can contact the committee clerk to find out. Members of the public have no automatic speaking rights at council meetings. You will have to ask for leave to speak in advance from your council committee services section.

Public question time

Many councils hold a public question time. This is a forum where any member of the public can ask questions of those councillors who make any decisions. They are generally held every few months and the details of each session will be advertised beforehand.

Public consultations

Public consultations are carried out by councils to consider the views of the local community. If the planning and decision-making process for your particular issue is at an early stage, this is a very useful way of airing your views.

There are currently around 20,000 county, district and borough councillors. They are elected for fixed four-year terms to small local areas known as 'wards' (rather than 'constituencies', which MPs represent). In London, all borough seats are contested together every four years. In the 36 metropolitan (big city) boroughs, one-third of the seats are contested each year, with county council elections in the fourth year. The non-metropolitan district and unitary councils choose either method.

Councillors are part-time and are paid expenses and attendance allowances only; they therefore tend not to be socially typical of the electorate, many of whom lack the time or money for local political involvement. Only around 29% of councillors are women. (However, this is higher than the 22% of women MPs at Westminster); 4% of councillors are from ethnic minorities. Councillors are usually party political, like MPs, but there are many more independents (around 10%) and there are many 'hung' councils where no one party has an absolute majority.

Table 9.1 shows the results of the 2011 local government elections, where 279 (out of about 500) councils were up for election – around 9,500 individual seats in total.

The Liberal Democrats suffered heavy losses, especially in the north of England – perhaps being punished for their role in the coalition government. Table 9.2 shows the percentages of votes won.

Table 9.1 Local government elections, 2011

Party	Councils	+/−	Councillors	+/−
Conservative	157	+4	4820	+81
Labour	57	+26	2392	+800
Liberal Democrat	10	−9	1056	−695
Other	55	−21	761	−199

Note: After 279 of 279 councils declared

Table 9.2 Local government elections, 2011, percentage of votes won

Party	Percentage vote	Percentage change
Labour	37%	+10%
Conservative	35%	0%
Liberal Democrat	15%	11%
Other	13%	+1%

Question...

9.1 What are the functions and powers of a local councillor? How do they differ from those of an MP?

(15 marks)

Local government is advised and administered by appointed officials who are full-time, paid and permanent. As with the central civil service, the distinction between advice, administration and policy making between politicians and civil servants may be blurred, and local officials are sometimes accused of having power without public accountability. The issue of 'politicisation' of these officials is, perhaps, even stronger at local than at national level.

Local government finance

Local government spending – e.g. on building and running schools, council housing, roads, and providing services like homes for the elderly, parks and gardens, plus the administrative costs of local government itself – totals around £180 billion – one quarter of all UK public expenditure.

- Capital spending – e.g. on new roads – is financed by borrowing from central government and banks etc., and by selling assets such as land.
- Expenditure (day-to-day running costs, wages etc.) is financed by:
  - Grants from central government. These provide about 60% of local revenue.
  - Public payments for services, e.g. council house rents.
  - Local taxation. Until 1989/1990, local rates were levied on business and domestic properties. These were replaced (by Thatcher's Conservative

government) by the community charge or 'poll tax' – a flat-rate charge paid by every adult, unconnected with property or income. This measure was highly controversial because it was unrelated to voters' ability to pay. It sparked a widespread campaign of civil disobedience (illegal non-payment), culminating in a violent anti-poll tax demonstration in London in 1990. It was one of the issues that helped to bring down Margaret Thatcher as Prime Minister in 1990; and her successor, John Major, was quick to replace the poll tax with a locally set, banded property tax per household – the 'council tax'. This provides about a quarter of local government funding. Like the poll tax, the council tax may be 'capped', i.e. central government can impose a ceiling on the maximum levied by each local council, which contradicts the principle of local responsibility and accountability for spending levels. It also undermines the 'mandate' of local authorities, and some councillors have said that if the levy is capped, they cannot then afford to provide mandatory (compulsory) local services. Capping is also perceived by its critics as being motivated by party politics.

- Business rates – a property tax on local businesses – have been removed from local authority control and replaced by the 'national non-domestic rate', centrally fixed and pooled, then redistributed to local councils. They provide around 20% of local government funding.

Controls on local government

- **Parliament:** local authorities are created by statute, and all powers must be granted by law.
- **Courts:** just as with central government, the courts may rule local authorities *ultra vires*, i.e. acting beyond their legal powers. For example, in 2011 the courts ruled council cuts in charity grants illegal, and also Birmingham City Council's plans to limit social care for disabled people.
- **Local quangos** such as the (unelected) Regional Development Agencies (RDAs), which are given resources and powers by central government, diverted from or in competition with elected local authorities. The 2010 coalition government announced plans to abolish the RDAs by 2012.
- **The Commissioners for Local Administration:** local ombudsmen, established in 1972, who investigate public complaints of maladministration against local authorities.
- **Central government**: intervenes to control overall public spending – hence, e.g. compulsory competitive tendering of some local services (this means that local councils are legally obliged to invite and accept competitive bids from private companies for the running of public services such as rubbish collection); also to ensure consistency of standards across the country e.g. in education; and to coordinate local functions e.g. planning. Methods include:
  - Financial control: grants, audits, capping, powers of veto over capital spending projects etc.
  - Ministerial approval is required in many policy areas, e.g. education.
  - Inspection by the relevant central department, e.g. police, fire, education.

- Appeals against local authority action, e.g. to the Secretary of State for the Environment against planning decisions.
- Inquiries into local councils set up by central government.
- Central government can remove local authorities' specific powers ('default') or, through parliamentary legislation, whole local authorities can be abolished.

It may be argued that all of this undermines local democracy and the mandate of local authorities. However, local elections are often about national parties, policies and issues; and the voter turnout is usually low (around 30–40%) – perhaps, of course, precisely because local councils are seen as weak and insignificant. Local government may be even more prone to sleaze and corruption than is central government and, therefore, in need of strict external control. For example, in the 1980s Westminster council was embroiled in the 'homes for votes' scandal: this involved the targeting of council house sales so to increase numbers of potential Conservative voters in key marginal areas, at a cost to the public purse of over £20 million. In his report, the district auditor condemned the policy as 'disgraceful and unlawful gerrymandering'. Protracted legal proceedings followed, until 2004, when the former Conservative leader of Westminster council, Dame Shirley Porter, finally paid £12 million of her substantial personal wealth in partial settlement of the dispute.

analyse this...

'Gerrymandering' usually means the redrawing of constituency boundaries for party political advantage. (The word comes from a corrupt nineteenth-century US governor, Elbridge Gerry, who created an electoral district shaped like a salamander, where his voters were located in the tail.)

Former electoral district

New electoral district

Questions

a Explain the term 'gerrymandering'.

b Since UK local councils do not have the power to reshape voting *boundaries*, what did the Westminster council do instead in the 1980s?

c Under 1980s statute law, local councillors can be 'surcharged' – that is, they can be held personally responsible for the financial losses of their councils through corruption or incompetence. Thus they must repay those losses from their own pockets. Do you think that MPs and government ministers should have the same personal, financial liabilities? Why or why not?

London

The 1997 Labour government promised to introduce an elected London council and mayor, and in 1998 a local, single-question referendum on this proposal produced a two-thirds majority in favour. However, the nature of the referendum was controversial because many voters wanted a council but not a mayor, or vice versa, but they were not given the choice. Voter turnout was only 34%. The new Greater London Authority (GLA) was the first local council to be elected on a system of proportional representation (Additional Member System [AMS]), in 2000.

Figure 9.1   London local authorities

Table 9.3   Greater London Authority election results, 2008

Party	Constituency seats	Top-up seats	Total seats
Conservative	8	3	11
Labour	6	2	8
Liberal Democrat	0	3	3
Green	0	2	2
BNP	0	1	1

Source: BBC News at bbc.co.uk/news

In the early stages of selecting a London mayoral candidate, Labour tried unsuccessfully to exclude the left-wing candidate Ken Livingstone – a move widely criticised as a 'stitch up'. (Meanwhile, the Conservatives' chosen candidate, Jeffrey Archer, was forced to stand down when he was charged and then jailed for perjury and perverting the course of justice. Steven Norris was chosen instead.) Ken Livingstone quit the Labour Party and won the mayoral election as an independent candidate.

By 2004, Livingstone looked very likely to win again, so Labour took him back into the party and ditched its own previous candidate. Opposition parties criticised both Labour and Livingstone for being opportunist rather than principled. It suited Labour to back a winner (when it was doing badly in other elections at the same time) and it suited Livingstone to have the political and financial support of central government for the next four years.

Livingstone stood again in 2008 but lost (on second preference votes) to the Conservative candidate, Boris Johnson. He will, nevertheless, contest the 2012 election as Labour's candidate. The main policy areas in dispute are London transport and policing.

Table 9.4 London mayoral election results, 2008

Candidate	Party	Votes
Johnson	Conservative	1,168,738
Livingstone	Labour	1,028,966
Paddick	Liberal Democrat	878,097
Berry	Green	409,101

Source: BBC News at bbc.co.uk/news

> **key term...**
>
> **Legislative devolution** The passing down of limited law-making powers from central to local or regional bodies, with the centre remaining sovereign – i.e. the state remains unitary.

Question...

9.2 What are the advantages and disadvantages of local government? *(20 marks)*

Devolution

> **key term...**
>
> **Federalism** A system of greater decentralisation, where the central and local powers are equal and autonomous, with mutual checks and balances between them – thus, there is no sovereign centre.

> **key term...**
>
> **Separatism** Complete political independence of a territory.

Devolution means the delegation – passing down – of some legislative and/or executive functions of central powers to local bodies, while the national power remains responsible for major national issues such as defence, foreign affairs and macro-economics. The local bodies are subordinate to the central legislature or executive, which can readily retrieve its powers. The system remains unitary because the centre is still sovereign. **Federalism**, on the other hand, entails greater local autonomy. Here the regions allocate certain national powers such as defence and foreign affairs to a central body, and they are, *de jure*, equal to it. The local powers have autonomy within their own, defined areas of decision making. Thus central government cannot increase its powers at the expense of the regions or federal states. The courts arbitrate in cases of conflict. The USA and Australia are examples of federal systems. **Separatism** means complete political independence.

The UK has long had elements of executive and administrative devolution in local government, and Scotland and Wales have their own secretaries of state with Cabinet status. Scotland's legal and educational systems have also long been quite different from those of England. Until 1999, however, there was no legislative devolution; Westminster was the sole UK legislature following the suspension, in 1972, of the Northern Ireland Parliament (Stormont) and the introduction there of 'direct rule' from Westminster because of the growing political conflict in Northern Ireland at that time.

Encouraged by the rise of nationalist feeling in Scotland and Wales, Labour and the Liberal Democrats advocated legislative devolution for Scotland and Wales from the 1970s on; and the Liberal Democrats also proposed elected local legislatures for the regions of England. A Labour government in 1977 introduced a Devolution Bill and held referenda on the issue in Scotland and Wales in 1979. Wales voted against; Scotland voted in favour, but the 'yes' vote amounted to only 32.5% of the total electorate, and the Devolution Bill required approval by at least 40% of the electorate (a backbench amendment), and so the issue was dropped.

Over the next two decades, support for the Scottish and Welsh nationalist parties increased, but the Conservative governments of that period were firmly opposed to devolution. In 1997, the Conservatives won no Westminster seats at all in Scotland or in Wales; and Labour came to power with a mandate to hold new referenda on the question of devolution.

Scotland

Scotland held a two-question referendum in September 1997: 74% voted in favour of a Scottish Parliament and 60% agreed that it should have tax-varying powers of up to 3p in the pound (turnout was 60%). The Scottish Parliament came into being in 1999, with 129 members (MSPs) elected by AMS: 73 elected by first-past-the-post and 56 'top-up' MSPs elected from closed regional party lists using the European parliamentary constituencies.

The Scottish Executive is responsible for the following policy areas:

Health
Education and training
Local government, housing and social work
Economic development
Employment
Transport
Law and home affairs
Police
Environment
Energy
Agriculture, forestry and fishing
Culture, sport and the arts
Administration of certain EU laws in Scotland (e.g. civil nuclear emergency planning)

Westminster remains responsible for foreign affairs, including relations with the EU, defence and national security, macro-economic and fiscal matters, immigration, railways, shipping, airlines, pensions, employment law, broadcasting and telecommunications and much else. Overall, the Scotland Act lists 19 pages of powers that are reserved to Westminster, including decisions on Scotland's own constitutional future; for example, independence (even if backed in a Scottish referendum) would still require the consent of the Westminster Parliament. In other words, devolution is a fairly limited form of decentralisation.

However, since the Scottish Parliament is elected by PR, this does change the party political balance, giving more representation to smaller parties such as the radical left-wing Scottish Socialist Party, which won six seats in 2003. (Left-wing politicians and politics have always been more successful in Scotland than in England, because Scotland has always been more economically disadvantaged.) The 1999 and 2003 Scottish Parliament elections produced a Labour–Liberal Democrat coalition executive in Scotland, and the 2007 election produced a minority Scottish National Party (SNP) executive.

Table 9.5 Scottish Parliament election results, 2011

Party	Constituency seats	Top-up/regional	Total	+/−
SNP	53	16	69	+23
Labour	15	22	37	−7
Conservative	3	12	15	−5
Liberal Democrat	2	3	5	−12
Other	0	3	3	+1

In 2011, the Scottish National Party won 69 out of 129 seats – the first-ever majority government in the Scottish Parliament. It will seek to win stronger powers from Westminster: for example, over financial and fiscal policy, such as corporation tax. It will hold a referendum on Scottish independence from the UK in the second half of the parliamentary term. Currently, around 28% of Scottish voters favour independence.

In the wake of their significant losses in the 2011 Scottish Parliament election, the Scottish Liberal Democrat, Labour and Conservative leaders all promptly announced their resignations.

Since its creation, the Scottish Parliament has voted to abolish tuition fees for Scottish students; to repeal Section 28 of the Local Government Act 1988 (which banned the promotion of homosexuality in local government and state schools), just after the House of Lords had blocked its repeal at Westminster; to support universal free personal care for the elderly; and to introduce free NHS prescriptions for Scotland – all clear examples of a devolved body flexing its muscle in the face of central opposition.

The devolution arrangements for Scotland did not address the 'West Lothian question' (so-called because it was first raised by the MP for that area, Tam Dalyell), namely, that Scottish MPs at Westminster continue to have law-making powers over areas of English policy such as health and education, while English MPs have no such power over Scotland because the Scottish Parliament now legislates on such matters. In 2004, for example, 46 Scottish Labour MPs voted with the Labour government at Westminster to push through top-up tuition fees for England on a total Westminster majority of just five votes – although the Scottish Parliament had already rejected tuition fees for Scotland.

Scotland has also had a disproportionate share of Westminster MPs, of Cabinet ministers and of central government finances across the UK. As English voters became increasingly aware of such imbalances, there were growing calls for fewer Scottish MPs at Westminster, reduced voting rights for Scottish MPs at Westminster, and/or elected assemblies for the regions of England, to parallel the Scottish Parliament.

A partial response to these constitutional imbalances was the reduction in the number of Scottish seats at Westminster from 72 to 59 for the 2005 general election. This did not resolve the West Lothian question.

A further controversy was the spiralling cost of the new Scottish parliamentary building (Holyrood), from an original estimate of £40 million to over £400 million.

The UK coalition government is (in 2011) putting a new Scotland Bill in the UK Parliament, to devolve some new tax and borrowing powers to Holyrood.

Wales

In Wales, the government held the devolution referendum one week after the Scottish vote in 1997, in the hope of giving the 'yes' side a boost. Despite this, the 'yes' vote scraped through with a 0.6% majority on only a 50% turnout. Although there has long been a sense of national Welsh culture, centred especially on the Welsh language, there is far less support for political nationalism in Wales than in Scotland because of the perceived economic and political benefits of the union with England. The 60-member National Assembly for Wales (also elected by AMS, with 40 first-past-the-post and 20 party list members) was therefore much weaker than the Scottish Parliament, with control over the spending of the £8 billion Welsh budget but with no taxation or primary law-making powers. It operated on the style of a local government committee system, with executive rather than legislative or fiscal powers – in effect, merely taking over the role of the Welsh Office in deciding how Westminster legislation is implemented in Wales, in the following policy areas:

  Economic development
  Agriculture
  Industry and training
  Education
  Local government services
  Health and social services
  Housing
  Environment
  Planning and transport
  Sport and heritage

However, in 2011 another referendum was held in Wales, on whether to give the Assembly primary law-making powers in the devolved policy areas (making it more similar to the Scottish Parliament). It won a 64% 'yes' vote, though on a turnout of just 35%. Nevertheless, this suggests a consolidation of nationalism in Wales.

The central government's Scottish and Welsh Offices have now been incorporated into a new department of Constitutional Affairs.

According to some critics, devolution in Scotland and Wales was an example of the Labour government's and Prime Minister's ambivalent attitudes towards power – namely, decentralising only on Labour's own terms and to its own advantage, as far as possible.

However, the 1999 and 2003 Welsh Assembly elections produced a minority Labour executive in Wales (which briefly formed a coalition with the Liberal Democrats, 2000–3), and the 2007 election produced a Labour–Plaid Cymru coalition. In the 2001 election Labour won 30 out of 60 seats – one short of an absolute majority. It sought informal cooperation with other parties, as a minority government.

Table 9.6 Welsh Assembly election results, 2011

Party	Constituency seats	Top-up/regional	Total	+/−
Labour	28	2	30	±4
Conservative	6	8	14	+2
Plaid Cymru	5	6	11	−4
Liberal Democrat	1	4	5	−1
Other	0	0	0	−1

Northern Ireland

At around the same time as the Scottish and Welsh referenda on devolution, but for different reasons (namely, the Northern Ireland peace process) an assembly for Northern Ireland was re-established at Stormont, for the first time since the abolition of the Northern Ireland Parliament in 1972, following the peace deal on 10 April (Good Friday) 1998. In May 1998 a referendum on the peace deal was held throughout Ireland and won strong support: in Northern Ireland 71% 'yes' on 81% turnout, and in the Irish Republic 94% 'yes' on 56% turnout.

The peace deal provided for a Northern Ireland Assembly of 108 seats elected by proportional representation (Single Transferable Vote), a 12-member executive chosen from within and by the Assembly in proportion to the parties' strength in the Assembly (thus, for example, Sinn Fein was guaranteed two seats on the executive). The first Northern Ireland coalition executive was formed in November 1999; the Unionists, in particular, had to adjust to the new realities when former IRA commander Martin McGuinness was appointed Education Secretary.

Thereafter, however, the Northern Ireland Assembly was repeatedly suspended by Westminster because of major policy deadlocks over, for example, the decommissioning of weapons by former 'terrorist' groups in Northern Ireland. This is an example of Westminster's ultimate sovereignty over the devolved bodies.

The 2007 election produced a historic five-party coalition led by the Democratic Unionist Party and Sinn Fein – the most radical unionist and republican parties respectively. This was also the first time that the nationalist parties had ever been represented in all three devolved governments. The five-party coalition was maintained after the 2011 election.

Table 9.7 Northern Ireland Assembly election results, 2011

Party	Assembly	+/−
Democratic Unionist Party	38	+2
Sinn Fein	29	+1
Ulster Unionist Party	16	−2
Social and Democratic Labour Party	14	−2
Alliance Party	8	+1
Other	3	0

talking point...

It is worth noting that, because of its unique history and political and religious divisions, Northern Ireland has an entirely different and more pluralist (multi-party) system than the rest of the UK. This should be mentioned if you are asked in an exam question to assess the nature of the UK's party system.

analyse this...

Table 9.8 Summary of devolved powers, 2011

Type of devolution	Powers	Scottish Parliament	National Assembly for Wales	Northern Ireland Assembly
Legislative	The power to pass, amend or repeal laws	✔	✔	✔
Financial	The ability to raise or lower taxes independently	✔	✕	✕
Administrative	The power to run services,	✔	✔	✔
	allocate funds	✔	✔	✔
	and organise administration	✔	✔	✔

Questions

a Summarise the differences between the powers of the devolved bodies.

b Why are tax-varying powers controversial?

c What has been the impact of devolution on the UK political system?

In 2004, a test referendum was held in the north-east of England on the proposal for an elected regional assembly. However, it was roundly defeated by 78% to 22% (on a quite respectable 48% turnout): perhaps because the assembly's proposed powers were conspicuously weak, or perhaps because the voters used it as an opportunity to express general dissatisfaction with the UK government. Regional devolution in England appears to be off the agenda for the foreseeable future.

Criticisms of devolution

Some parties have criticised devolution for going too far; for others, it has not gone far enough. In summary:

- **The Conservative Party:** was originally against devolution on principle – it is unionist and favours politically strong, centralised government and feared that devolution might be the first step down the slippery slope towards the complete break-up of the United Kingdom. However, largely for political and pragmatic reasons, the party would not now reverse it, and the UK coalition government is extending it in some significant ways.
- **The Labour Party:** favoured devolution to different degrees in different parts of the UK – which, critics say, was a largely self-serving agenda. It also tried (not always successfully) to control the leaderships of the new institutions. However, it does not favour any greater degree of decentralisation, such as UK federalism.
- **The Liberal Democrat Party:** favours federalism, i.e. greater local autonomy, in a consistent pattern across the whole UK. For it, Labour's programme of devolution did not go far enough.
- **The nationalist parties (SNP, Plaid Cymru, SDLP and Sinn Fein):** ultimately favour separatism, – i.e. the complete independence of Scotland, Wales and Northern Ireland from the UK. However, they are content to accept devolution for the foreseeable future.

Note: A broader list of the advantages and disadvantages of devolution, for exam purposes, would be very much the same as the 'advantages and disadvantages of local government' listed earlier in this chapter.

Quiz

1. Suggest two reasons why voter turnout for local council elections is usually low.
2. Explain one way in which the central Labour government changed the structure of local government after 1997.
3. What was the turnout for the 1998 London referendum on a directly elected local mayor and London authority?
4. Define 'devolution'.
5. How does devolution differ from federalism?
6. Give three distinct legislative decisions made by the Scottish Parliament.
7. Describe the powers of the Welsh Assembly.
8. How do these powers compare with those of the Scottish Parliament?
9. Why is the Northern Ireland party system entirely different from that of the rest of the UK?
10. Why might devolution threaten the territorial integrity of the UK?

True or false?

1. Local councillors are elected for fixed four-year terms
2. Nationalist sentiment is stronger in Scotland than in Wales.
3. Devolution does not affect England.
4. Scotland separately elects both members to the Scottish Parliament (MSPs) and members to the sovereign Westminster Parliament (MPs).
5. The 'West Lothian question' means that MSPs can vote on English affairs.

Answers to questions

Note: The following are notes for guidance only and are not intended to be taken as model answers.

9.1 *What are the functions and powers of a local councillor? How do they differ from those of an MP?*   *(15 marks)*

A councillor is a member of a local executive body, whereas an MP is a member of the national legislature. Both are elected to represent a local area; but a council ward is smaller than a parliamentary constituency and, whereas a councillor is purely local, an MP is expected to represent both constituency and national interests (especially according to the traditional conservative view). An MP is a sovereign law maker and local councils (like everyone else) should work within the law of the land. MPs may pass laws (such as the Local Government Act 2000, which extended the system of directly elected mayors) which can alter the structures or powers of local councils, or even abolish them completely. MPs are also meant to scrutinise and control the executive, both central and local; councillors are therefore subordinate to MPs. The only kind of law which councillors may make is delegated (secondary) legislation, e.g. local government by-laws. Their functions are executive and administrative rather than legislative – they decide on and provide local services such as education, housing, refuse collection, fire and police, roads and harbours, leisure and social services. Some of these are 'mandatory', i.e. local government is obliged by law to carry out certain functions, such as housing the homeless; others are 'permissive', i.e. optional, such as providing local libraries and nurseries.

9.2 *What are the advantages and disadvantages of local government?*   *(20 marks)*

Advantages of local government:
- Is more responsive to the needs of local areas (knows what the issues are, can act more quickly).
- Allows an element of local democracy and added tier of political participation and representation.
- Is closer to the people and therefore more accessible.
- Is more accountable and subject to public control because it is closer to the people it serves.
- Imposes checks and balances on the centre.
- Upholds liberal democratic principles of decentralisation and pluralism.

- Some areas, e.g. Scotland and north of England, are often not well represented by Westminster and Whitehall.
- Allows regional parties access to power.
- Provides training and recruitment ground for the centre.
- Relieves the centre of some workload and pressure.
- May be more efficient and cost-effective than central bureaucracy.
- Is more legitimate because it is based on more tangible local culture and reflects regional, not national, political attachments.

Disadvantages of local government:
- May thwart mandate of central government and provoke damaging conflicts between the centre and the regions.
- May mean inconsistent, uncoordinated and unjust provision of services across the country.
- May be unduly costly, bureaucratic or even corrupt.
- May mean local 'elective dictatorship' of one strong and/or radical and/or irresponsible party on a minority vote.
- Strong local government is contrary to the constitutional principles of a unitary state; too much decentralisation may even threaten the unity of the UK
- Alternatively, if it is too weak, it may not provide adequate checks and balances on central government and may, instead, simply generate voter apathy.

Quiz

1. The structure of local government in the United Kingdom is a bit complicated and, at the same time, local councils do not have very much real power in Britain's centralised system.
2. Labour introduced directly elected local mayors.
3. 34%.
4. 'Devolution' is the passing down of limited law-making powers from central to local or regional bodies, with the centre remaining sovereign – i.e. the state remains unitary.
5. Devolution entails the passing down of limited decision-making powers and the centre remains sovereign; federalism entails much stronger decision-making powers for local bodies and the central power is no longer sovereign.
6. The abolition of university tuition fees, foundation hospitals and prescription charges in Scotland.
7. The Welsh Assembly had, until the 2011 referendum, only limited local executive and administrative powers. It now has primary law-making powers.
8. Until 2011, the Welsh Assembly had no primary legislative or tax-varying powers, unlike the Scottish Parliament. It still has no taxation powers.
9. Because of Northern Ireland's unique history, political and religious divisions.
10. Conservative critics of devolution fear that it might be the first step towards the complete break-up of the United Kingdom, if the nationalist parties were to gain more strength.

True or false?

1. True.
2. True.
3. False.
4. True.
5. False.

Sample questions

Short

- What is local government?
- Distinguish between devolution and federalism.
- Describe the powers of the Scottish Parliament.

Medium

- What factors explain the differences in parliamentary representation in different parts of the UK?
- Explain what is meant by the 'West Lothian question' and why it is politically controversial.
- Outline the views of the main UK political parties on the devolution process.

Long

- Evaluate the case for stronger local government in the UK.
- Has devolution created more problems than solutions in the UK?
- To what extent has Scottish independence become a more important issue, and why?

Useful websites

www.bbc.co.uk/news
An excellent, wide-ranging and impartial source for topical news items and archive articles.

www.bbc.co.uk/news/scotland/scotland_politics
The BBC News website for Scottish politics.

www.bbc.co.uk/news/wales/wales_politics
The BBC News website for Welsh politics.

www.bbc.co.uk/news/northern_ireland/northern_ireland_politics
The BBC News website for Northern Ireland politics.

www.london.gov.uk
The official website of the Greater London Authority (Mayor and London Assembly)

10 The European Union

Aims of this chapter

- To outline the history and development of the EU.
- To outline the UK's changing attitude and relationship to the EU.
- To assess the nature and balance of 'sovereignty'.
- To explain the institutions of the EU and their functions.
- To explain the UK parties' views on the EU.
- To outline and evaluate the impact of the main EU treaties.
- To debunk some EU myths.

History and issues

The (then) European Economic Community (EEC) was formed in 1957, by just six countries: France, Germany, Italy, Luxembourg, the Netherlands and Belgium.

Britain, Denmark and Ireland joined in 1973; Greece joined in 1981; then Spain and Portugal (1986); then Finland, Sweden and Austria (1995). Norway had also planned to join in 1995 but its voters rejected membership in a referendum. More recently, ten more (mostly former communist) states joined in 2004: Cyprus, the Czech Republic, Estonia, Hungary, Latvia, Lithuania, Malta, Poland, Slovakia and Slovenia. Bulgaria and Romania joined in 2007. There are now 27 member states in the EU, and a population of 495 million.

The original creation of the EEC was intended to establish a common free market, economic and monetary union and 'an ever closer union among the peoples of Europe'. Thus the visions of a single market and a federal Europe date from the 1950s (not from the 1980s or 1990s, as is sometimes suggested today). These goals were inspired by a desire for lasting peace and security after two world wars; awareness of growing economic and social interdependence and a desire for greater international cooperation between European countries; the advantages of large-scale markets; greater world influence; and the wish to challenge the blocs of the USA and the then USSR. The main economic principle enshrined in the 1957 Treaty of Rome was free trade – the removal of barriers and the establishment of common tariffs and policies (especially in agriculture, fishing, coal and steel) across Europe.

In 1967, the EEC became the European Community (EC). When the Maastricht Treaty came into effect in 1993, this institution became the European Union (EU). The changing labels are clearly illustrative of the broadening and increasingly integrated embrace of the EU.

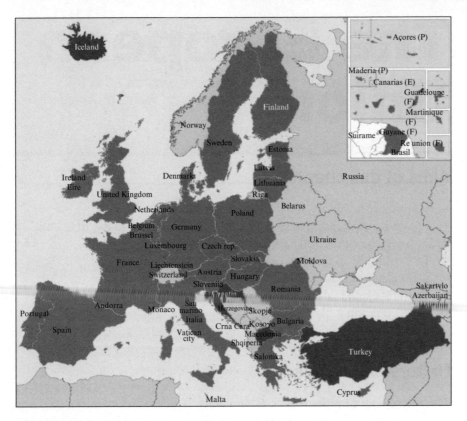

Figure 10.1 The European Union, 2011

The EU is a **supranational** institution, i.e. not just an intergovernmental fraternity, but a sovereign power over member states with a body of law that takes precedence over national laws.

The changing attitude of the UK towards Europe

Britain initially refused to join the EEC in the 1950s for a number of reasons: a sense of superiority and national pride after victory in war; a hankering after lost imperial status; Britain's international status and links with the USA and Commonwealth; a sense of political and geographical difference – an island mentality; xenophobia (and mistrust especially of Germany and France); for the right wing of the Conservative Party, especially, fear of loss of sovereignty and 'national' identity; and for the left wing of the Labour Party, dislike of the free market capitalist nature of the EEC. By the 1960s, however, it was clear that the EEC was an established success.

Britain eventually joined in 1973, under Ted Heath's Conservative government. When the Labour Party came to power in 1974 it was very divided on the issue, so Prime Minister Harold Wilson held the first-ever UK-wide referendum in 1975, on the question of staying in the EC. He lifted 'collective responsibility' and allowed his dissident left-wing Cabinet ministers (such as Tony Benn) publicly to divide on the issue. Two-thirds of the UK electorate voted to stay in Europe, thus legitimising Wilson's own support for the EC.

> **key term...**
>
> **Supranational institution**
> A sovereign body over member states with laws that take precedence over national laws.

talking point...

Note that there was no UK referendum on *joining* the EC in 1973 – only on staying in it, in 1975. This is a common source of confusion – and sometimes criticism.

UK elections to the European Parliament were first held in 1979.

The issue of sovereignty

The question of sovereignty is multi-dimensional.

The main issue since 1973 has been Parliament's 'legal sovereignty', which has been effectively negated (overruled) by the primacy of EU laws and treaties. Even on entry in 1973, the British Parliament had to accept 43 volumes of existing EU legislation. This loss of sovereignty to Europe has since increased, with the growing scope of European intervention and with reforms of European voting procedures. The most important reform was the change from unanimous voting in the EU Council of Ministers (i.e. any one country could effectively veto any policy) to **Qualified Majority Voting (QMV)** under the Single European Act 1986 (introduced, ironically, by the Eurosceptic Prime Minister Margaret Thatcher), whereby several countries must now band together in order to veto a policy, on a growing range of issues.

Between 15% and 50% of UK legislation now originates from the EU; the exact figure is hard to calculate, and Europhobes and Europhiles pick their figures to suit their arguments.

No other member state has (or had) parliamentary sovereignty, because they all have written constitutions and supreme courts; therefore this issue matters more to the UK. However, observers might be forgiven for being sceptical about UK *governments'* expressed concerns about the loss of sovereignty to Europe, since the 'elective dictatorships' of some recent British governments have done more than Europe ever has to undermine Westminster's real power, from within.

UK governments are generally more concerned about their own loss of 'national sovereignty', i.e. their ability to pursue their own policies without external interference. From another perspective, however, the primacy of EU law has curbed the dangers of 'elective dictatorship' of a single-party majority UK government within a 'sovereign' Parliament. The European Court of Justice has protected many civil liberties of UK citizens against British law, for example in relation to retirement ages, working hours and workers' holiday entitlements, food and water standards and the pension rights of part-time workers.

'Economic sovereignty' has become an important issue, especially with the creation of the single European currency. However, it has actually long been undermined in the UK by foreign ownership of businesses and industries, and especially by Britain's dependence on the health of the US economy – apparently with little hostility from the traditional right-wing Eurosceptics.

key term...

Qualified Majority Voting (QMV)
A weighted system of voting (according to countries' population sizes) used in the EU Council of Ministers (see below) where several member states must vote together to block a decision, across a growing range of policy areas.

Moreover, the Labour government's granting to the Bank of England of independent control of interest rates (immediately after the 1997 general election) was a willing surrender of a key economic power which brought Britain into line with one of the conditions for joining the euro.

The 'political sovereignty' of the electorate has, arguably, been undermined by the 'democratic deficit' created by the EU: namely, that the only directly elected EU institution – the European Parliament – is also the weakest. However, the European Parliament is rapidly gaining political strength; it has given UK voters an added tier of democratic representation (via pure PR); and the issue of Europe did set the precedent, in the UK, for the holding of referenda on major constitutional issues.

A more positive view of EU membership argues that national governments benefit from pooling sovereignty to achieve policy goals which would be unattainable alone; and that EU decision making helps to strengthen national governments by reducing the impact of domestic constraints.

Table 10.1   UK policy and EU power

Policy areas wholly or largely under EU jurisdiction	Policy areas wholly or largely outside EU jurisdiction
Trade	Education
Agriculture	Health
Fishing	Social security
Competition control	Law and order
Employment law	Personal taxation
Consumer law	UK political structures
Regional development	Local government services

Questions...

10.1 Define the concept of sovereignty. *(5 marks)*

10.2 Outline two ways in which the EU has limited UK sovereignty. *(10 marks)*

The institutions of the European Union

The Council of Ministers

The Council of Ministers is the ultimate EU policy-making body, and comprises the foreign ministers of all member states (with other ministers in topic sub-committees when appropriate). Before 1986, Council voting had to be unanimous on every issue. Since then, QMV on a growing range of issues has meant a loss of power by individual states to Europe.

The European Commission

Each member state has one Commissioner, appointed by its government for a five-year renewable term. Commissioners are usually former – some critics would say 'failed' – politicians, diplomats or senior civil servants. They present policy proposals to the Council of Ministers, have significant powers of delegated legislation (each year the Commission passes 4,000–5,000 pieces of secondary legislation), carry out decisions made, administer most of the EU's budget and investigate breaches of the rules – thus they can impose fines on offenders and take member states to the European Court of Justice.

In sum, the Commissioners have significant executive, administrative and even legislative powers. Since they are not elected, this annoys Eurosceptics.

Each Commissioner has a small team of personal advisors and officials appointed by the Commissioners themselves, which allows scope for 'cronyism'.

talking point...

Brussels bureaucrats

The Commission has a civil service of about 18,000. Although the EU is frequently criticised for being overly bureaucratic, this is remarkably small and generally efficient by comparison with the bureaucracy of some member states (for example, Britain's Ministry of Defence alone has 70,000 civil servants).

However, in 1999 the Commission's officials were at the centre of a major scandal about fraud, corruption, nepotism and cronyism, in which three or four of the Commissioners – most notably France's Edith Cresson – were also implicated. The European Parliament came close to sacking all 20 Commissioners (because it lacked the power to dismiss individuals). Following the publication of a highly critical report from the European Committee of Independent Experts in 1999, which concluded that 'It is difficult to find anyone who has even the slightest sense of responsibility', all 20 European Commissioners resigned – an unprecedented crisis in the history of the EU. Most, however, were promptly reappointed by their national governments (although not Cresson, who was charged with corruption).

The European Council

The European Council, established in 1974, is made up of the heads of each government, and meets twice a year in European summit meetings – e.g. the Maastricht Treaty was signed by John Major at a European Council meeting in December 1991, with opt-outs on the single currency and Social Chapter;

and in 1997 Tony Blair signed the Amsterdam Treaty by which the UK signed up to the EU Social Chapter. Some summits have weighty programmes, for example, about EU enlargement in 2004 or about military action against the Libyan regime in 2011. Other summits, however, may be little more than media events.

The European Parliament

This is the only directly elected body of the EU but it has, arguably, relatively little power (however, see below). It has 736 seats, of which Britain has 72. Germany (the biggest country in the EU) has 99 seats. Other countries have fewer seats, roughly in proportion to their populations, ranging down to Malta with 5 seats.

Table 10.2   Number of seats per state (2009–14 parliamentary term)

Austria	17	Latvia	8
Belgium	22	Lithuania	12
Bulgaria	17	Luxembourg	6
Cyprus	6	Malta	5
Czech Republic	22	Netherlands	25
Denmark	13	Poland	50
Estonia	6	Portugal	22
Finland	13	Romania	33
France	72	Slovakia	13
Germany	99	Slovenia	7
Greece	22	Spain	50
Hungary	22	Sweden	18
Ireland	12	UK	72
Italy	72		
Total			**736**

Members of the European Parliament (MEPs) are elected every five years. In 1999 the Labour government changed the UK electoral system for European elections (without holding a referendum) from first-past-the-post to the Closed Party List system, a form of pure PR where the party leaders, rather than the voters, choose the MEPs to fill the seats. The main criticism of this system is that the voter has no say in who are the actual MEPs, who are likely to be loyal party placemen. The House of Lords rejected the closed list system for EU elections a record *six* times, but the government in the Commons pushed it through nevertheless. Some independent-minded and popular MEPs – e.g. Labour's Christine Oddy (Coventry and North Warwickshire) – were pushed so far down the party lists as to be effectively deselected by the leadership, with the voters having no say in the process.

The European Parliament is a forum for debate; it is consulted on major policy issues and can suggest amendments which the Commission often accepts; it can veto certain forms of legislation; can modify or reject the EU budget (as it did five times in the 1980s); can investigate public complaints of European maladministration (with an EU Ombudsman since Maastricht); can veto EU Commissioners' appointments; and can, in theory, dismiss the entire Commission by a two-thirds majority (never yet done, but it was pressure from MEPs which forced the Commission's collective resignation over allegations of sleaze and corruption in 1999).

talking point...

The whole European Parliament commutes each month between Brussels and Strasbourg, at a cost to European taxpayers of almost £200 million per year. France will not agree to its staying permanently in Brussels.

The European Parliament's profile is fairly low and many voters are apathetic or cynical about it. In the 2004 elections turnout reached a record low, with just 45% of EU voters casting ballots. It was especially low for many of the ten new member states, which averaged a mere 26%. The lowest turnout was in Slovakia, where fewer than 17% cast their votes. Turnout in the UK was 38%.

analyse this...

EUROPE'S CINDERELLA OR UGLY SISTER?

Adapted from an article by Paul Reynolds, News Online world affairs correspondent

The European Parliament (EP) is perhaps the most misunderstood and, mainly in Britain, probably most reviled institution in the European Union.

It seems to be in the news solely when there are expenses scandals or when someone takes a shot at it for being an expensive and pretentious talking shop. In fact, it has acquired a significant amount of power over the last 20 or so years so that it now stands as a co-equal to the Council of Ministers, that is the member states, in making decisions about many European laws.

This power of "co-decision", as it is called in eurospeak, means that, largely unnoticed by most of the populations which vote in its members, it can make or break many pieces of legislation which affect the ordinary lives of European citizens.

Some examples illustrate how and why the Parliament now counts.

- Working time directive. This introduced limits on the hours employees can be made to work, and regulates rest periods, annual leave and night work.

- Cosmetics directive. This regulates what industry can do to test cosmetics on animals, and banned animal testing of cosmetics after 2009.
- Takeovers directive. This establishes standard EU rules on takeover bids, and restricts the tactics companies can use to avoid foreign takeovers.
- GM food regulation: This governs the amount of genetically modified products which are allowed in food and the labelling required to alert the consumer.

It affects the food you eat, the air you breathe, your workplace, your health and safety and your environment.

Quite often the European public is unaware that laws passed by their national parliaments began life in Brussels.

In the UK, the government has introduced a ban on age discrimination in the workplace – without widely advertising the fact that it stemmed from an EU directive.

'When it is seen as a good news thing, they want to claim credit for it,' says Kirsty Hughes, of the Centre for European Policy Studies. 'If it is something controversial, they blame it on Brussels.'

The struggle for recognition by the European Parliament has been a long one. It is not over yet. Somehow it has not overcome its poor image to be accepted for what it wants to be – a democratic workhorse at the heart of the European Union.

Zvl ý l A# l J #Jl ~z#h{# i j 5̆ v5 r&̆l ~z

Questions

a What are the merits and demerits of the UK's voting system for the EU Parliament?

b Suggest reasons why the turnout for EU elections is so low.

c Should the European Parliament have more or less power than it has now?

Questions...

10.3 What are the powers of the European Parliament? *(20 marks)*

10.4 Does the European Parliament need reform? *(20 marks)*

The European Court of Justice (ECJ)

This comprises judges appointed by member states for six-year renewable terms, and is based in Luxembourg. It interprets and enforces EU law, which takes precedence over national law for every member state. UK courts are therefore obliged to refuse to enforce domestic Acts of Parliament which contravene European law (a principle established by the 1990 *Factortame* case about fishing rights in British waters). The workload of the ECJ has increased from 79 cases in 1970 to over 2,000 per year now. In 2009, the ECJ passed 377 judgments against member states for failing to fulfil their obligations, including 9 against the UK.

EU decision making – a summary

At its simplest: the Commission makes a proposal; the Parliament offers its opinion and agreement; the Council of Ministers makes a decision; the Court of Justice interprets and enforces the decision; the member countries administer the decision.

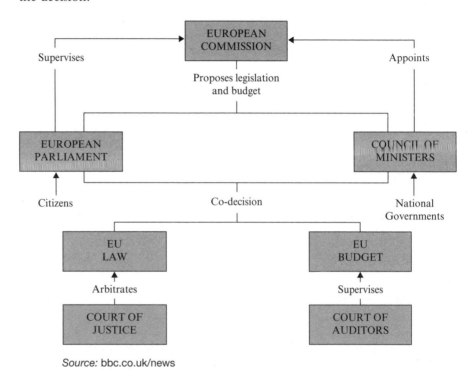

Source: bbc.co.uk/news

Figure 10.2   Summary of EU decision-making processes

The impact of the EU on British political parties

Membership of the EU has profoundly divided the two main British political parties: Labour especially in the 1970s, and the Conservatives especially since the 1980s. Left-wing Labour MPs have always been hostile to the EU, which they perceive as a free market 'capitalist club'. The 'new' Labour government was more Europhile (pro-European), but retreated from joining the euro.

The Conservatives, under Margaret Thatcher, became increasingly suspicious of the EC in the 1980s, as they saw it extending beyond a free trade community to a supranational political power (which, in fact, it always was). Since 1990, divisions within the Conservative Party over Europe were primarily responsible for: Thatcher's prime ministerial defeat in 1990; the temporary withdrawal of the whip from several Conservative Eurorebels, which eradicated John Major's small majority; Eurosceptic John Redwood's leadership challenge against Major in 1995; the defection from the Conservative Party of pro-European MPs to the Liberal Democrats or Labour, such as Robert Jackson in 2005; and the defection of some anti-Europeans to increasingly influential Europhobic parties such as the UK Independence Party (UKIP), such as Bob Spink, who defected in 2008 and subsequently lost his seat to the Conservative candidate in the 2010 general election.

The Conservative Party's current policy on joining the euro is 'never'. Of the three main parties, only the Liberal Democrats are fully committed to the development of a federal Europe.

Euroscepticism in the UK has also generated the creation and rise of some minor parties: most notably, the UKIP, which dented the main parties' vote in the 2004 and 2009 EU elections, pushing the Liberal Democrats (in 2004) and Labour (in 2009) down the list. The UKIP seeks complete withdrawal from the EU – a prime example of a protest vote. The Greens held their two UK MEPs.

Table 10.3   EU Parliament elections (UK), 2009

Party	% votes	% seats	Seats won
Conservative	27.7	36.1	26
UKIP	16.5	18.1	13
Labour	15.7	18.1	13
Liberal Democrat	13.7	15.3	11
Green	8.6	2.8	2
BNP	6.2	2.8	2
SNP	2.1	2.8	2
Plaid Cymru	0.8	1.4	1
Sinn Fein	0.7	1.4	1
DUP★		1.4	1
Others	8.5	0.0	0
Total UK seats			72

★Voting figures not shown because Single Transferable Vote was used rather than the party list system.

Key events in the development of the EU

The Single European Act (SEA) 1986
The SEA developed the idea of a single European market with a commitment to advancing economic integration. The Single European Market officially came into being on 1 January 1993, establishing the 'four freedoms' of movement for goods, capital, services and persons, although Britain refused to scrap frontier controls for the movement of persons.

The Maastricht Treaty 1993
The Maastricht Treaty created a European Union with common citizenship and set out a timetable and procedure for creating a single currency.

The ratification in the British House of Commons was a very fraught process and was only achieved when John Major made the issue a vote of confidence in his government. He also ensured the deletion of every reference to federalism ('the F-word') from the treaty, because the word 'federalism' has been used, inaccurately, by Eurosceptics to imply the complete absorption of member countries into a European 'superstate'. In fact, of course, 'federalism' means the ordered division of sovereignty between central and local powers, with constitutional guarantees of mutual spheres of autonomy. Thus the Maastricht treaty established the principle of **subsidiarity**, whereby decisions should be taken 'at the lowest possible level' compatible with efficiency and democracy. This was an attempt to return to member states some power previously lost to Brussels; and Scottish and Welsh nationalists argued that it also implied greater devolution of power *within* the UK.

key term...

Subsidiarity The principle (enshrined in the 1993 Maastricht Treaty) whereby decisions should be taken 'at the lowest possible level' compatible with efficiency and democracy, i.e. encouraging decentralisation down to member states.

The single currency

The Maastricht Treaty bound member states to work towards a single currency (the euro), starting in 2002, with the exceptions of Britain, Denmark and Sweden, which secured an 'opt-out'. A European Central Bank was established in Frankfurt to regulate interest rates.

The first stage for each country was to enter its currency into the Exchange Rate Mechanism (ERM), whereby currency values were tied to each other within certain bands of flexibility. Britain joined the ERM in 1990, but was humiliatingly forced out on 16 September 1992 (so-called 'Black Wednesday') when currency speculation on the international financial markets forced the devaluation of the pound below the floor of its ERM band. Conservative Chancellor Norman Lamont eventually – and reluctantly – resigned in 1993 over Britain's fall-out from the ERM. (A young David Cameron, then a special adviser to Lamont, was, famously, seen with him in the 1992 TV interviews.)

Successive UK governments have since resiled from joining the euro and, as Euroscepticism predominates, membership seems unlikely in the near future.

The case for a single currency

European integration and a truly 'single market' require a single currency; it would enhance Europe's competitiveness against the USA and other major economies; currency transaction costs would be eliminated; currency speculators would be weakened; business stability and certainty would be enhanced, as would price transparency and, hence, lower costs for consumers.

The case against a single currency

Practical difficulties in aligning the very diverse economies and currencies of member states; loss of national sovereignty; loss of governments' ability to adjust currency values against external shocks; loss of wealth, employment and power from weaker to stronger member countries, including probable domination by the European Central Bank.

The Social Chapter

The Maastricht Treaty also bound member states – except Britain, which again secured an 'opt-out' – to the Social Chapter, an agreement incorporating minimum employment wages and rights, sexual equality, freedom of information and other social improvements throughout the EU. The then Conservative government's main argument against it was that such added constraints and costs on British businesses would increase unemployment and decrease profits. The Labour government signed up to the Social Chapter in 1997. The minimum wage has since been accepted by all main parties, and it has increased over time.

Maastricht's other 'pillars'

The two other pillars of the Maastricht treaty were based on intergovernmental cooperation rather than supranational integration, and also on unanimous voting rather than QMV; therefore the British government did not feel threatened by them. The Maastricht Treaty's 'second pillar' deals with foreign and defence policy cooperation; the 'third pillar' concerns cooperation on interior and justice affairs, e.g. toughening rules against drug smuggling, terrorism, immigration and asylum seekers from outside Europe, but relaxing restraints against movement of persons within Europe.

The Amsterdam Treaty 1997

This agreement (signed by Prime Minister Blair early in his first term of office) signed the UK up to the Social Chapter and provided for the gradual introduction of common policies on immigration, asylum and visa laws. It also extended QMV to such areas as employment, sexual equality, public health and customs cooperation.

True or false?

1. Norway is not a member of the EU.
2. The UK held a referendum on joining the EU in 1975.
3. The EU court is the European Court of Human Rights.
4. The European Parliament is the only directly elected institution of the EU.
5. The Conservative Party seeks withdrawal from the EU.

The Nice Treaty 2000

The aim of the Nice Treaty was to decide how power should be distributed within the European institutions after EU enlargement to 25 member states in 2004: e.g. changing the number of seats in the European Parliament and the size of the Commission, and extending QMV. The result was the proposed EU constitution.

The proposed EU constitution 2004–5

With the enlargement of the EU to 25 member states, it was agreed that a written EU constitution was necessary, for the first time, so as to clarify and coordinate the rules of procedure. Agreement on the content of the constitution proved difficult, with smaller states (such as Spain and Poland) resisting control by larger states. The then UK Labour government at first insisted that the new constitutional treaty was simply a 'tidying up exercise'; but, under pressure from the Conservatives, Liberal Democrats and a largely Eurosceptic press, Prime Minister Blair made a major U-turn in 2004 and accepted the principle of a referendum on the new EU constitution – at some unspecified time in the future.

The EU constitution sought to create:

- A new (non-elected) EU President for two-and-a-half year terms.
- A new (non-elected) EU Foreign Minister accountable to member governments.
- New powers for national Parliaments to block Commission proposals.
- Further extension of QMV, with new weighting amongst member states.
- A new Charter of Fundamental Rights.

The French and Dutch voted against it in 2005, negating the need for any referendum in the UK.

The Lisbon Treaty 2009

The Lisbon Treaty was a modified version of the previously proposed EU constitution. It was rejected, and hence blocked, by an Irish referendum in 2008; but was accepted in a second Irish referendum in 2009, to the fury of Eurosceptics. It contained most of the same provisions as the proposed constitution, but did not attempt to replace all previous EU treaties and start afresh.

The UK government defended most of its 'red lines' (national vetoes) on tax and economic policy, justice and home affairs, defence and foreign affairs; and it has not signed up to the Charter of Fundamental Rights. However, it has accepted majority voting in areas such as social security, in return for the removal of the veto from agricultural and fishing policies.

EU myths

Never let the facts stand in the way of a good story. This is a deeply held principle in the cynical world of journalism, and the EU has long been a victim of it. Below are listed just a few of the classic EU myths, all of which are untrue. Some of them are based on half-truths, on misunderstandings about the role of different European organisations, or on confusion between UK and EU law; and there are many which are complete fantasy and fibs. Perhaps the most famous is the bendy banana myth.

- Bananas must not be excessively curved (*Sun*, 4 March 1998).
- Brandy butter is to be renamed 'brandy spreadable fat' (*The European*, 6–12 April 1998).
- The EU has decreed that condom dimensions should be harmonised across the seamless Continent (*Independent on Sunday*, 12 March 2000).
- Due to new European safety directives, firemen must walk down the stairs instead of sliding down a pole (*Daily Mail*, 16 June 2002).
- Mother Christmas outfits: politically correct Eurocrats say Santa must be a woman (*Sun*, 24 October 2001)
- Eurocrats are to demand that the Queen's crest is wiped from British passports and replaced by the yellow stars of the EU (*Mail on Sunday*, 29 August 2000).
- The EU constitution means 'signing away a thousand years of British sovereignty' (*Sun*, 18 June 2004.)
- 'Brussels will gain extensive powers over foreign, defence and employment laws' under the new constitution (*Daily Mail*, 19 June 2004).
- 'We will have to surrender our place at the international top table – in NATO, in the UN and at the G8 summits' (Nigel Farage, UKIP MEP, 4 June 2004).

- 'A secret clause in the constitution would give Brussels control over our oil' (*Sun*, 12 November 2003).
- 'The constitution confers on the EU the power to tax' (*The Times*, 13 April 2004).
- The constitution is 'a gateway to a country called Europe' (Michael Ancram, Shadow Foreign Secretary, 20 June 2004).

The European Commission's website (www.cec.org.uk/press/myths) provides a lengthy (and fully explained) A–Z list of such myths which, though often amusing, raises serious questions about the integrity of some UK press and politicians.

Question...

10.5 Assess the advantages and disadvantages of European integration *(25 marks)*

The future – a Europe of nation states or a United States of Europe?
The EU has grown from six states at its origin in the 1950s to 27 states in 2011, with almost 500 million citizens. The two main British parties have always been divided on the question of Europe; the Conservatives have become increasingly Eurosceptic since the 1980s, and Labour has had to deal with growing hostility to Europe amongst voters since 1997. By contrast, most other European countries are more pro-EU. It seems likely that the EU will both deepen and widen in the future, and Britain will have to decide whether it genuinely wishes to be 'at the heart of Europe' or to be side-lined and left behind.

However, the EU is not about to become a 'super state'. The intense national arguments over the drafting of the EU constitution in 2004 – and its ultimate failure – demonstrated how much the EU is still a fragmented coalition of self-interested member states fighting to defend their own national interests. In fact, the constitutional arrangements of the Lisbon Treaty actually return more powers to national parliaments and governments – for better or worse.

Quiz

1. When was the EEC formed?
2. Where was the treaty signed that created the EEC?
3. Name two European states which are not members of the EU.
4. Give one-sentence definitions of the following terms:
   a. Sovereignty
   b. Subsidiarity
   c. Supranationalism.
5. Give two reasons why the idea of a more united Europe gained strength in the post-1945 era.
6. Give two reasons why Britain initially refused to join this process.
7. In what year did Britain join the (then) EEC?

8. In what year was the British referendum on staying in Europe?
9. In what year were UK elections to the European Parliament first held?
10. a. What is QMV?
    b. When was it introduced?
    c. What impact has QMV had on the balance of power between Europe and individual member states?
11. Why has the left wing of the Labour Party traditionally been hostile to the EU?
12. Why has the right wing of the Conservative Party been hostile to Europe?
13. Give one argument for, and one argument against, a single European currency.
14. What is the Social Chapter?
15. Why are there 12 stars on the European flag?

Question...

10.6 Discuss the impact of the European Union on British political processes.

(25 marks)

Answers to questions

Note: The following are notes for guidance only and are not intended to be taken as model answers.

10.1 *Define the concept of sovereignty.* *(5 marks)*

'Sovereignty' means the legitimate location of power of last resort over any community. It may be defined purely in legal terms as the power to make binding laws which no other body can set aside or overrule. It may also be viewed as the autonomous power of a community to govern itself – a territorial concept relating to the powers of independent states. The voters are said to have the 'political sovereignty' to rule themselves and elect and remove governments, i.e. the 'people power' at the root of the legitimacy of the UK Parliament and government which justifies the democratic claims of the British political system. The location of sovereignty is not always easy to pinpoint, e.g. in federal systems such as the USA.

10.2 *Outline two ways in which the EU has limited UK sovereignty.* *(10 marks)*

The most obvious legal limitations are: that by signing EU treaties – Rome, SEA, Maastricht, Amsterdam, Nice, Copenhagen – the UK has subordinated itself to the dictates of EU laws, regulations and directives. The *Factortame* case is an example, together with its implications for the qualitatively new role of the British courts in being able to veto UK statutes when they conflict with EU law. There has been a loss of control over many areas of economic policy – e.g. agriculture, tariffs and trade, the EU ban on the world-wide export of British beef (1996–2006), etc. Other areas include fishing, the environment, conditions of work (the minimum wage etc.). Territorial sovereignty has been limited by the 'four freedoms': freedom of movement across the EU of goods, workers, capital and services. The UK's resulting inability to control immigration from the EU has generated particular controversy. Given QMV, loss of sovereignty is a matter of degree.

10.3   *What are the powers of the European Parliament?*   *(20 marks)*

The European Parliament is composed of 736 MEPs. It performs some similar functions to the British House of Commons – representation, debate and scrutiny – but it has more limited legislative powers. It can veto the EU budget – and in the 1980s it rejected the budget five times. It can dismiss the Commission with a two-thirds majority. The Parliament can also suggest amendments to draft legislation from the Commission, about 70% of which are accepted by the Commission. The Maastricht Treaty gave it more powers: for example, to veto certain forms of legislation, to veto Commissioners' appointments and to investigate voters' complaints of EU maladministration. Its powers have increased with each new EU treaty – for example, the 2009 Lisbon Treaty gave it powers over the entire EU budget. Many new laws in member states now stem from the need to implement EU legislation.

10.4   *Does the European Parliament need reform?*   *(20 marks)*

The Parliament is the only directly elected body of the EU but has fairly limited powers – hence, say critics, the 'democratic deficit' at the heart of the EU. Paradoxically, as it stands, the EU (through the Council of Ministers) strengthens national governments and bureaucracies at the expense of national Parliaments and voters. If the European Parliament were to be given more genuine law-making power and ability to control the Commission and Council, that would further democratise the EU, on the one hand, and reduce the potential for 'elective dictatorship' within Britain, on the other. The European Parliament should also remain in Brussels; and the much-abused system of travel expenses and other perks for MEPs should be scrapped, to save millions of pounds for the taxpayers – who might, then, have more respect for the European Parliament.

True or false?

1. True.
2. False.
3. False.
4. True.
5. False.

10.5   *Assess the advantages and disadvantages of European integration.*   *(25 marks)*

Advantages:

- Lasting peace and security after two great European wars.
- A common free market and free trade.
- The advantages of large-scale markets.
- Enhanced economic competitiveness and consumer rights.
- Greater world influence in the global economy through 'pooled' sovereignty.

- An added tier of democratic representation.
- Curbs on national 'elective dictatorship' and more power for UK regions.
- Protection of the environment, health and safety and UK workers' rights.
- Further civil rights through the ECJ.
- Enhanced collective security against international crime and terrorism.
- 'An ever closer union among the peoples of Europe.'
- Cultural diversity and choice, from food to fashion.

Disadvantages:
- Loss of sovereignty in its various forms.
- (Perception of) loss or dilution of national and cultural identity.
- Loss of emotive national symbols, such as the pound or imperial system of measurement.
- Economic imbalances and drains between richer and poorer member states.
- Widespread consequences of any future euro instability or weakness.
- Difficulties of EU management and coordination, especially with enlargement.
- Over-centralisation and ignorance of diverse needs of local regions.
- EU inadequacies in foreign policy, conflict and crisis management – e.g. Kosovo.
- Risks and costs of waste, inefficiency and corruption.
- Disadvantages to non-EU states and their trading partners (e.g. the Commonwealth and the UK) of protective EU trade agreements.
- The 'democratic deficit' created by the non-elected institutions of the EU.

Quiz
1. 1957.
2. Rome.
3. Norway and Switzerland.
4. a. Ultimate authority and power.
   b. The principle established by the Maastricht Treaty that, within the EU, 'decisions should be taken at the lowest possible level compatible with efficiency and democracy'.
   c. The creation of a sovereign authority over and above member states.
5. Desire for peace and security after two wars; awareness of growing economic and social interdependence and desire for greater international cooperation; advantages of large-scale markets; greater world influence; challenge to USA and other major economies.
6. A sense of superiority and national pride after victory in war; hankering after imperial status; international status and links with USA and Commonwealth; sense of political and geographical difference; left-wing dislike of capitalist aspects of EU; right-wing xenophobia.
7. 1973.
8. 1975.
9. 1979.
10. a. Qualified Majority Voting, in the Council of Ministers.
    b. The Single European Act 1986.
    c. Member states have lost further power to the Council.
11. They see it as a bastion of free market capitalism.
12. They fear loss of sovereignty and 'national' identity.

13. For: European economic integration requires a single currency; it would enhance Europe's competitiveness against the USA, China and India; currency transaction costs would be eliminated; the currency speculators would be weakened; business stability and certainty would be enhanced. Against: Loss of national sovereignty; loss of governments' ability to adjust currency value against external shocks; loss of wealth, employment and power from weaker to stronger member states.

14. Agreement on minimum employment rights, sexual equality, freedom of information and other social improvements throughout the EU.

15. It is a number that represents perfection and completeness.

10.6 *Discuss the impact of the European Union on British political processes.* *(25 marks)*

The EU (then the Common Market) was formed in 1957 by six states. It now has 27 member states.

The UK joined in 1973. This meant that the British Parliament lost 'legal' or legislative sovereignty both de jure and de facto (i.e. both in law and in practice) in areas where European law took precedence. This loss of sovereignty has since increased, with the growing scope of European intervention and with reforms of European voting procedures. The most important reform was the change from unanimous voting in the Council of Ministers (i.e. any one country could veto any policy) to Qualified Majority Voting, under the Single European Act 1986, signed by UK Prime Minister Margaret Thatcher. For example, in 1993 Britain was overruled on the principle of a 48-hour working week.

In 1975 a national referendum was held on Britain's continuing membership of the then EC. Technically, this was merely 'advisory', and so, in theory, Parliament's legal sovereignty was not affected. In practice, however, Parliament could not have ignored the referendum result, which was a two-thirds 'yes' vote. The EU has, therefore, provided the impetus for more 'direct democracy' within the UK. Similarly, in theory, Westminster could legislate to leave the EU at any time, but in political practice that seems difficult and unlikely. From another perspective, the primacy of EU law has curbed the dangers of 'elective dictatorship' of a single-party majority UK government within a sovereign Parliament; e.g. the EU has obliged the UK government to extend national holiday laws and rights for part-time workers.

Since British and European courts are required to enforce European law rather than domestic law when there is conflict between the two, Parliament has also lost some legal sovereignty to both the British courts and the ECJ. For example, in 2011 the ECJ banned the use of gender differentiation in underwriting insurance premiums, implying higher car insurance costs for women.

Elections to the European Parliament were first held in 1979, adding a new layer of representative democracy to the British political system. However, the European Parliament – the only elected institution of the EU – is still relatively weak. Since the main decision-making bodies of the EU – the Council of Ministers and the European Commission – are not elected, membership of the EU has also meant some loss of the 'political' sovereignty of the British electorate – the so-called 'democratic deficit'.

The sheer quantity of EU law and its impact upon Britain has given the

British constitution an increasingly codified and rigid character, as well as modifying its unitary nature.

Membership of the EU has increased the powers of British Prime Ministers: for example, in membership of the European Council with its twice-yearly summits; in signing EU agreements such as the Maastricht, Amsterdam and Lisbon treaties; and in appointing European Commissioners and civil servants.

Membership of the EU has also increased the policy-making powers of UK Foreign Secretaries in the Council of Ministers; and it is widely held to have increased the power of UK civil servants.

Most obviously, membership of the EU has profoundly divided the two main British political parties: Labour especially in the 1970s, and the Conservatives especially in the 1980s and 1990s. Also, the rise of small parties which are more or less hostile to the EU, such as the UKIP, has dented the main parties' votes in secondary elections (i.e. local, London and EU elections). However, this has had a lot to do with PR electoral systems; the small (and sometimes single-issue) parties have had much less impact in general elections.

The ECJ has protected many civil liberties against British law, for example in relation to minimum wages, retirement ages, food and water standards and the employment rights of part-time workers.

The emphasis on 'subsidiarity' in the Maastricht Treaty has encouraged devolution and decentralisation within the UK.

Finally, many British pressure groups are increasingly focusing their attention on EU rather than domestic decision-making institutions – a reliable indicator of the shifting balance of power and influence. For example, the Committee of Professional Agricultural Organisations (COPA), comprising most of the national farmers' organisations, including Britain's National Farmers' Union, is based in Brussels, where it can effectively lobby the relevant EU institutions, especially the Commission. Similarly, most British local authorities – especially those which receive EU financial aid – now have a European office in order to maintain effective contacts, again, especially with the Commission; and local authority by-laws (e.g. on weights and measures) are often based on EU regulations.

Whether the impact of the EU upon British political processes has been, on balance, positive or negative is a matter of highly subjective and sometimes very emotive assessment. It has certainly done more to divide the main parties than any other issue for the last half century; but it may have done more to enhance the rights and freedoms of UK citizens than have any of those parties.

Sample questions

Short

- What is meant by a 'supranational' organisation?
- Explain what is meant by Qualified Majority Voting in the EU.
- Describe the role of the European Court of Justice.

Medium

- Outline the views of the main UK political parties on the UK's relationship with the EU.

- Describe the powers of the European Parliament.
- In what ways has the UK lost sovereignty to the EU?

Long
- To what extent has membership of the EU benefited democracy in the UK?
- Discuss the view that a 'federal Europe' is a threat to the United Kingdom.
- Is the enlargement of the European Union desirable?

Useful websites

www.bbc.co.uk/news
  An excellent, wide-ranging and impartial source for topical news items and archive articles.

http://europa.eu
  The official website of the European Union.

www.europarl.europa.eu/en/headlines
  The official website of the European Parliament.

www.bbc.co.uk/programmes/b006tt0f
  The website of *The Record Europe*, a regular BBC programme that takes an in-depth look at the politics of Europe.

www.eu.org
  A site that provides free European internet domain names (has no official connection to the European Union).

Glossary

Administrative law	The body of laws which apply to executive and other public bodies.
Adversary politics	A period when the two main parties have polarised philosophies and policies.
Anarchism	Rejection of all forms of coercive power, especially of the state.
Anti-constitutional	Seeking the complete overthrow of the constitution.
Anti-parliamentary	Seeking the complete overthrow of the parliamentary system.
Authoritarianism	A system of rule based on coercive power rather than consent.
Authority	Rightful, legitimate power based on consent.
Autonomy	Self-government, independence from external control.
Bias	Prejudice or partisanship that sways or distorts mind and judgement.
Bicameral legislature	A Parliament with two chambers/houses.
Bill of Rights	A legal document enshrining citizens' entitlements against each other and the state.
Block vote	Method of trade union voting at Labour Party conferences where a majority union vote for an option results in 100% of that union's votes counting towards that option.
Bureaucracy	The large-scale, professional administration of any organisation, business or government.
By-election	An election held in a single constituency (e.g. when an MP dies).
Cabinet government	Collective policy making and accountability by all senior ministers, with the Prime Minister *primus inter pares* (first among equals).
Capitalism	An industrialised economic system based on private ownership of the means of production for private profit.
Case law	Judge-made law as interpreted by the courts in significant test cases.
Charisma	Personal magnetism and charm as a basis for personal authority.

Citizenship	Legal membership of and recognition by a state of an individual, entailing mutual rights and duties.
Civil disobedience	Law-breaking, usually peaceful and public, as a deliberate act of political protest.
Civil/legal rights	Citizens' entitlements (e.g. to freedom or equality) granted by the state.
Class	A social group sharing the same economic characteristics of wealth or income. Marxist definition: a group sharing the same relationship to the means of production.
Closed shop	An occupation or workplace where an individual must belong to the appropriate union or association in order to work in that particular trade or profession.
Coalition government	Two or more parties in government, ruling together.
Coercion	Compulsory force.
Collectivism	Broadly, a belief in the primacy of some kind of group or collective over the individual; narrowly, a 'left wing' belief in collective economic ownership and equality.
Collective ministerial responsibility	Based on the assumption of collective Cabinet policy making, therefore all ministers are collectively accountable for government policies, and should publicly and unanimously support those policies, or otherwise should resign.
Common law	Law based on custom and precedent rather than on statute.
Communism	Theory of economic equality through common ownership of property and wealth, e.g. Marxism.
Consensus politics	A period when the two main parties share similar policies, e.g. the 1960s economic boom.
Constitution	A set of rules and principles by which a state is governed.
Constitutional law	Law that regulates the powers of the various branches of the state.
Constitutional monarch	An impartial and largely symbolic hereditary head of state whose powers are largely exercised by ministers, subject to the will of Parliament and the people.
Constitutionalism	Advocacy of, or acting within, a set of clear and enforceable rules which set limits to the power of state and government.

Conventions	Unwritten rules of the constitution which have become so through traditional practice, but which have no legal force.
Corporatism	The tripartite involvement and consultation of government, employers and workers in economic planning and policy making in a private-enterprise economy to promote industrial harmony, productivity and profit.
Cross-benchers	Peers in the House of Lords who are independent of any party.
Delegate	An elected representative who acts in accordance with the wishes of the voters.
Delegated legislation	Law made by bodies other than Parliament (e.g. local authority by-laws) under powers passed down by the sovereign Parliament.
Devolution	The passing down of limited executive or legislative powers from the sovereign centre to subordinate local bodies – i.e. a more limited form of decentralisation than federalism. Neither entails complete local autonomy.
Elective dictatorship	Hailsham's thesis of excessive executive power, between elections, over Parliament and public.
Elitism	Belief in rule by a superior minority as desirable and/or inevitable.
Extra-parliamentary	Any political body or activity outside of Parliament.
Faction	A group within a party which favours and seeks to promote a particular school of thought within the party's broader ideology.
Federalism	Division of power between central and local executive and legislative bodies, with both, in theory, supreme in their particular fields, i.e. there is shared sovereignty and the centre cannot override the local bodies. Contrasts with a unitary system, where there can be devolution but no genuine regional autonomy.
Feminism	A perception of women's inequality and a desire to reduce or eradicate it.
Flexible constitution	One that needs no special legal process for change, i.e. not rigid.
Franchise	The right to vote.
Functional representation	Political representation and decision making based on occupational, industrial or interest groups rather than on parties.

Gerrymandering	The manipulation of electoral boundaries for party political advantage.
Government	Narrowly: the executive, policy-making branch of state; broadly: the whole machinery of state – legislature, executive and judiciary.
Green Paper	A consultative document of diverse ideas and options published prior to a Bill; more tentative than a White Paper.
Guillotine	A time limit on parliamentary debate of a Bill in the committee stage, imposed by the government.
Ideology	A comprehensive and more or less coherent package of doctrines, beliefs and values which provides a guide to political action.
Impartiality	Objectivity and the absence of bias.
Impeachment	A formal process for removing a politician from office, e.g. for wrongdoing.
Imperialism	The political and/or economic takeover and control of one country by another.
Individual ministerial responsibility	Based on the assumption that ministerial heads of department are the chosen representatives of the people (while the non-elected civil servants are anonymous administrators); thus ministers should be publicly accountable for the actions of their department and of themselves and should resign in the event of serious departmental or personal error.
Individualism	A belief in the primacy of the individual over any group, society or state.
Influence	Persuasive effect on others' ideas or actions.
Judicial review	Court hearings against the actions of central or local government or other public authorities.
Justice	Fairness and equity.
Laissez-faire	Free market private enterprise economy with minimal state intervention.
Law	Rules of state enforceable by the courts.
Legitimacy	Rightful authority.
Liberal democracy	A system of individual representation and protection of individual rights based on free, regular and competitive elections.
Mandate	Authority to govern, granted by the electorate; strictly, the authority or obligation of the government to implement its manifesto proposals.
Manifesto	A booklet of policy proposals issued by each party before a general election.

Mechanistic theory	Likens state and society to a machine created by individuals to serve them, with the parts interchangeable and more important than the whole.
Meritocracy	A system where people rise to the top and rule due to personal skill, intelligence and effort (term coined by Michael Young in *The Rise of the Meritocracy* [1958]).
Minority government	Executive with fewer than 50% of seats in the House of Commons.
Monism	The opposite of pluralism; a unitary state with a single ideology, party and leader – a feature of totalitarianism.
Morality	Ethical ideas of good and evil, right and wrong.
Nationalism	A sense of common culture based on, e.g. language, religion, traditions and history, usually entailing the desire for (maintenance of) a nation-state.
Natural/human rights	Entitlements which should, in theory, accrue to everyone simply by virtue of being human.
Negative freedom	Unrestrained liberty, without state help or hindrance.
New Right	Thatcherite Conservatives (as distinct from traditional political Conservatives) who advocate a free market economy (derived from nineteenth-century *laissez-faire* liberalism), combined with strong moral and social authoritarianism.
Oligarchy	Political elitism, or rule by the few.
Ombudsman	An official of Parliament who investigates public complaints of government maladministration.
Open government	Non-secretive government, with public access to official papers, policy making processes and decisions.
Organic theory	Likens state and society to a natural organism whose parts are unequal but interdependent and harmonious and less important than the whole.
Parliamentary government	A system based on overlap rather than separation of powers, i.e. the executive is chosen from the legislature and is, in theory, subordinate and accountable to the legislature – as opposed to a presidential system.

Parliamentary privilege	The exemption of MPs and peers from some ordinary laws, notably slander and libel when addressing the chamber.
Parliamentary sovereignty	Parliament has supreme law-making power and can make, amend or repeal any law without challenge from any domestic body. Thus it cannot be ruled illegal or unconstitutional, it can legalise illegality and no Parliament can bind its successors. However, it is (since 1973) formally overridden by the EU.
Party system	Political representation and power on the basis of formal, organised groups of people who put up candidates for election on a common policy programme.
Paternalism	The exercise of 'fatherly' power or authority over others to protect them from harm or to promote their welfare, usually usurping individual responsibility and freedom of choice – a doctrine of traditional conservatism.
Patriarchy	A power structure dominated by men in both the public, political sphere and the private, family sphere.
Patriotism	Love of one's country, which may or may not be a nation-state.
Patronage	Powers of appointment – granting of jobs, honours or titles.
Pluralism	Diverse and competing centres of power, especially many parties and pressure groups, many centres of economic power and various checks and balances throughout the system. Contrasts with monism/totalitarianism.
Police state	A state where control is maintained by arbitrary and oppressive law enforcement – or illegal repression – by the police, who are themselves largely above the law, with extensive powers of detention, secret surveillance and use of force; i.e. no 'rule of law'.
Political elite	A small, dominant, usually privileged decision-making and power-holding group.
Positive freedom	Real ability to achieve one's autonomy and potential, with state help where necessary (e.g. through welfare, civil rights legislation etc.).
Power	The ability to do, or make others do, something based on the capacity to coerce.

Pragmatism	Practical adaptation to concrete circumstances, rather than attachment to abstract or rigid theory or ideology.
Presidential system	A system where the executive is separately elected from the legislature and the two bodies are *de jure* equal, possessing checks and balances against each other.
Pressure group	An organisation seeking to promote a cause or protect a section of society, often by influencing government, Parliament or the public.
Primary election	The election of a candidate for further election to political office.
Private Bill	A Bill which affects only specific individual or group interests, rather than the general public.
Private member's Bill	A Bill introduced by an individual back-bench MP (of any party), rather than by the government.
Proportional representation	Umbrella label for systems of election which produce seats in proportion to the parties' votes.
Quango	Quasi-autonomous non-governmental organisation – a body appointed by government but not a formal part of government, and meant to be impartial, to perform some administrative or regulatory function.
Racialism/racism	A perception of innate biological castes within human society which can be ranked in a hierarchy; a perception used to rationalise discrimination and/or domination.
Reactionary	Desire to turn the clock back to an earlier *status quo ante*.
Referendum	A vote by the electorate directly on a specific issue; may be either advisory or binding.
Representation	A form of indirect democracy reflecting the views, interests and/or typical social background of the electorate.
Responsible (party) government	Executive accountable to Parliament and the public (through party system, manifesto and mandate); or wise and sensible government in the best interests of the people.
Rights	Entitlements, e.g. to some kind of freedom or equality.
Rigid constitution	One which requires a special legal process for change.
Royal prerogative	The legal powers of the Crown.

Rule of law	A principle which seeks to ensure 'just' law which is applicable to all – thus there should be legal equality, clear, consistent and impartial law and an independent judiciary.
Safe seat	A constituency which one particular party is virtually certain to win, regardless of the candidate.
Scientism	The application of criteria of scientific method to the study of human society – hence objective, empirical, logical, rational, determinist, classificatory, quantifiable and verifiable.
Select committees of the House of Commons	All-party committees of backbench MPs whose task is to scrutinise the activities of government departments and issues of public interest.
Separation of powers	An arrangement (favoured by liberal democratic thinker Montesquieu) whereby the personnel and structures of the legislature, executive and judiciary do not overlap with each other.
Separatism	(Desire for) complete break-away and independence of a local region to form a sovereign state.
Sequestration	The freezing and/or seizure of a trade union's assets by the courts as a penalty for contempt of court over illegal industrial action.
Socialisation	The instilling of political attitudes and values through agencies such as family, media, education, peer group, church etc.
Sovereignty	Ultimate legal and political power and authority.
Standing committees of the House of Commons	All-party committees of backbench MPs whose task is to scrutinise and amend Bills.
State	The formal, abstract, sovereign political power over a given territory, usually comprising legislature, executive and judiciary and usually possessing a legal monopoly of coercive power.
Subsidiarity	The principle enshrined in the EU Maastricht Treaty that power should be exercised at the lowest possible level compatible with efficiency and democracy.
Supranationalism	The establishment of a sovereign power over member states.
Surcharging	The personal fining of a local councillor by the courts to the amount of money illegally spent.

Toleration	Acceptance of diverse views and actions.
Totalitarianism	A twentieth-century concept (devised by Italian fascism) of total control by a monist state of both the public and private spheres based on mass, active consent as well as coercion.
Ultra vires	Literally 'beyond legal powers' – phrase used when actions by central or local government bodies are ruled illegal by the courts.
Unconstitutional	Breaking any rule of the constitution.
Unicameral legislature	A parliament with only one chamber/house.
Unitary constitution	A constitution based upon a single, sovereign, national legislature.
Unwritten/uncodified constitution	Set of rules and principles of government (some written), but not contained in a single, legal document.
Veto	The power to block a decision through refusal of consent.
Welfare state	Provision by government and public authorities of money, goods and services to those deemed in need.
White Paper	A draft Bill, for public consultation, before publication of the Bill.

Index

Page numbers in **bold** refer to figures, page numbers in *italic* refer to tables

Abraham, Ann 116
absolute majority 40
absolute monarchy 124
Act of Settlement 1701 124
Action on Smoking and Health (ASH) 90
active citizen, the 12
Acts of Parliament (statute law) 17–18
additional member system (AMS) 48
administrative law 145, 148
administrators 123
adversary politics 74, 127
Advisory, Conciliation and Arbitration
    Service (ACAS) 91
Alternative Vote (AV) 45–6, 73
alternative vote plus (AV+) 10
Amsterdam Treaty 1997 186, 192, 199
Anarchist Federation 90
anarchists 99
Animal Liberation Front 90, 94
anti-capitalism 10, 95–6
anti-terror law 116–17, 153, 154–5
Anti-terrorism, Crime and Security Act 2001
    116–17, 154
Ashdown, Paddy 73
Ashley, Jack 82
Asquith, Herbert 136
Atkin, Lord 151
authority 1–2, 13, 135

backbench revolts 28, 117
backbenchers 76
Bagehot, Walter 125, 126
Belgium 10
Benn, Tony 71
bicameral legislature 23, 105
big business 27
Big Society, the 12, 71, 137
Bills 78–80, 105, 110–13
Black Wednesday 191
Blair, Tony 19, 29, 53, 71, 71–2, 75, 107, 108,
    115, 117, 118, 131, 134, 135, 136–7, 186,
    192
block vote 100
bound/closed lists 49
British citizenship 11–12
British National Party 73, *74*, *76*, 97, *190*
British political culture *9*, 9–10
Brown, Gordon 53, 72, 115, 134, 137
Burke, Edmund 6, 78, 82
Butler Report 137
by-elections 38
Byers, Stephen 71
cabinet, the 19, 123, 125–30, 132; collective
    ministerial responsibility 127–8, *128*;

functions 126; functions of ministers 126–7;
    individual ministerial responsibility 127,
    128–30, *129–30*
Cabinet committees 133, 133–4, *133–4*
cabinet government 125–6, 132, 136
Cable, Vince 127–8
Cameron, David 12, 69–71, 107, 115, 134,
    137, 149, 152, 191
Campaign for Nuclear Disarmament (CND)
    90, 94
capital punishment 89, 155–6
case law (judge-made law) 18, 147–8
cash for questions scandal 82, 118
cause groups 89
Charter of Fundamental Rights 193
Chief Whip, the 78
Churchill, Winston 155
citizenship 11–12
civil courts **146**
civil disobedience 10, 94–6, 143, 145, 152,
    168
civil law 143
civil liberties 8, 10; judicial protection of
    153–5; protection 155–6, 160, 183
civil rights 8, 152–3; judicial protection of
    153–5
civil servants 123, 137–8
civil service 137–8, **138**, 139
civil service anonymity 137, **138**
civil service neutrality 137, **138**
class 10, 51–2
class dealignment 52
Clause Four of the Labour Party constitution
    71
Clegg, Nick 73
closed shop 100
Coalition Committee *133*, 133
coalition government 28, 47
Coalition Government, the 19, 38, 56,
    73, 74, 107, 117, 118, 126, 127, 149,
    174
codified constitution 20, 30
collective influence 98
collective ministerial responsibility 127–8,
    128
collective responsibility 64
Commissioners for Local Administration
    168
commissions of inquiry 151
Committee of Professional Agricultural
    Organisations (COPA) 93, 199
Committee on Public Standards 75
Committee on Standards in Public Life 82
common culture 8
common law 18

Commons Public Accounts Committee (PAC) 114
community charge 168
Confederation of British Industry 97
conscience 82
consensus politics 74, 90
consent 1, 6
Conservative Party 68, 69–71, 74; criticisms of devolution 177; and the EU 189–90, 194; financing 75; greening 88; membership 74; organisation 74–5; party conference 81; peers 107
constituencies 38, 169
constituency party 81
constituents 76, 81
constitution 17. *see also* UK constitution, the; codified 20, 30; federal **21**, 21; flexible/unentrenched 20; rigid/entrenched 20; uncodified 20, 31–2; unitary 20–2, **21**; unwritten 33
Constitutional Affairs, Department of 175
constitutional monarchy 124–5
Constitutional Reform and Governance Act 2010 109
constitutional reforms: Coalition Government 29; Labour, 1997–2010 28–9
constitutional writings 18
constitutionalism 8
conventions 18–19
corporal punishment 155–6
corporatism 91, 100
Council of Ministers (EU) 184, 199
council tax 168
councillors 165–6, *167*, 178
Country courts **146**
Countryside Alliance 94
Court of Appeal **146**
courts, the 145–9; civil and criminal courts 145, **146**; European 145–7; and the executive 148–9; and local government 168; and Parliament 147–8
criminal courts **146**
Criminal Justice Act 1994 144
criminal law 143
cross-benchers 106, 107
Crossman, Richard 132
Crown, the 123, 124
Crown courts **146**
crown immunity 125
Crown Prosecution Service (CPS) 143

delegated legislation 113
democracy 2, 2–4, 6–7, 13–14; British 9; and consent 6; criticism 14; direct 2–3, 56; E-democracy 4–5; indirect/representative 3; liberal 7–8; and pressure groups 98–9
democratic participation 3–4
democratic socialists 71
Democratic Unionist Party 175, *176*
departmental select committees 114–16
devolution 29, 112, 171–2; criticisms of 177; Northern Ireland 172, 175, *176*, 177;

regional 177; Scotland 172, 172–4, 175, 177; Wales 172, 174–5, *175*, 177
Devolution Bill, 1977 172
devolved powers *176*
Dicey, A.V. 20
dictatorship 63
direct action 92
direct democracy 2–3, 56
discrimination 152
Disraeli, Benjamin 81
doctrine of the mandate 64, 65
dominant party system 68
double jeopardy rule 148–9

economic sovereignty 183–4
E-democracy 4–5
elections 7; turnouts 43, *45*,
elective dictatorship 27–8, 48, 63, 64, 68, 98, 108, 116–17, 183
electoral deposits 39
electoral systems 38–50; additional member system (AMS) 48; the alternative vote (AV) 46–7; alternative vote plus (AV+) 48; first-past-the-post **40**, 40–5, *41*, **42**, independent candidates 42–3; mixed proportional systems 48; non-PR systems 39, 45–6; proportional representation 39, 41, 46–50, 50–1; the Second Ballot 46; the supplementary vote (SV) 46; United Kingdom 39
Employment Acts 91
environmental crisis 12
equality 7, 152
EU constitution 192–3
EU Social Chapter 29, 185–6, 191–2, *192*
euro, the 190, 191
European Commission 185, 186–7, **189**, *189*
European Convention on Human Rights 29, 145–7, 152, 155
European Council 185–6, 199
European Court of Human Rights (ECHR) 19, 27, 37, 145–7
European Court of Justice (ECJ) 145, 183, 188–9, 199
European integration: advantages 196–7; disadvantages 197
European Parliament 49, 184, 186–8, 189, **189**, *190*, *190*, 196, 198
European Union (EU): budget 187; citizenship 12; Commission 185, 186–7, 189; constitution proposals 192–3; Council 185–6, 199; Council of Ministers 184, 199; decision making process **189**, *189*; enlargement 192–3; foreign and defence policy cooperation 192; future 194; history and development 181–2, 190–3; impact on British political parties 189–90, 194; impact on British political processes 198–9; institutions 184–9; legislation 112, 183; membership **182**; myths 193–4; Parliament *186*, 186–8, 189, 196, 198; single currency 191, 198; the Social Chapter 29,

185–6, 191–2, 192; sovereign power 182;
  sovereignty question 183–4, *184*, 195–6,
  198; UK attitude towards 182–3
European Union law 17, 21–2, 27, 147, 198,
  199
Eurosceptics 69, 183, 190, 194
Exchange Rate Mechanism (ERM) 191
executive **22**, 22–3, 29, 123–4; and the courts
  148–9; judges and 151; parliamentary
  control 113–16
executive agencies 137

Factortame case 188, 195
federal constitution 21, **21**
federal systems 171
federalism 171, 191
fire services 165
first-past-the-post electoral systems 40–5, **42**
flexible/unentrenched constitution 20
franchise 2, 9, *9*, 37–8
freedom 152–3
Freedom of Information Act 156
functional representation 101

general elections 38; 1997 52; 2005 69; 2010
  4, 41, 42–3, 49–50, *66–7*, 71, 72; results,
  1970–2010 *43–5*; turnouts 43, *45*, *54*;
  winning parties, 1974–2010 *41*
gerrymandering 169
good citizen, the 11–12
government 8
government departments 123–4
government finance 114
Grant, Wyn 90
Greater London Authority (GLA) 165, *170*,
  170–1
Green Paper 111
Green Party 73, *74*, *75*, 97, *190*
Greenpeace 98–9
Griffith, John 150, 151

Hague, William 53
Hamilton, Neil 82
Heath, Edward 182
Hemming, John 118
Her Majesty's Opposition (HMO) 67, 68,
  113–14
hereditary peers 106
High Court **146**
historical documents 18
House of Commons: backbench revolts 117;
  controlling the executive 113–16; elective
  dictatorship 116–17; law-making 110–
  13, 119–20; reform 118; representation
  117–18
House of Lords: attendance allowance 109;
  composition 106–8; criticisms 109; defence
  of 108–9; law-making 112, 119–20;
  powers 108, 119–20; reform 107, 118;
  representation 109
Howard, Michael 107, 138
Human Rights Act 1998 29, 71, 146–7, 148,
  152, 155, 156, 158–60

hung parliament 47
Hurd, Douglas 98

independent candidates 42–3
indirect/representative democracy 3
individual ministerial responsibility 127,
  128–30, *129–30*
influence 1
initiatives 51
Innocent until proved guilty 144
insider groups 90, 93, 99
interest groups 82, 89
internment 34, 154, 156
Iraq 49
Israel 8, 49
issue groups 89

Johnson, Boris 71, 171
judge-made law (case law) 18, 147–8
judges 150–1
Judicial Appointments Commission 106
judicial bias 144
judicial independence 149, 150–1, 158
judicial neutrality 150–1, 158
judicial review 148, 149, 157–8
judiciary 8, **22**, 22–3, 29, 150–1
just law 144
justice 144, 145
Justice Secretary 150

Kinnock, Neil 53, 71
kitchen cabinets 126

Labour Party 68, *71*, 71–3; criticisms
  of devolution 177; and the EU 189,
  192–3, 194; financing 75; foundation
  97; greening 88; membership *74*, 75;
  organisation 74–5; party conference 81; and
  trade unions 91
Lamont, Norman 191
Law Lords 106, 116, 145, 148, 151, 154
law-making 110–13, 119–20
laws 17, 17–18, 143; EU 147; retrospective
  26–7, 148–9; unconstitutional 19–20
legal certainty 144
legal citizenship 11
legal equality 143–4
legal sovereignty 26–7
legislative devolution 171
legislature **22**, 22–3
legitimacy 1
legitimate power 1
Liaison Committee 115
liberal democracy 7–8
Liberal Democratic Party 68, *71*, 73, *75*;
  criticisms of devolution 177; and the EU
  190; membership *74*
life peers 106, 107, 109
limited government 8
Lisbon Treaty 2009 56, 193, 194, 199
Livingstone, Ken 170–1
Lloyd George, David 106
lobbying 93, 98

local government 163; advantages 178–9; contacting 165–6; controls 168–9; councillors 165–6, *167*, 178; disadvantages 179; elections 166, *167*, 169; finance 167–8; functions 164–5; London *170*, **170**, 170–1, *171*; officials 167; parish and community councils 164, 165; representation 166; single-tier system 163–4, 164; sleaze and corruption 169; structure 163–7; two-tier system 164, 164–5

London, local government *170*, **170**, 170–1, *171*

Lord Chancellor 106, 150

Maastricht Treaty (1992) 12, 112, 181, 185, 190–2, 199

MacDonald, Gus 19

McGuinness, Martin 175

Macmillan, Harold 136

Magistrates' courts **146**

Major, John 20, 82, 134, 135, 168, 185, 189, 190–1

majoritarian representation 38

majority government 27–8

mandarins 137–8

mandate 20, 45, 64, 65

manifesto 19

Marr, Andrew 137

media, the 27, 53

Members of the European Parliament (MEPs) 186, *190*, 196

Miliband, David 72

Miliband, Ed 72–3

miners strike, 1984–85 91, 151, 152

ministerial responsibility 19

ministers 80, 126; appointment 124; functions 126–7; individual ministerial responsibility 128–30, *129–30*; resignations 127, *128*, 128–30, *129–30*; scandals 129

Ministers of the Crown Act 1937 127

minority government **24**, 28, 40

mixed proportional systems 48

mobocracy 2

monarch, the 124

monarchy, the 124–5

money Bills 108, 110

morality 145

MPs 41, 76–83; backbench revolts 117; backbenchers 76; conscience 82; contacting 81; as controller of executive 80; expenses scandal 83, 118; interest groups 82; as legislator 78–80; loyalties 81–2; personal fees 82; recall 51, 82–3; representation 77, 77, 80, 84, 84–5; responsibility 77; roles 78–80, 84; Scottish 173–4; sponsored 93; as trainee minister 80; women *71*

multi-party system 67–8

Murdoch, Rupert 91, 127

nation 8

National Assembly for Wales 112, 174, *175*, 175, *176*

National Audit Office (NAO) 114

national interest 82, 151

national sovereignty 183

nationalism 10

natural rights 152

Nazi Germany 6

Neill Committee on Public Standards 56

neo-conservatives 69

neo-liberals 69

New Labour 71, 71–2, 74, 75, 91, 189

New Right 11–12, 69

newspapers 53

Nice Treaty 2000 192

Nolan Commission 82

non-violent action 94

Northern Ireland: devolution 172, 175, *176*, 177; local government 163; party system 68

Northern Ireland Assembly 48–9, 175, *176*

Northern Ireland Parliament (Stormont) 172

obligations 12

oligarchy 3

Ombudsman, the 115

open government 8

Opposition, the 67, 68, 113–14

Orders in Council 113

outsider groups 90

parish and community councils 164, 165

Parliament 10; authority 20–1; balance of power 27–8; and the courts 147–8; departmental select committees 114–16; elective dictatorship 116–17; functions 105–6; government subordination to **24**; history 105; House of Commons 110–18, 119–20; House of Lords 106–10, 112, 118, 119–20; and local government 168; representation 117–18; supremacy of 26, 34; term 38

Parliament Act 1949 108

parliamentary government **23**, 24, **24**, 32–3, 34

parliamentary privilege 110, 118

parliamentary sovereignty 19, 20, 25–8, 98, 110, 120, 147, 156, 183

participation 3–4

parties 63; 2010 general election participants *66–7*; comparison with pressure groups 97, 101; and the EU 189–90; financing 75, *75–6*; funding *75–6*, 93; image and policy 53; leadership 53; membership *74*, 74, 75, 101; methods 64; MP loyalty to 81; organisation 74–5; public opinion polls 87–8; single-issue groups 97

partisan dealignment 52

party conferences 81

party system 63, 83; advantages 63–4; disadvantages 64; United Kingdom 65–8, *66–7*

party whip 78, 78–80

party/regional list system 49

Peel, Sir Robert 131

people power 2, 3, 92, 101

Permanent Secretaries 137–8

pluralism 7–8, 38, 48, 98

police, the 156, 165
political activism 3–4, 10
political culture 9; British *9*, 9–10
political equality 7
political socialisation 6–7
political sovereignty 27, 184
poll tax 168
power 1, 13
presidential government **23**, 32–3
presidential system 136–7
presidentialism 29, 136–7
pressure groups 4, 27, 89–90, 134; causes
 of success 102–3; civil disobedience
 94–6; comparison with parties 97, 101;
 and democracy 98–9; methods 93–6, 99;
 mobilisation of public opinion 94; numbers
 101; power 98–9, 100; use of the courts 94
primaries 51
Prime Minister 18, 118, 123, 125, 126;
 1945–2010 *130–1*; accountability
 115; appointment 131; authority 135;
 Cabinet committee system 133–4, *133–4*;
 constraints on 135–6; policy advice 134;
 policy examples 134, power 132–3, 135–6;
 powers 131–2; reform proposals 135; status
 132
prime ministerial government 132, 135–6
Prime Minister's Question Time (PMQT)
 114, 118
Private Bills 111
Private Members' Bills 93, 110–11
professional associations 91
promotional/cause/issue/ groups 89, 90, 99,
 100
proportional representation 39, 41, 46–50;
 advantages 46–7; consequences of 50–1;
 disadvantages 47–8; mixed systems 48;
 party/regional list system 49; single
 transferable vote (STV) 48–9; systems
 48–50
protective/sectional/interest/groups 89, 98,
 100
Public Bills 110
public disorder 10
public expenditure 167
public opinion 6, 7, 64, 87–9, 94
public opinion polls 87–8
public spending 114, 168–9

Qualified Majority Voting (QMV) 183, 184,
 192, 198
quangos 108, 115, 168
Question Time 114

recall provisions 51, 82–3
referenda 2, 18, 55–6, 59–60; advantages and
 disadvantages 56–7, 60–1; United Kingdom
 55–6, 56, 60
Reform Act, 1832 37
representation 6, 77, 77, 80, 84, 84–5, 109,
 117–18, 166
representative democracy 3
representative government 25

responsibility 6, 77
responsible government 6, 25
retrospective law 26–7, 148–9
rights 147, 152–3
rigid/entrenched constitution 20
royal assent 105, 112
royal prerogative 124, 125
rule of law 34, 118, 143–5, 150
Russia, legislature 23

safe seats 40, 42
Scotland 10, 12; constituencies 38; devolution
 172, 172–4, 175, 177; local government
 163; MPs 173–4; parliamentary elections
 47; party system 67–8; Scottish Parliament
 elections 173, *173*; voting behaviour 52
Scotland Act 172–3
Scottish Executive 172
Scottish Nationalist Party 67–8, 73, *74*, *76*,
 173, 173, 177, *190*
Scottish Parliament 23, 29, 112, 172, *173*, 173,
 174, *176*
Second Ballot 46
sectional groups 89
select committees 114–16
separation of powers 23, 113, 150
separatism 171, 177
sequestration 91, 101
Shadow Cabinet 73
simple majority 38
single currency, the 191, 198
Single European Act (SEA) 1986 112, 183,
 190, 198
single transferable vote (STV) 48–9
single-issue groups 97
Sinn Fein 175, *176*, 177
Skinner, Dennis 80, 82
sleaze 117–18, 135, 169
Smith, Tim 82
social citizenship 11
Social Contract, 1973–78 90–1
social democrats 71
socialisation 6–7
society 8
sovereignty 8, 26, 33–4, 195; economic 183–4;
 and the EU 183–4, *184*, 195–6, 198; legal
 26–7; national 183; parliamentary 19, 20,
 26, 98, 110, 120, 147, 156, 183; political 184
spin doctors 7
sponsored MPs 93
Standing committees 111
state, the 8
statute law (Acts of Parliament) 17–18, 105
statutory instruments 113
Steel, David 93
Stop the War 90
strikes 91, 92
subsidiarity 191, 199
supplementary vote (SV) 46
supranational institution 182
supremacy of Parliament 26–7, 34
Supreme Court 106, **146**, 148, 149
Supreme Court Justices 151

surveillance 156
Switzerland 2, 49, 55

Thatcher, Margaret 69, 74, 91, 107, 131, 134,
    135, 138, 168, 183, 189, 198
Thatcherism 69, 100–1
third-party vote 40
trade unions 82, 89, 90–2, 100–1; legal
    curbs on 91; protection of individual
    workers 92; public hostility to 92;
    sponsored MPs 93
Trade Unions Congress 97
Traditional political conservatives 69
trustee model 6
two-and-a-half party system 68
two-party system 40, 68
two-tier councils 164, 164–5
tyranny of the majority 2, 56

UK constitution, the 17; contradictions
    20; conventions 18–19; criticism 32;
    laws 17–10, parliamentary sovereignty
    26–8; principles 33; reforms 28–30;
    sources and features 17–22, **21**, 32; system
    of government 22–5; twin pillars of 20;
    unconstitutional action 19–20; weaknesses
    33
UK Independence Party (UKIP) 73, *74*, *75*,
    97, 190
uncodified constitution 20, 34
unconstitutional action 19–20

unitary (single-tier) councils 163, 164
unitary constitution 20–2, **21**
United Kingdom 8
United States of America 2, 7, 171; Bill
    of Rights 148, 155; Constitution 20;
    legislature 23; President 135, 136;
    presidential government **23**; presidential
    system 25; separation of powers 23
unwritten constitution 17, 33

violence, legal monopoly on 8
vote, the 37–8, 41
voter turnouts 10
voting ages *5*, 9, 37
voting behaviour 57; abstentions 54; factors
    influencing 51–4
voting rules 4

Wales 10, 12, 73; constituencies 38; devolution
    172, 174–5, *175*, 177; local government
    163; voting behaviour 52
Wapping revolution, the 91
welfare state 11
West Lothian question 173–4
Westminster council 169
White Paper 111
Wilson, Harold 47, 182
women: franchise 9; MPs 70, *71*; voting
    behaviour 52
workers' power 92
written constitution 17